A DICTIONARY OF COOKING

Books by Ralph De Sola:

ABBREVIATIONS DICTIONARY

A DICTIONARY OF COOKING

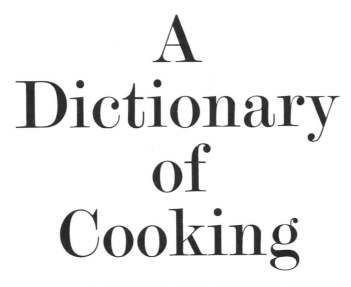

A
Dictionary
of
Cooking

APPROXIMATELY EIGHT THOUSAND DEFINITIONS
OF CULINARY INGREDIENTS, METHODS,
TERMS, AND UTENSILS

Compiled by Ralph and Dorothy De Sola

with an introduction by Peg Bracken

MEREDITH PRESS   *NEW YORK*

SBN: 696-58012-8

Library of Congress Catalog Card Number: 74-93838

Manufactured in the United States of America for Meredith Press

Preface

Because American cookery derives from the cultures of all nations, particularly western European countries whose peoples settled here, many entries reflect these across-the-border and overseas culinary terms. The names of favorite dishes, important words such as bread, fish, fowl, meat, and water are included, as well as things we encountered while dining out or traveling.

This dictionary includes the terminology of baking, cooking, culinary arts, and dining.

Entries include ales, appetizers, appliances, beverages, breads, cakes, candies, cereals, cheeses, condiments, cookies, crackers, dairy dishes, desserts, eggs, fruits, game, herbs, ices and ice creams, jams and jellies, ketchups, kippers, liquors, lobsters, meats, milk, nuts, oranges, oysters, poultry, puddings, quinces, rice, rum, salads, sandwiches, seafoods, sauces, soups, stews, teas, turkey, utensils, vegetables, waffles, Xmas cookies and many other entries under X, yams, yeast, yogurt, and items ranging from *zabaglione* to *Zwieback*, and even zmurgy.

Just about everything pertaining to beverages and foods of popular appeal should be found. Every effort was made to make this dictionary as comprehensive as possible without allowing the material to become tedious or going too far afield.

Readers are urged to send suggestions for other entries to the authors for use in future editions.

M. Josef Herweg, *escoffier extraordinaire,* gave his expert advice in a free and friendly manner. Our good friends Marjorie Brooks and Doris Sadoski supplied considerable research material.

And last but not least to be mentioned is Phil Polito, who gave us much of the good music played in the background while this dictionary was being compiled.

Sincere thanks to all these good people.

Ralph and Dorothy De Sola

Kissing' don't last; cookery do!

— GEORGE MEREDITH

Introduction

I usually question the value of an Introduction. Either the book is there to speak for itself, or it isn't and doesn't. Still, I remember the case of the multilingual bird that a sailor sent home, from some exotic port, to his mother. When the sailor eventually arrived home too, his first question was, "How did you like the bird?"

"Delicious!" said his mother.

And the sailor said, "But that bird could speak eleven languages!" And his mother shrugged, "So why didn't he say something?"

Clearly, an introduction would have been helpful in that instance. And so an Introduction does, perhaps, serve an occasional purpose, if only to point with pleasure, as I must do now, in the direction of Ralph and Dorothy De Sola's *Dictionary of Cooking*. According to Boswell, a dictionary is a prodigious warehouse. But this one is also a prodigious pantry. And a bountiful buffet. And a long, long, long menu.

— Not a *Larousse Gastronomique*, with its recipes and histories, the emphases classical and the accent French. No, this is a dictionary, pure though not necessarily simple, ranging from international to local, well spiced with the vernacular and the homely.

I warn you that merely dipping into it can be a chastening experience. Whoever thinks he has cooking down cold, or hot as the case may be, is apt to emerge dripping and a bit shaken. For it's all here — dishes, ingredients, expressions, processes, containers, but mainly food and drink from *aal* to *zythos*, a treasure trove for the dedicated and nondedicated cook alike, as well as for the uneasy bystander.

Well, it's high time! For we're hip-high in cookbooks — books on the alleged joys of cooking, and its certain frustrations; recipes from seafood to soul-food, from *la haute cuisine* to the backyard barbecue to The Toddler's 101 New Tricks with Graham Crackers Besides Rubbing Them into the Furniture. And finally, now, to help make sense of them all, this book, the De Solas' labor of scholarship, food lore, and — surely — love, with solid gold nuggets on every page.

Where else would you learn about fannie daddies, or foo foo? Or how Liederkranz was invented, though you may still be wondering why. Or what a runcible spoon actually is. Or a tansy pudding. Or peanut soup. Where else would you find out what a Xerophagist does? Or that a bilberry is precisely the same as whortleberry? Learning that fact alone has relieved my mind no end.

A maker of dictionaries surely needs to make a thousand small decisions invisible to the naked eye, but vital to the usefulness of the book. *How basic should I be?* he must ask himself. *Should I, for instance, include fish as an entry?*

I applaud the authors' sound answers. No, they decided here, and wisely, apparently figuring that anyone who must look up *fish* isn't quite ready for a dictionary yet. But varieties of foodfish, oh my, yes; from the broadbill to the buckling to the sterlet (small sturgeon of the Caspian Sea and its tributaries, great caviar producer).

Nor is the book cross-indexed to a fare-thee-well — another great plus. I don't know if the casual reader is aware of it, but shrewd cross-referencing can make one entry take the space of six, thus giving the book a far more comprehensive look than it deserves.

The De Solas don't stoop to such nonsense, except when necessary. A French chestnut, they explain, is a Spanish chestnut, which — if your hand is still in the air — is a large, sweet chestnut grown along the shores of the Mediterranean.

Or take the guanabana. The guanabana is a soursop, the book says. Which may be information enough for some people, but not for me. However, I merely looked up soursop to learn that it is a — but no, I don't think I'll tell you. Look it up yourself and you'll remember it better. Though I'll give you one hint: it is related to the sweetsop. Now run with it.

I appreciate, too, the fact that the authors were not frightened by brand names which have become accepted words in themselves — Coke, Imo, Fig Newton, Aplets. . . . And I like the poetry that is here, for certainly there is poetry in food, as well as solider nourishment. Earth apple, the old name for the Jerusalem artichoke or for the cucumber. And greenlings. And mad apple, which they called the eggplant, long ago. And, best of all, merrythought, which was the old, old name for the wishbone.

This is a book of many uses. It will settle arguments and win bets. It will help translate menus, from Filipino to Mexican-Spanish to the ancient Egyptian, should you be so unfortunate as to be faced with one. It will help translate one's gourmet friends' merry prattle on their return from wherever it was, and it will help translate ordinary books. (For you know how it is with writers these days, especially novelists. They travel a lot, which would be all right if they'd keep it to themselves. But they seldom do, preferring to one-up the reader with colorful bits like "Pass the *achar*,' said Mukji." It is a comfort, at these times, to be able to find out quickly that Mukji only wants some more pickles.)

Mainly, this is a lovely book to keep handy and dip into, like a box of chocolates. To anyone intrigued for whatever reason with the spiced, savory, multi-flavored, many-faceted world of food, a world that even I am faithful to, after my fashion, I commend it unreservedly.

— *Peg Bracken*

A DICTIONARY OF COOKING

aal: (Afrikaans or Dutch—eel)

Aal: (German—eel)

aal i gélé: (Danish—jellied eel)

aalsoep: (Dutch—eel soup) National soup of the Netherlands, available in cans at gourmet counters.

Aalsuppe: (German—eel soup)

AAN: Abbreviation for American Academy of Nutrition.

A and B: Applejack and benedictine served in a small liqueur glass.

aardappel: (Dutch—potato)

aardappel puree: (Dutch—mashed potatoes)

aardappelsoep: (Dutch—potato soup)

abacate: (Portuguese—avocado)

abacaxi: (Portuguese—pineapple)

abaisse: (French—pie crust)

abalone: Edible rock mollusk prized for its tender meat.

abalone chowder: Stew made of abalone, corn, milk, onions, potatoes, and seasoning, served with oyster crackers.

abat-faim: (French—hunger killer) Large plate of appetizers or a big bowl of soup served before the rest of the meal.

abatis: (French—giblets) Edible entrails: heart, intestines, kidneys, liver, lungs; sometimes the term includes head and feet.

abatis d'oie: (French—goose giblets)

abatis en ragoût: (French—giblet stew)

abatte: Thick double-edged knife used to flatten meat, from *battre* (French—to beat).

abattoir: (French—slaughterhouse)

abbacchio: (Italian—baby lamb)

abelmosk: Indonesian herb for flavoring coffee.

Abendessen: (German—evening meal; supper)

aberdeen: Rich and creamy cheese originally made around Aberdeen, Scotland.

Aberdeen Angus: Breed of black hornless cattle originating in Scotland and improved in the U. S.

abernethy biscuit: Hard biscuit flavored with caraway seeds.

abertam: Czechoslovakian sheep's-milk cheese.

abondance: (French—abundance) Diluted water-and-wine mixture.

a brasileira: (Portuguese—in Brazilian style)

abricot: (French—apricot)

abricotine: Brandy liqueur infused with apricot extract.

abricot-pêche: (French—apricot-peach) Nectarine.

absinthe: Green alcoholic liqueur formerly made of wormwood, anise, and various aromatics; because wormwood brings about blindness, delirium, and idiocy its use in this concoction is prohibited.

abstainer: Anyone abstaining from drinking alcoholic beverages.

abstergent: A cleansing agent.

Abzugsabfüllung: (German) Wine bottled where the grapes were grown.

acacia-blossom ratafia: Acacia-blossom liqueur.

acacia gum: Basis of gum arabic taken from acacia and babul trees found in many parts of the tropics; water-soluble gum arabic is used in making gum drops, cough drops, and many chewy candies.

acaju: (Brazilian Portuguese—cashew nut)

acarajé: (Portuguese) Beans covered with shrimp sauce in the Brazilian manner.

acciuga: (Italian—anchovy)

accolade: (French—embrace) Arrangement on a serving platter of two chickens, fish, or ducks back to back; sometimes the two are facing but separated by asparagus stalks or boiled brussels sprouts.

accote-pot: (French—three-legged trivet)

aceite: (Spanish—oil)

aceitunas: (Spanish—olives)

acepipes: (Portuguese—hors d'oeuvres)

acetic acid: Chief acid of vinegar obtained from fermenting ciders and wines.

aceto: (Italian—vinegar)

aceto-dolce: (Italian—sour-sweet) Hors d'oeuvres of fruits and vegetables pickled in vinegar but preserved in jars containing honey and mustard.

achaia: Sweet Greek wine from Achaia in the Peloponnesus.

achar: (Hindi—pickle)

achara: (Filipino—pickle)

achiote: Annatto seeds crushed into powder and used in West Indian cooking to give a golden-yellow color to foods such as rice.

achras: Large fruit from a tropical American tree related to the sapodilla.

acid drop: Sourball hard candy flavored with tartaric acid; English hard candies packed in glass jars are often known by this name.

acid foods: Cereals, cheeses, eggs, fish, meats, and seafood, that leave an acid residue because they contain varying amounts of chlorine, phosphorus, or sulfur.

acid ice: Mixture, similar to meringue, made of beaten egg whites, lemon juice, and sugar.

acidophilus milk: Lactic-acid fermented milk culture resembling a well-emulsified clabber, sometimes served with carbonated water.

acorn squash: Acorn-shaped winter squash filled with orange-yellow flesh.

acqua: (Italian—water)

acqua bianca: (Italian—white water) Liqueur containing flaked silver floating in alcohol flavored with cinnamon, cloves, and nutmeg.

acqua d'oro: (Italian—gold water) Liqueur containing flaked gold floating in alcohol flavored with angelica, cinnamon, cloves, lemon peel, etc.

acqua minerale: (Italian—mineral water)

acquette: Liqueur containing flakes of gold leaf, somewhat like *Danziger Goldwasser*.

açúcar: (Portuguese—sugar)

ADA: Abbreviation for American Dietetic Association.

Adam and Eve on a raft: Slang for bacon and eggs on toast.

Adam's ale: Slang for water.

addled eggs: Rotten eggs.

ade: Any beverage consisting of fruit juice and sweetened water such as lemonade, limeade, orangeade, etc.; some are artificially flavored and colored.

adipose: Fatty.

admiralty ham: Slang for corned beef.

adobo: (Filipino—stew) Beef, chicken, and pork simmered in water before frying.

adobo a la monja: (Filipino-Spanish—nun-style *adobo*) Chicken adobo plus pineapple and tomatoes.

adobong labong: (Filipino—adobo containing bamboo shoots, pork, and shrimp)

adobong pusit: (Filipino—adobo made of squid)

advocaat: Dutch drink consisting of egg yolks, sugar, and vanilla; Dutch liqueur made with brandy, egg yolks, sugar, and vanilla.

æble: (Danish—apple)

æblegrød: (Danish—applesauce)

æblekage: (Danish—apple cake)

æbleskive: (Danish—apple disk)

æg: (Danish—egg)

æg og sild: (Danish—egg and herring)

aerated bread: Dough raised by mixing with water charged with carbon dioxide.

aerated flour: Self-rising flour.

aerated water: Carbon-dioxide-charged water such as club soda, seltzer, soda water, the basis of many soft drinks.

afd: Abbreviation for accelerated freezing and drying, process for preserving cooked or raw foods at extremely low temperatures and vacuum drying with radiant heat.

affriolé: (French—fresh from the garden; fresh fruits or vegetables)

african ginger: White ginger grown in Africa, India, and other tropical places; pickled and preserved in India for overseas export.

african peanut: Domestic peanut introduced from West Africa.

african saffron: Orange-colored vegetable dye extracted from saffron flowers, used in coloring rice dishes and in flavoring other foods.

after-dinner coffee: Demitasse—extra-strong and served in little cups.

after-dinner drinks: Liqueurs such as anisette, benedictine, chartreuse, curaçao, kümmel, or any of the many cordials.

aftertaste: Flavor lingering after certain beverages and foods are swallowed.

agar: (Malay—agar-agar) Gelatinous colloid extracted from boiled red seaweed; used in canning and as a thickener in making ice creams, jellies, soups, and stews; also called chinese gelatin, chinese isinglass, or japanese gelatin.

agateware: Porcelain-enameled iron or steel kitchenware, an easy-to-clean and relatively unbreakable material used for cups, dishes, kettles, pans, plates, pots, skillets, etc.; first produced in grayish mottle resembling agatestone but now available in many colors.

agave: Plant native to southwestern United States, the spine-covered but pulpy stems of which are cut, mashed, fermented, and bottled as pulque and mescal in Mexico and along its borders.

agemono: (Japanese—fried food)

ägg: (Swedish—egg)

aglio: (Italian—garlic)

agneau: (French—lamb)

agnello: (Italian—lamb)

agora: (Greek—marketplace)

agua: (Spanish—water)

água: (Portuguese—water)

aguacate: (Spanish—avocado)

aguacates batidos: (Spanish—whipped avocados) Panama-style avocados blended with lime juice and sugar.

aguamiel: (Spanish—honey water) Sweet juice of the agave, aloe, century plant, maguey, or sotol —desert plants of the American Southwest and Mexico; fermented *aguamiel* is called pulque; distilled pulque becomes mescal; redistilled mescal produces tequila.

aguardiente: (Spanish—firewater) Latin American alcoholic distillate of molasses or wine, a colorless ginlike intoxicant served straight or in cocktails.

agurkesalat: (Danish—cucumber salad)

agurksalat: (Norwegian—cucumber salad)

AHEA: Abbreviation for American Home Economics Association.

'ahi: (Hawaiian—tuna) Pacific yellowfin tuna.

aigrefin: (French—haddock)

aholehole: (Hawaiian—ahole) Tasty young perchlike fish found in brackish lagoons and streams of the Hawaiian Islands.

ai ferri: (Italian—grilled)

aigre-doux: (French—sour-sweet)

aiguillette: (French—long slice of meat)

ail: (French—garlic)

aile: (French—wing)

aillade: (French—garlic sauce)

AIN: Abbreviation for American Institute of Nutrition.

aïoli: (French—thick garlic sauce)

air: (Malay—water)

aitchbone: Slang for H-bone, or hipbone, cut of beef.

ait-jannock: Scotch oatmeal shortbread.

aj: Slang abbreviation for apple juice.

ají: (Spanish—green pepper) Hot capsicum pepper common to Andean countries of South America; Colombian hot sauce is made of this pepper.

ajo: (Spanish—garlic)

akala: Hawaiian plant yielding a berry that tastes something like the raspberry.

akvavit: Scandinavian liquor distilled from cereal grains, potatoes, or even from sawdust, and flavored with caraway seeds; akvavit is often served before meals as an appetizer and quickly quenched with a glass of beer.

ål: (Danish, Norwegian and Swedish—eel)

à la: (French—in the style of)

à la bayonnaise: (French—in the style of Bayonne) Garnished with braised onions and gherkins; sometimes anchovy fillets are added.

à la béarnaise: (French—in the style of Béarn) Thick sauce of eggs, butter, and mustard.

à la Beauharnais: (French—in the style of Beauharnais) Garnished with artichokes in tarragon sauce, named for the family of the Empress Josephine.

à la bellevue: (French—beautiful view) Served in aspic.

à la bigarade: (French—in Seville-orange style) Served with sour-orange sauce, usually on poultry or venison.

à la boulangère: (French—baker's wife style) Served with fried onions and potatoes.

à la bourgeois: (French—townsman style) In plain family style.

à la broche: (French—on a skewer or spit)

à la brochette: (French—on a small spit)

à la calédonienne: (French—Caledonian) Baked with dressing of butter, parsley, and lemon juice)

à la campagne: (French—in country style)

à la carte: (French—according to bill of fare) Ordering dish by dish from a menu instead of from a set combination or *table d'hôte* (French—landlord's table).

à la casserole: (French—in casserole style)

à la châtelaine: (French—in the style of the lady of the castle) Garnished with celery, artichoke hearts, baked tomatoes, and sautéed potatoes.

à la Clermont: (French—in the style of Clermont) Garnished with fried onions and stuffed potatoes and named for a town in northern France.

à la Condé: (French—in Prince of Condé style) Cooked fruit prepared in syrup with rice.

à la coque: (French—in the shell) Term applied to boiled eggs.

à la cordon bleu: (French—blue-ribbon style) Stuffed with ham and cheddar cheese and crowned with creamed mushrooms, usually a veal cutlet.

à la crapaudine: (French—toad style) Poultry broiled and flattened and trussed to resemble a toad.

à la créole: (French—in créole style) With onions, peppers, tomatoes, and seasoning.

à la Croissy: (French—Marquis de Croissy style) With carrots and turnips.

à la dauphine: (French—in the style of the dauphin's wife) Garnished with *duchesse* potatoes combined with *pâté à chou* pressed into balls before frying.

à la diable: (French—in devil style) Deviled or seasoned with spices.

à la duchess: (French—in duchess style) If a fish: served with oyster sauce; if a meat: with braised lettuce and *duchesse* potatoes; if in a sauce: with ham and mushrooms; if a soup: with asparagus tips and truffles in chicken stock.

à la fermière: (French—in farmer's-wife style) Usually a roast prepared with turnips, carrots, celery, and onions.

à la financière: (French—in the style of the banker's wife) Garnished with cucumbers, mushrooms, and olives; brown sauce with mushrooms and truffles; also a soup with goose-liver cream and croutons.

à la flamande: (French—in Flemish style) With braised cabbage, carrots, potatoes, and pork.

à la florentine: (French—in the style of Florence) Garnished with spinach.

à la forestière: (French—in the style of the forester's wife) Served with mushrooms and potato balls browned in butter.

à la française: (French—in the French style) Garnished with mixed vegetables, potatoes, and hollandaise sauce; also a sauce of béchamel and crayfish.

à l'africaine: (French—African style) Curried and spiced.

à la génevoise: (French—Geneva style) Served with red wine sauce, usually fish.

à la génoise: (French—in Genoa style) Fish served with red wine sauce similar to *Genevoise*.

à la gitane: (French—in gypsy style) Usually with tomato sauce, Spanish style.

à la Godard: (French—in the style of Godard) Garnished with truffles and mushrooms and named for a 19-century composer.

à la godiveau: (French—in force-meat-pie style) With minced-veal meatballs.

à la grecque: (French—in Greek style) With oil, rice, and olives.

à la Holstein: (French—in Schleswig-Holstein style) Fried food topped with fried eggs.

à la Hong Kong: (French—in Hong Kong style) With noodles and rice.

à la hongroise: (French—in Hungarian style) Served with paprika and sour cream.

à la Houmy: (French—in Comtesse de Houmy style) Buckwheat groats fortified with mushrooms, onions, and paprika.

à la impératrice: (French—in empress style) A cold dessert of rice, fruit, and kirsch.

à la jardinière: (French—in gardener's wife style) With cooked vegetables.

à la julienne: (French—in Juliana style) Served with thin strips of vegetables.

à la king: Creamy white sauce containing mushrooms and red pimentos or mushrooms and green peppers.

à l'algérienne: (French—in Algerian style) Garnished with oil-braised tomatoes and sautéed sweet potatoes.

à la liégeoise: (French—in Liége style) Flavored with juniper.

à la livournaise: (French—in Leghorn style)

à l'allemande: (French—in German style) Garnished with potatoes, wine-stewed prunes, or sauerkraut.

à l'alsacienne: (French—in the Alsatian style) Garnished with pickled herring, potatoes, and thinly sliced apple.

à la luzonia: (French—in Luzon style) With pork and rice.

à la lyonnaise: (French—in the style of Lyons) Served with sliced fried onions.

à la macédoine: (French—in Macedonian style) Served with diced fruits or vegetables.

à la Maintenon: (French—in the style of the Marquise de Maintenon) Garnished with mushrooms and sauce soubise.

à la Malgache: (French—in Madagascar style)

à la maltaise: (French—in Maltese style)

à la maréchale: (French—in the style of the marshal's wife) Dipped in egg and bread crumb and fried in butter, usually scallops or breasts and wings of chicken.

à la Marengo: (French—in Marengo style) Served with sauce made of mushrooms, olives, olive oil, tomatoes, and wine, named for a village in northern Italy where chicken *à la Marengo* was served Napoleon by the villagers after his victory there in 1800 over the Austrians.

à la marseillaise: (French—in Marseilles style)

a la Maryland: American term meaning served with butter-and-cream sauce, as with baked chicken.

à l'américaine: (French—in American style)

à la meunière: (French—in the miller's wife style) If a fish dish: sautéed in butter, dipped in flour, served with butter sauce and lemon; if a soup: prepared with white sauce and croutons.

à la Meyerbeer: (French—in the style of Meyerbeer) Shirred eggs served with kidneys and truffle sauce and named for a 19th-century composer.

à la milanaise: (French—in Milan style) Dipped in egg, bread crumbs, and Parmesan cheese, and fried.

à la militaire: (French—in military style)

à l'amiral: (French—in the style of the admiral) A term usually applied to seafood dishes.

à la mode: (French—in the fashion of; in the style of) In America, with ice cream, as pie à la mode; in France, hot or cold braised beef.

à la mode de Caen: (French—in the fashion of Caen) Prepared with leeks, vegetables, and wine, a Norman method of serving tripe.

à la moscovite: (French—in Moscow style) Garnished with caviar.

à la napolitaine: (French—in Neapolitan style) If a meat: served with eggplant and tomatoes au gratin; if spaghetti: with tomato sauce and cheese.

à la navarraise: (French—in Navarre style)

à l'ancienne: (French—in old-fashioned style) Served with a mixed garnish of some kind, usually said of a stew.

à l'andalouse: (French—in Andalusian style) If a consommé or soup: with eggplant, red pepper, and rice; if a garnish: with rice and tomatoes; if a salad: with cucumbers, eggs, olive oil, onions, tomatoes, and vinegar; if a sauce: with mayonnaïse, red peppers, and tomatoes.

à la neige: (French—in snowy style) Served with beaten egg whites or boiled white rice.

à la Newburg: American term meaning served in sauce made of butter, cream, egg yolks, and wine (madeira or sherry); crab and lobster are often prepared à la Newburg.

à l'anglaise: (French—in the English manner) If breaded cutlets: with boiled potatoes; if eggs: poached or shirred; if a garnish: cabbage, carrot, boiled potato, or turnip.

à la Normande: (French—in Norman manner) Braised in white wine, usually said of fish; dishes *à la Normande* are usually garnished with *sauce Normande.*

à la parisienne: (French—in Parisian style) Garnished with tiny sautéed potatoes and braised celery.

à la Parmentier: (French—in the style of 18th-century economist Antoine-Auguste Parmentier) Served with potatoes and named in honor of this economist who introduced the potato into France and made it a popular food.

à la périgourdine: (French—in the style of Périgord) With truffles or truffle sauce.

à la piémontaise: (French—in Piedmont style)

à la polonaise: (French—in Polish style) Served with chopped hard-boiled egg and parsley, usually a vegetable dish.

à la Pompadour: (French—in Madame Pompadour style)

à la portugaise: (French—in Portuguese style) With garlic, olive oil, onions, and tomatoes.

à la printanière: (French—in springlike style) With spring vegetables.

à la provençale: (French—in Provençale style) With mushrooms, tomatoes, olive oil, garlic, and onions.

à la ravigote: (French—in a cheering-up style) With herbs, mustard, and tarragon vinegar.

à la reine: (French—in the queen's style) Method of preparing chicken to the queen's taste, often with truffles and mushrooms.

à l'Argenteuil: (French—in the style of Argenteuil) Usually meaning a course served with asparagus; most of the asparagus in France comes from this town near Paris.

à la Richelieu: (French—in the style of Cardinal Richelieu) Garnished with artichokes, braised lettuce, mushrooms, and potatoes, or with an allemande sauce enriched with tomatoes.

à l'arménienne: (French—in Armenian style) With rice pilaf.

à la Romaine: (French—Roman style)

à la Rossini: (French—in the style of Rossini) Served with rich sauce of madeira wine, mushrooms, *pâté de foie gras,* and truffles; Gioacchino Rossini, 19th-century composer, devoted much of his adult life to devising tasty dishes, many of which are named in his honor.

à la royale: (French—in royal style)

à la russe: (French—in Russian style)

à la Sainte-Menehould: (French—in the style of this town in northern France)

à la Saint-Germain: (French—in the style of this town west of Paris) With peas.

à la savoyarde: (French—in Savoy style)

à la sicilienne: (French—in Sicilian style)

alaska pollack: Walleyed pollack, a codlike food fish common in the North Pacific from Alaska to California.

à la soubise: (French—in onion-purée style)

à la suédoise: (French—in Swedish style)

à la suisse: (French—in Swiss style)

à la tartare: (French—in Tartary style) Served raw with capers and parsley and with a raw egg yolk, said of minced beef.

à la toulousaine: (French—in Toulouse style)

à la turque: (French—in Turkish style)

à l'autrichienne: (French—in Austrian style)

à la vénitienne: (French—in Venetian style)

à la Vichy: (French—in the style of this spa of central France) With carrots.

à la viennoise: (French—in Viennese style)

à la villageoise: (French—in cottager style; in villager style)

à la Viscaina: (French—in Vizcayan or Biscay style)

albacore: Deep-sea tuna, the source of most canned tuna; bonito and bluefin are also called albacore.

albana: Very dry white Italian wine from Lake Albano region near Rome.

albaricoque: (Spanish—apricot)

albedo: White pith forming inner peel of citrus fruit, the source of pectin.

Albemarle: Greenish-yellow cooking apple; also known as Newtown Pippin.

albicocca: (Italian—apricot)

albóndiga: (Spanish—meatball; fishball)

albumen: Egg white.

albumins: Sulfur-rich proteins such as egg-white, meats, milk.

al burro: (Italian—in butter style)

alcachofa: (Spanish—artichoke)

alcarraza: Unglazed pottery jug of Hispano-Moresque design, used for cooling liquids.

alcazar: Spanish pastry with almonds and apricot jam.

alcohol: Intoxicating ingredient of beers, whiskeys, wines, etc.; alcohol is produced by fermentation of grapes, apples, corn, molasses, potatoes, rice, and many other fruits and grains; the ferments are then distilled into purer and more volatile forms such as whiskey and gin.

alcool: (French—alcohol)

al dente: (Italian—in toothy style) Macaroni or spaghetti cooked just enough to be somewhat firm rather than completely soft.

Alderney: Cattle of type bred on Alderney in Channel Islands off the north coast of France.

ale: Bitter beer brewed by rapid top-fermentation process in preference to longer-lagering technique; ale is higher in alcoholic content than most beers, although in England "ale" and "beer" are practically synonymous terms.

a l'écossaise: (French—in the Scots style)

alecost: Aromatic herb—costmary.

alegar: Ale + vinegar = vinegar derived from ale.

à l'egyptienne: (French—in Egyptian style) Served with lentils.

à l'espagnole: (French—in Spanish style)

alewife: Popular Atlantic Coast food fish of the herring family, also known as allice, and round pompano; its name "alewife" supposedly comes from its big belly, because many women who kept alehouses, like male tavern keepers, had beer bellies.

alexander: Cocktail frappé consisting of finely shaved ice, crème de cacao, sweet cream, and brandy or gin.

al fresco: (Italian—in fresh-air style) Outdoor dining, as on a deck, in a garden, on a porch, or along a sidewalk.

a l'habitant: (French—in the inhabitant's style) In the style of French-Canadian cooking.

alho: (Portuguese—garlic)

al horno: (Spanish—oven-baked)

à l'huile: (French—in oil style) With olive oil.

alicante: Wine grape originally cultivated in the province of Alicante, Spain.

alimentary paste: Flour paste (pasta) in all shapes: macaroni, noodles, spaghetti, vermicelli, etc.; most are made from semolina flour which provides a tough dough.

à l'indienne: (French—in East Indian style) With curried sauce allemande or with curried rice.

à l'irlandaise: (French—in Irish style)

à l'italienne: (French—in Italian style) Garnished with artichoke bottoms and macaroni croquettes, or with brown sauce and ham, herbs, mushrooms, tomatoes and truffles.

alivenca: (Rumanian) Cottage-cheese dessert.

à l'ivoire: (French—in ivory style) Served with an ivory-white sauce.

alla: (Italian—in the style of)

alla carbonara: (Italian—in peasant style) Spaghetti served with bits of prosciutto and eggs.

alla marinara: (Italian—in sailor's style) Served with marinara sauce.

alla Marsala: (Italian—in the style of Marsala)

alla Parmigiana: (Italian—in Parmesan style) Served with parmesan cheese.

all-day sucker: Big piece of hard candy or oversize lollipop.

allemande: (French-German) Yellowish sauce made by mixing egg yolks with veal stock, called allemande because of its blond color.

alle vongole: (Italian—in mussel style) With Italian clam sauce.

alligator pear: Avocado.

all-purpose flour: Flour made of a mixture of hard and soft wheats and used in all kinds of baking.

allspice: Flavor-filled berry of the allspice tree, so named because it seems to combine flavors of cinnamon, cloves, and nutmeg; it is used whole for pickling or for seasoning fish and meat, used ground for cakes, fruit preserves, puddings, and relishes.

allumette: (French—match) Short rectangle of puff pastry filled with chopped chicken, fish, shrimp, etc., baked, and served as an *hors d'oeuvre*.

alma torte: Apple cake named in honor of Allied victory at the Alma River during the Crimean War.

almeja: (Spanish—clam)

almejón: (Spanish—mussel)

almendra: (Spanish—almond)

almendrado: (Spanish—macaroon)

Almerias: Greenish-white grapes grown in California from vines brought from Spain.

almôço: (Portuguese—luncheon)

almond: Nutlike kernel of the almond tree, usually boiled and blanched or roasted and salted, thinly sliced to garnish fish dishes, seafoods, and chop sueys; almonds also are made into candied paste for confections and flavoring.

almond butter: Butter flavored with almonds.

almond-butter frosting: Cake icing made of butter, confectioner's sugar, salt, and almond extract.

almôndega: (Portuguese—meatball)

almond extract: Alcoholic flavoring extract prepared from almond kernels.

almond icing: Almond paste with which cakes are coated before they are iced.

almond mill: Device for grinding dried almonds after they are blanched.

almond paste: Paste made of finely ground blanched almonds, confectioner's sugar, egg white, and almond extract.

almond sauce: Brown blanched almonds in white sauce.

almond syrup: Emulsion of ground kernels of sweet and bitter almonds and barley or sugar syrup, often flavored with orange-flower water.

almuerzo: (Spanish—lunch)

à l'Orléans: (French—in Orleans style)

à l'Orly: (French—in Orly style) Fried in batter.

alosa: (Spanish—shad)

alose: (French—shad)

à l'Ostende: (French—in Ostend style)

aloyau de boeuf: (French—sirloin of beef)

alpes: Soft creamy French cheese of the pungent variety.

alphabet soup: Thin consommé or soup containing small letter-shaped bits of macaroni.

al pomodoro: (Italian—in tomato style) With tomato sauce.

al punto: (Italian—to the point) Medium-well done.

al sangue: (Italian—in bloody style) Rare, with the blood running.

Alse: (German—shad)

al sugo: (Italian—with sauce)

alter Kuhkäse: (German—old cow cheese) Sour-milk cheese.

alum: Ammonium or potassium aluminum sulfate, astringent chemical used in pickling cucumbers, green beans, melons, and onions, as it keeps them crisp.

aluminite: Fireproof earthenware used for cooking utensils.

aluminum foil: Thin foil available in roll form for covering, baking, freezing, and wrapping all kinds of foods.

amande: (French—almond)

amande amère: (French—bitter almond)

amande cassée: (French—shelled almond)

amande douce: (French—sweet almond)

amande pralinée: (French—burnt almond)

amandine: Served with almonds; the almonds may be blanched and thinly sliced or roasted kernels or tiny almond chips.

amaretto: (Italian—macaroon)

amaretto: Italian liqueur of bitter almonds.

amazake: Japanese sweet wine.

ambassadrice: (French—ambassador's wife or ambassadress) Sauce made with madeira wine and veal gravy.

amberjack: A large fish of the genus *Seriola* found in the western Atlantic.

ambigu: (French—ambiguous) Buffet meal at which various dishes are served.

ambrosia: Mythical food eaten by Greek and Roman gods; also a name applied to fruit compote topped with shredded coconut or whipped cream or both, or a nickname for any tasty food.

amêijoa: (Portuguese—clam)

american cheese: Domestic cheddar cheese also known as store cheese or trap cheese.

american cherry: Black-cherry cordial.

américaine: (French—American style)

american fried potatoes: Hashed brown potatoes.

American lobster: Large-clawed lobster found chiefly along the North Atlantic coast and also known as Maine lobster.

americano: Cocktail of angostura bitters, soda water, and vermouth.

American or Canadian service in the home: Service in which the host carves and then passes filled plate to the guests who help themselves to vegetables from serving dishes.

American plan: Board and meals included in the price of a lodging.

American watercress: Thin-leaved herb of the mustard family, only distantly related to true watercress; it is found in mountain streams of the eastern United States, and is excellent in salads and soups.

American white walnut: Butternut.

American wine: Any wine made in the United States including the products of California, New York, Ohio, and Virginia.

amér piçon: (French) Bitter liqueur made in France and most commonly drunk as an apéritif.

ammonia water: Solution of ammonia (a gas) in water; it is a strong household cleaning detergent.

amontillado: Pale dry sherry, originating in Spain.

amourette: (French—love affair) Croquette or fritter made with calf marrow taken from the spinal bones.

amphitryon: French term for the host, named for Amphitryon, Greek hero and foster father of Hercules, satirized by Molière.

Amstel: Dutch beer brewed in Amsterdam.

añada: (Spanish—vintage wine)

anak ajam: (Malay—baby chicken) Indonesian chicken dish.

analeptique: (French—analeptic; health giving) Light but rich food such as chocolate, milk, and wine.

ananá: (Spanish—pineapple)

ananas: (French—pineapple)

Ananas: (German—pineapple)

ananasso: (Italian—pineapple)

anchoa: (Spanish—anchovy)

anchois: (French—anchovy)

ancholivette: Anchovy-stuffed olive.

anchovy: Small Mediterranean fish of the herring family; anchovy is available canned, dried, or pickled, and is used in pizzas, salads and fish pastes for cocktail canapés.

anchovy paste: Preserved anchovies mashed into a paste and used in making canapés and other appetizers.

anchovy spear: Small plastic or wooden fork used for spearing anchovies and similar hard-to-handle appetizers.

anchoyade: (French — anchovy *hors d'oeuvre*)

Ancona: Black-and-white mottled domestic poultry of a type originally bred around Ancona, Italy.

Andalusian: Domestic poultry of a type first developed in Andalusia, Spain.

andouille: (French—a kind of pork sausage) Norman delicacy sometimes featured in *hors d'oeuvres.*

angel cake: Angel food, a white spongelike cake made with egg whites.

angelica: European herb of the carrot family; the leaves and stalks are boiled or served raw in salads; the rootstalks are candied, and the roots yield an oil used for flavoring.

angel food: Angel cake.

angel pie: Baked meringue shell filled with berries and whipped cream over a layer of white fluffy cheese filling.

angel's kiss: Cocktail similar to *pousse-café,* concocted of layers of colored liqueurs such as green *crème de menthe,* brown *crème de cacao,* red cherry liqueur, etc.

anglaise: (French—English style) Without sauce.

Angobert: Large cooking or stewing pear.

angostura: Bitter flavoring extract used in making cocktails; bitters are extracted from the bark of certain tropical trees found in Brazil, the Guianas, and Venezuela.

anguila: (Spanish—eel)

anguilla: (Italian—eel)

anguille: (French—eel)

anhydrated potatoes: Cooked, peeled, and dehydrated white potatoes reduced to dry flakes; instant mashed potatoes are made by adding anhydrated potato flakes to boiling hot water.

anhydrated vegetables: Cooked, peeled, and thoroughly dehydrated vegetables reduced to dry flakes; vegetables so processed are quickly reconstituted by mixing with boiling water.

anice: (Italian—anise)

anijs: (Dutch—anise)

animal crackers: Animal-shaped arrowroot crackers popular with children.

anís: (Spanish—anise)

anise: Herb seeds used in flavoring cakes, cookies, liqueurs, and pastry; the flavor is similar to licorice; anise oil or aniseed oil often used in cooking and baking.

aniseed cake: Baked biscuit or cake flavored with anise seeds.

anisette: Anise-flavored liqueur, usually colorless and usually served after dinner.

anisina: (Italian) Anise-flavored liqueur.

anitra: (Italian—duck)

Anjou: Large wine-flavored yellow pear popular for eating, canning, or cooking.

anna potatoes: Thin round slices of potato cooked in butter.

annatto: Yellowish-red food coloring derived from a tropical tree, the annatto.

annette potatoes: Finely shredded potatoes cooked in butter.

anon: Sweetsop.

ANS: Abbreviation for American Nutrition Society.

ansjos: (Norwegian—anchovy)

antepast: Appetizer drunk or eaten before a meal.

antipasto: (Italian—before the meal) A side dish similar to *hors d'oeuvres*.

apéritif: (French—appetizer) Cocktail, liqueur, or wine taken before the meal to stimulate the appetite.

aperitivo: (Portuguese—appetizer)

Apfel: (German—apple)

Apfelmost: (German—cider)

Apfelmus: (German—applesauce)

Apfelsine: (German—orange)

Apfelsuppe: (German—apple soup)

Apfelwein: (German—cider)

apio: (Spanish—celery)

aplets: Confection made of apples, cloves, cinnamon, nuts, nutmeg, and gelatin, a specialty of the State of Washington.

à point: (French—medium)

Apollinaris: Tasteless effervescent mineral water originally imported from German spring of the same name.

apothecary jar: Wide-mouthed ceramic or glass jar made in the style of apothecary shops of long ago; today such jars are used mainly to hold kitchen herbs.

appel: (Dutch—apple)

appelbol: (Dutch—apple dumpling)

äppelkaka: (Swedish—apple cake)

appelmoes: (Dutch—applesauce)

äppelsoppa: (Swedish—apple soup)

appeltaart: (Dutch—apple pie)

äppelvin: (Swedish—cider)

appelwijn: (Dutch—apple cider)

appenzeller: Cow's-milk cheese from Appenzell Valley of Switzerland, marinated in cider or white wine before it is aged.

appetitost: (Danish—appetite cheese) Buttermilk cheese first made in Denmark but now produced by many Danish-American communities.

appetizer: Foods or drinks served before meals to stimulate the appetite, generally salty or spicy; *antipasto* precedes Italian-style meals; canapés and *apéritifs* are served at cocktail parties; *hors d'oeuvres* are served before French-style meals.

appetizer wines: Dry sherries and vermouths served before meals, either by themselves or in cocktails.

apple: Tree of the rose family yielding a luscious pomaceous fruit, red, yellow, or streaked; apples are eaten raw, cooked in a variety of ways, or made into apple brandy or applejack.

apple brandy: Whiskey distilled from apple cider.

apple butter: Sauce or jam made by stewing apples in cider.

apple cider: Beverage made from apple juice; hard cider is alcoholic, sweet cider is nonintoxicating; fermented cider is cider vinegar.

apple corer: Utensil for removing apple cores; some apple corers are combined with an apple peeler or a device for simultaneously sectioning apples into quarters or into eighths.

apple dumpling: Small apple-filled mass of dough cooked by baking or steaming.

apple fritter: Cut-up apples fried or sautéed in batter.

apple gin: Greenish gin containing apple mash produced during cider making.

applejack: Apple brandy produced by freezing hard cider; in England applejack is the name for an apple dumpling or a pastry made of sliced apples.

apple juice: Beverage obtained by pressing ripe apples and chilling the juice so extracted.

apple mint: Apple-flavored true mint brewed as a digestive tea or used for flavoring.

apple pandowdy: Deep-dish apple pie made with molasses.

apple pie: Pie made with apples.

applesauce: Sauce made of peeled and chopped apples stewed and flavored with cinnamon, lemon juice, and sugar.

applesauce fluff: Applesauce-and-gelatin mixture whipped until light and fluffy.

apple snow: Applesauce mixed with meringue or whipped cream.

apple tansy: Apple rings fried in butter-and-egg batter before being served with cream.

apple toddy: Warm alcoholic drink containing cooked apple pulp.

apricoat: To cover a cake with a layer of apricot jam flavored with apricot liqueur.

apricot: Golden-yellow fruit somewhat smaller than a peach or plum, eaten dried, raw, or stewed, and used in making brandy, in baking, and in many preserves.

apricot brandy: Sweet cordial flavored with apricots.

apricot gin: Apricot-flavored liqueur.

apron: Protective overgarment usually tied around the waist with strings, the kitchen costume of the careful cook.

apry: French liqueur characterized by its apricot flavor.

aqua vitae: (Latin—water of life) Distilled liquor such as aquavit or the French brandy called eau-de-vie.

arabian coffee: Coffee brewed with cardamom seeds, honey, rose water, and sometimes with brown sugar instead of honey.

arabique: (French—Arabian) Gracefully garnished.

arachis oil: Peanut oil.

aragosta: (Italian—lobster)

arancia: (Italian—orange)

aranciata: (Italian—orangeade)

arenque: (Spanish—herring)

'arf an' 'arf: Cockney English for half ale and half porter.

argentine beef: Canned beef imported from Argentina.

aringa: (Italian—herring)

arista: (Italian—roast loin of pork)

armagnac: Brandy from the Armagnac area in southern France.

armored cow: Slang for canned milk.

armoricaine: (French—Amorican) Prepared in the style of Brittany, the peninsula of northwestern France.

arm pot roast: Beef cut from midchuck or forefront.

arm steak: Veal cut made just above the forelegs.

army strawberries: Slang for prunes.

aromatic: Fragrant herb or spice.

arrack: Tropical intoxicant distilled from coconut juice, rice, molasses mash, sugar cane juice.

arrosto: (Italian—roast)

arrowroot: Nutritious and easily digested starch from finely ground tuberous rootstalks of the arrowroot plant found in many parts of tropical America; arrowroot is used in making biscuits, crackers, custards, and puddings, and for modifying milk.

arroz: (Spanish—rice)

arroz con bacalao: (Spanish—rice with codfish)

arroz con frijoles: (Spanish—rice with beans)

arroz con pollo: (Spanish—rice with chicken) Dish seasoned with garlic and colored with annatto or saffron.

ARS: Abbreviation for Agricultural Research Service (of the U. S. Department of Agriculture).

artichaut: (French—artichoke)

artichoke: Member of the thistle family yielding an edible flowering head, which is boiled in seasoned water, sometimes with olive oil added; artichokes are served with mayonnaise or melted butter, and are widely cultivated in many parts of the American Southwest.

aruba roast: Highly spiced kid or lamb roast served with freshly shredded cucumbers; it was first popularized on the Dutch West Indian island of Aruba.

asado: (Spanish—roast, roasted)

asciutto: (Italian—dry; thin) Term applied to dry wines.

ash bread: Cornbread wrapped in cabbage leaves and baked in hot ashes or embers.

ashcake: Cornbread baked in hot ashes.

asiago: Italian cheese made from partly skimmed milk; asiago has a dark surface, creamy body, and spicy flavor.

asitia: Lack of appetite or loathing for food as induced by motion sickness, overeating, stomach disorders.

asopao: (Spanish—Puerto Rican-style chicken and rice)

asparago: (Italian—asparagus)

asparagus: Edible shoots of asparagus plant, which are boiled or steamed under pressure, and served cold in salads or hot with hollandaise sauce, melted butter, or grated cheddar cheese.

asparges: (Danish—asparagus)

aspargessuppe: (Danish—asparagus soup)

asperge: (French—asparagus)
aspergesoep: (Dutch—asparagus soup)
aspic: Meat-juice jelly or tomato-juice jelly used as a relish and often molded in the shape of a fish or vegetable; aspics are also made from fish, fowl, fruit, and vegetable juices in combination with gelatin.
assaisonnement: (French—seasoning)
assaisonner: (French—to mix; to season)
assam: Indian tea famous for its pungence.
asti spumanti: (Italian—sparkling asti) Effervescent wine made from sweet muscat grapes originally grown in the Asti region of northwestern Italy.
athole brose: Scots' honey-and-whiskey drink.
atka fish: Alaskan food fish sometimes called atka mackerel; it is related to the Pacific greenling.
Atlantic coast hard-shell clam: Thick-shelled American clam found in the Atlantic Ocean; the largest ones are called cape cods; the medium-sized, cherrystones; and the smallest, littlenecks.
attelet: (French—skewer)
attereau: (French—skewered meat)
atum: (Portuguese—tuna)
atún: (Spanish—tuna; tunny)
au: (French—to; in; with [singular])
auberge: (French—inn)
aubergine: (French—eggplant)
au beurre noir: (French—with black butter) In browned butter sauce, usually served with fish courses.

au blanc: (French—in white style) Cooked white or with a white sauce or cooked very gently so foods will not brown.
au bleu: (French—in blue style) Fish blued by being cooked in vinegar.
au brun: (French—in brown style) Cooked in brown sauce.
au cari: (French—in a curry)
and man's milk: Scots eggnog.
Auflauf: (German—swelling) Soufflé.
au four: (French—in oven style) Oven-baked.
Aufschnitt: (German—cut) Cold cut, sliced cold meat.
au gras: (French—in the fat) Cooked in broth or gravy.
au gratin: (French—with a crust) Crusted with bread crumbs or grated cheese and slightly charred before serving.
au jus: (French—with juice) Served in its own juice.
au lait: (French—with milk or cooked in milk)
au maigre: (French—in lean style) Served lean, without fat.
au naturel: (French—in natural style) Food served in its natural state—raw, uncooked, or unseasoned.
au rhum: (French—with rum)
aurum: Italian orange-flavored liqueur.
Auslese: (German—selection) Vintage produced from selected grapes.
Auster: (German—oyster)
Australian banyan: Moreton Bay fig.
Australian baobab: Cream-of-tartar tree.
Australian nut: Macadamia nut.
Australian steak: Slang for mutton.

automat: Cafeteria-type restaurant where most beverages and foods are vended from coin-operated devices.

au vin blanc: (French—with white wine) Made in or served in white wine.

aux: (French—to; in; with [plural])

aux croûtons: (French—with crusts) Croutons.

aux fines herbes: (French—with chopped herbs) Served with a mixture of chervil, chives, onions, parsley, shallots, and sorrel, all finely minced.

aux hâtelets: (French—with skewers) Bread crumbs and egg sauce.

avdp: Abbreviation for avoirdupois, meaning the pounds-ounces-tons system in use in English-speaking countries.

ave: (Portuguese and Spanish—bird or fowl)

aveline: (French—filbert; hazelnut)

avellana: (Spanish—hazelnut)

avercake: English oatcake.

avern: Scots for a wild strawberry.

avgolemono: (Greek—broth thickener) Chicken soup thickened with eggs and flavored with lemon juice.

avocado: Tropical American tree yielding pulpy pear-shaped fruit also called alligator pear; the yellow fruit is used chiefly in cocktail dips and salads.

avondeten: (Dutch—supper)

a votre santé, bonheur, et prospérité: (French—to your health, happiness, and wealth) A toast.

azeitão: Portuguese sheep's milk cheese.

azeitona: (Portuguese—olive)

azúcar: (Spanish—sugar)

azymous: Unleavened.

baalies: Lightly baked thin oatmeal cakes popular in Scotland and found in some gourmet shops in America.

baba: (French—soft cake) Cake with leavened dough and usually baked in a fluted mold.

baba au rhum: (French—soft cake with rum) Yeast-leavened cake soaked in rum.

babeurre: (French—buttermilk)

baboy: (Filipino—pork)

baby beef: Meat cut from a yearling heifer or steer.

baby foods: Fruits, vegetables, and meats puréed, and usually sold in small jars or cans.

baby gouda: Smooth yellow cheese originally from the Netherlands, shaped like a somewhat flattened cannonball and covered with red wax.

bacalao: (Spanish—codfish)

bacalhau: (Portuguese—codfish)

bacalhau do céu: (Portuguese— heavenly codfish) Codfish dressed with hard-boiled eggs, onions, olive oil, and sauce *béchamel* plus potatoes.

bacardí: Cuban-type rum originally distilled in Cuba by the Bacardí family.

bacardí cocktail: Mixed drink containing bacardí rum, sugar, lime juice, and grenadine syrup.

baccalà: (Italian—codfish)

Bachforelle: (German—brook trout)

bacillus bulgaricus: Essential element in yogurt and other fermented milks; the culture was named *bulgaricus* in honor of Bulgarian centenarians who insist their longevity is due to eating much yogurt.

back bacon: Canadian bacon.

backbone: Spinal column or spine.

Bäckerei: (German—bakery)

Backhendl: (Austrian German dialect—fried chicken)

Backpflaume: (German—dried plum; prune)

backspan: Scots oatcake baking plate.

back spittle: Long-handled wooden baking spatula.

Backsteiner: (German—brick) Brick-shaped German cheese similar to Limburger.

Backwert: (German—pastry)

bacon: Pig's side after removal of the spareribs, soaked in brine and smoked; some bacon is merely salted and smoked without soaking in brine.

bacon and cheese: Open-face sandwich combination often served with sliced cucumbers, sliced tomatoes, and potato chips.

bacon dish: Covered platter for holding bacon strips and keeping them warm until served.

bactericide: Anything capable of destroying bacteria; hot soapy water is a good bactericide.

badderlocks: Edible seaweed found along coasts of British Isles, and European continent, where it is used in stews or eaten as a vegetable.

badian: Anise-flavored fruit from China.

badiane: Drink made of brandy, bitter almonds, spices and lemon peel.

badminton cup: Claret cup containing carbonated water, herbs, and sugar.

bagel: Doughnut-shaped roll boiled in water and glazed with beaten egg yolk before baking; bagels are usually served buttered, with smoked red salmon and cream cheese.

bagoong: (Filipino—shrimp paste)

bagration: French-style soup or salad named after 19th-century Russian general—Prince Pëtr Bagration.

baht: (Turkish—good luck) A toast.

baie: (French—berry)

bain-marie: (French—water bath) Double boiler or multiple double saucepan.

baiser: (French—to kiss) Small meringues joined by thick cream or other filling.

baka: (Filipino—beef)

bake: To cook over dry heat, usually in an oven, between 250 and 450 degrees Fahrenheit.

bakeboard: Large wooden board on which dough is kneaded and rolled.

baked alaska: Meringue-covered sponge cake filled with ice cream, briefly browned in a high oven, and often topped with rum and served flaming.

baked apple: Cored apple with core replaced by white or brown sugar before baking; baked apples often served with sour cream or with whipped sweet cream.

baked beans: Boston specialty consisting of brown beans soaked, seasoned with molasses and salt pork, and baked slowly in a special pot.

baked beef bones: Low-calorie dietetic item favored by overweighters and others who enjoy the baked lean meat left adhering to the bones as well as the marrow within them.

bakehouse: Bakery.

bakemeat: Meat pie.

baker: Specialist in preparing and baking all kinds of breads, cakes, and pastries; the term is also applied to a vegetable serving dish without a cover.

baker's cheese: Skimmed-milk cheese softer and finer grained than cottage cheese which it resembles.

baker's dozen: Twelve plus one— extra one given to keep customers returning.

baker's yeast: Maximum-growth yeast used for leavening dough.

bakery: Place where bread and cakes are baked and sold.

bakeware: Heat-resistant utensils suitable for use in baking; today most bakeware is made of pyrex glass or porcelainized steel.

baking powder: Leavening agent used in cakes and biscuits, a mixture of baking soda (sodium bicarbonate), some acid substance (alum, calcium phosphate, cream of tartar, or their combination) and a base of flour, cornstarch, and salt; once wetted, the dough containing the baking powder rises during baking; tartrate powders are faster acting than alum or phosphate powders.

baking-powder biscuits: Biscuits made with baking powder, flour, milk, salt and shortening.

baking soda: Bicarbonate of soda (sodium bicarbonate).

baklava: (Turkish—leaf-thin pastry) Dessert consisting of very thin sheets of buttered dough filled with ground nuts and honey, and rolled before baking.

bakverk: (Swedish—pastry)

Baldwin: Round reddish winter apple popular when cooked, when served in salads, or eaten raw.

Ballantine: Brand of American ale or beer brewed in Newark, New Jersey.

ball cheese: Pennsylvania-German sour-milk cheese.

ball jar: Glass jar fitted with hermetic top and rubber gasket, used for canning and preserving; the name is generic but at one time was a trade name: Ball Jar.

ballotin: (French—small ball) Boned fish, flesh, or fowl rolled into a small stuffed ball.

balm: Aromatic herb with fragrant lemon odor, used in fruit drinks, punches, teas, and wines; it is also used for flavoring meats and salads.

baloney: Smooth pinkish sausage meat served thinly sliced; the name is a corruption of Bologna in northern Italy where the sausage originated.

balsam herb: Costmary.

balthazar: Outsize wine bottle holding about 13 quarts.

Baltimore beefsteak: Military slang for broiled liver.

balyx: (Russian—salted or smoked sturgeon)

bamboo cocktail: Mixture of bitters, sherry, and vermouth.

bamboo juice: Rice wine sold in a section of bamboo.

bamboo shoots: Oriental vegetable delicacy, obtained from the leaf buds of the bamboo, a tropical arborescent grass; bamboo shoots are cooked alone or with other vegetables.

banana: Gigantic herb native to Asia but grown throughout tropical America where it yields a soft pulpy fruit growing in bunches; bananas are eaten raw or cooked.

banana bread: Banana-flavored cakelike bread baked from dough containing mashed ripe bananas.

banana chips: Thinly sliced fried and baked banana chips popular throughout the tropical world from the Philippines to Puerto Rico.

banana chutney: Chutney made with riced bananas, powdered curry, dates, crystallized ginger, and other ingredients.

banana cream pie: Baked pie shell filled with bananas in a custard mixture plus a topping of whipped cream.

banana flour: Flour made from dried ripe bananas; it is easily digested and highly nutritious.

banana fritters: Bananas dipped in batter and fried in deep fat.

banana ice cream: Vanilla ice cream blended with banana pulp.

banana split: Split bananas topped with ice cream, chopped nuts, whipped cream and maraschino cherries.

banana squash: Taper-ended variety of winter squash.

banane: (French—banana)

Banane: (German—banana)

bananes flambées: (French—flaming bananas) Sliced bananas heated in syrup, sprinkled with rum, and set alight before serving.

banania: Banana-flavored French liqueur.

banbury cheese: Very rich English cheese sold in small soft rounds.

banbury tart: Raisin-filled triangular tart.

b and b: Slang abbreviation for benedictine and brandy.

bandes des cervelas: (French—sausage strings)

b and s: Slang abbreviation for brandy and soda.

b and w: Slang abbreviation for bread and water.

bang: Ale and cider mixture spiced with ginger and nutmeg; often sweetened with sugar and may be fortified with large jiggers of gin or whiskey.

bannock: Unleavened Scottish bread made of barley meal or oatmeal and cooked on a griddle.

banquet: Elaborate dinner consisting of many courses, usually held to honor some event or person; the meal is traditionally concluded with entertainment, speeches, and toasts.

bantam: Very small domestic or wild fowl; bantam is a corruption of Banten in Java where the wild dwarf breed was first domesticated.

banyuls: Ruby-red dessert wine first grown near Banyuls in southern France.

bap: White flour-coated breakfast roll made in Scotland.

bar: Counter where drinks are mixed.

bar: (French—bass)

barack: Hungarian apricot brandy.

bara lawr: Welsh bread made with seaweed.

barbacoa: (Spanish—barbecue)

barbados cream: Spicy liqueur containing cinnamon, citrus fruit peel, cloves, mace, and brown sugar.

barbados water: Cordial flavored with orange and lemon peels.

barbarone: Barbera-type red table wine produced in California.

barbecue: To roast on racks or spits over live coals or in an oven.

barbecue pit: Trench for holding live coals and food to be barbecued.

barbecue rack: Metal rack supporting a spit for turning fish, fowl, or meat above a bed of live coals; chops, ears of corn, hamburgers, etc., are often grilled on the rack itself.

barbecue sauce: Highly seasoned basting sauce used in barbecuing; most barbecue sauces have a tomato base, and some feature a hickory-smoked flavor.

barbera: Italian red wine made from barbera grapes of northern Italy.

barberey: Small soft French cheese resembling camembert, sometimes known as *fromage de Troyes.*

barberry: European shrub long grown in many parts of New England where it was introduced; the tart red berries used in jellies and preserves.

bar-b-q: Slang abbreviation for barbecue.

barbread: Slang for barley bread.

barcelona nut: Spanish-type filbert.

bard: To cover meat with strips of bacon or pork.

bardé: (French—larded with bacon)

bar de mer: (French—sea bass)

bardolino: Italian dry red table wine.

bar-le-duc: Preserve of seeded white currant originating in France.

barley: Cereal grass widely cultivated for its seeds and used in breakfast cereals, soups, and beverages; barley is also malted and used to brew beer and distill whiskey.

barley banger: British barley cake.

barley flour: Ground hulled barley for blending with other flours in baking bread, cakes, cookies, pancakes, etc., and also in infant feeding and restricted diets.

barley grits: Whole, hulled barley cracked into small particles and used in casseroles, cereals, meat loaves, hamburgers, and soups.

barley sugar: Transparent confection made by melting and cooling cane sugar; the name is derived from the time barley water was used in its preparation.

barley water: Mixture of boiled barley and ice water sweetened with brown sugar.

barley wine: Strong ale brewed from barley.

Barnevelder: Dual-purpose fowl producing large eggs and tender meat, originally raised in Barneveld, Holland.

bar noir: (French—black bass)

barolo: Fine red table wine originating in the Piedmont area of northern Italy.

baron of beef: Two sirloins and part of the ribs usually prepared as a roast.

barquette: (French—small boat) Oval-shaped tartlet shell.

barquillo: (Spanish—rolled wafer)

barracuda: Fierce fighting fish of the Caribbean which is sometimes eaten; the smaller and less voracious Pacific species has a tasty flesh often broiled, fried, smoked, or steamed.

bar rayé: (French—striped bass)

barsac: White wine from Bordeaux region in southwestern France.

bar spoon: Long-handled stirring spoon used when mixing drinks.

bar syrup: Simple syrup.

barszcz: (Polish—beet soup)

bartend: To prepare and serve alcoholic drinks.

bartender: Person tending bar in a barroom, cocktail lounge, restaurant, tavern, etc.

bartender's shaker: Two-compartment shaker used to keep ice

and liquid separate until ready for pouring.

Bartlett: Large, yellow, bell-shaped eating pear developed in France and England, named after American importer Enoch Bartlett.

basic foods: Foods such as fruits, milk, and most vegetables which leave an alkaline or base residue because they contain varying amounts of calcium, magnesium, potassium, and sodium.

basil: Aromatic herb of the mint family used in salads and to flavor eggs, fish, meats, soups, and sauces.

basil thyme: Name applied to basil balm and to field balm; the dried leaves are used in cooking and salad making.

basket-fired tea: Green tea grown chiefly in Japan; the name refers to the method of preparing the leaves for market.

basketware: Dining and kitchen accessories made of wicker—bread, fruit, and wine baskets, etc.

Bass: English ale bottled in London.

bass: Popular name applied to many different freshwater and saltwater fishes; Atlantic Ocean black bass and Pacific Ocean white bass are popular food fishes.

bastaple: Irish soda bread.

baste: To moisten fish, meat, or poultry with their own juices while they are being roasted.

basted eggs: Whole eggs fried on one side and basted with shortening until tops are set.

baster: Syringelike device for basting roasts by sucking up and expelling gravy or juice.

basting brush: Long bristle brush for basting roasts with gravy or other cooking juices.

batata: (Portuguese—potato; Spanish—sweet potato)

batch flour: Coarse flour.

bath bun: Round egg bun containing candied citrus peel originating around 1700 at the fashionable English spa of Bath.

bâton: (French—stick) Breadstick.

battelmatt: Emmenthaler type of cheese originating in northern Italy and Switzerland.

batter: Flour-and-liquid mixture used in making biscuits, cakes, and pancakes, and as coating for batter-fried foods.

batterbread: Spoonbread.

battercake: Flapjack.

batterie de cuisine: (French—kitchen battery) All the utensils needed in a kitchen down to the last pot and pan.

batter pudding: Baked unsweetened pudding made of cream, eggs, flour, and milk.

battery acid: Slang for coffee.

bauden: Austro-German sour-milk cheese.

Bauernbrot: (German—farmer's bread) Usually a dark bread.

bauple: Macadamia nut.

bavarian cream: Dessert made of flavored gelatin and whipped cream.

bavaroise: (French—Bavarian) Served with bavarian cream.

baya: Philippine rice wine.

baya: (Spanish—berry)

bay leaf: Aromatic leaf of a shrub of the laurel family used in seasoning.

b/b: Abbreviation for bottled in bond.

B-boy: Busboy or mess sergeant.

bbq (BBQ): Abbreviation for barbecue.

beaked parsley: Chervil.

beaker: Wide-mouthed goblet.

bean: Edible seed of various leguminous herbs of the bean family; broadbeans (string beans and wax beans) are eaten in the pod; shellbeans (kidney, lima, mung, etc.) are eaten shelled.

bean curd: Vegetable cheese popular in many Oriental countries.

beanery: Slang for a cheap or low-class restaurant.

bean flour: Flour made from dried beans.

beano: British slang for a cocktail party.

bean oil: Soybean oil.

bean pot: Covered crockery pot used for baking beans.

bean sprout: Sprout of a legume seed, such as soy or mung.

beat: To mix by stirring rapidly by hand or mechanically with a mixer at high speed.

beaten biscuit: Biscuit made with shortening, flour, salt, and sugar, and beaten with a mallet until thoroughly flat.

beater: Utensil operated manually or by electricity for beating, mixing, stirring, or whipping.

beaujolais: Red wine first produced near Beaujolais in the Burgundy region of France.

beb: Slang abbreviation for best ever bottled.

béchamel: (French) Basic white sauce made with milk, flour, butter, and meat stock; variations of this white sauce are named *mornay, sauce aurore, velouté.*

bêche-de-mer: (French—spade of the sea) Edible sea slug of the South Seas also known as trepang; this invertebrate is eaten by many Pacific Islanders as well as Orientals who prepare them in many ways.

Beck's: German beer brewed in Bremen.

beechnut: Sweet triangular fruit of the beech tree used to flavor confections.

beech oil: High-quality oil extracted from beechnuts.

beef: Meat of any adult bovine; in the United States beef usually means heifer or steer meat—invariably so if stamped: *U.S. Inspected and Passed;* bull, cow, and stag meat is inferior to meat from animals specially bred and raised for beef; U.S. Department of Agriculture grades beef in descending order of fatness and tenderness: prime, choice, good, standard, commercial, utility, cutter, and canner.

Beefaroni: Beef and macaroni served in tomato sauce.

beef bacon: Beef cured by soaking in brine or by smoking just as pig bacon is prepared.

beef bread: Pancreas of a cow or steer.

beefburger: Hamburger made of ground beefsteak.

beef cattle: Meat-producing breed such as Aberdeen-Angus, Hereford, black and white-faced Shorthorn; beef cattle are generally shorter and stockier than dairy breeds.

beef essence: Beef juice seasoned with salt, used in making beef stock.

beef extract: Beef-tea tonic made of beef juice and other soluble parts of beef meat; beef extract is used in many sauces and stews.

beef glaze: Concentrated beef stock boiled down to syrup consistency.

beef half: Carcass half bought for butchering and deep-freeze storage.

beef jerky: Beef cut into long strips and dried in the sun; sometimes beef jerky is prepared by seasoning and smoking; jerky is said to be corruption of the Indian word *charqui,* "smoked meat."

beef juice: Liquid produced by quickly boiling bits of raw beef and expressing the juice with a beef-juice press.

beef-juice press: Utensil for extracting beef juice from boiled beef.

beef marrow: Fatty filling of beef bones; in the British Isles and many parts of Europe marrow is spread on bread or used in baking and cooking.

beef ragout: Spicy beef stew.

beef roulade: Slice of meat rolled and sometimes stuffed before braising or sautéing.

beefsteak: Choice hindquarter cut of beef which is broiled or fried.

beefsteak mushroom: Large red variety of edible fungus whose beefsteak consistency is regarded by many as a delicacy.

beef stroganoff: Meat dish made with onions, mushrooms, and sour cream, and named for Count Stroganoff, a 19-century Russian diplomat.

beef tea: Beverage produced by boiling lean beef or by adding hot water to beef extract; beef tea is often served to children, invalids, and passengers recovering from seasickness.

beer: Alcoholic beverage produced from brewing fermented hops and malt; rice, spruce, ginger, sassafras, and other substances are also occasionally made into beer.

beer comb: Bone or plastic spatula for scooping foam off tops of beer glasses and mugs.

Beere: (German—berry)

beeregar: Beer vinegar.

Beeren Auslese: (German—berry selection) Vintage produced from specially selected grapes.

beer-pull: Dispensing-tap handle of a beer barrel.

beer yeast: Brewer's yeast.

beet: Succulent herb of the goosefoot family whose ruby-red root is used as a vegetable; beet leaves are often used in salads.

beet sugar: Sugar produced from the white roots of sugar beets.

beignet: (French—fritter)

beignets de fromage: (French—cheese fritters)

belgian hare: Small chestnut-colored breed of rabbits often served in rabbit ragouts and stews.

belgian loaf: Boat-shaped bread loaf with four or five cuts on the top and a very crusty bottom.

belgian pastry: Layered pastry.

bellelay: Soft rennet cheese, originating in the Abbey of Bellelay, Bern, Switzerland; it is also called monk's-head cheese.

bell pepper: Bell-shaped green pepper.

bel paese: (Italian—beautiful country) Creamy dessert cheese of mild flavor.

Beltsville small white: Small white turkey developed by the U.S. Department of Agriculture in its laboratory at Beltsville, Maryland.

beluga: White sturgeon fished from the Black and Caspian seas for its roe, which is used in making caviar.

ben cotto: (Italian—well done)

benedictine: Herb-flavored liqueur of syrupy consistency, originally distilled by Benedictine monks.

bengal gram: Chick-pea or indian gram.

benzoate of soda: Food preservative.

berenjena: (Spanish—eggplant)

bergamot: Any of several aromatic herbs of the mint family; bergamot also refers to a variety of pear and to a species of pear-shaped orange whose skin is used in making some perfumes.

bergamot mint: True mint of the genus *Mentha* noted for its faintly orange scent.

berinjela: (Portuguese—eggplant)

Berkshire: Medium-size white swine with black markings, originally developed in Berkshire, England.

Berliner Kuhkäse: (German—Berlin cow cheese) Soft hand cheese flavored with caraway seeds.

Berliner Pfannkuchen: (German—Berlin-style pancakes)

bermuda onion: Large sweet variety of onion.

berry: Small pulpy edible fruit such as the blackberry, blueberry, or dewberry; botanists define grapes and tomatoes as berries but exclude raspberries and strawberries.

berry basket: Cardboard, plastic, or shaved-wood container for berries, fruits, and vegetables; berry baskets come in half-pint, pint, and quart sizes.

berry spoon: Big-bowled spoon for serving berries, juicy fruits, and salads.

berry sugar: Finely granulated sugar.

beschuit: (Dutch—biscuit)

betterave: (French—beet)

between the sheets: Cocktail consisting of equal parts of brandy, curaçao, and rum; lime juice is sometimes added.

beurre: (French—butter)

beurre d'anchois: (French—anchovy butter)

beurre fondu: (French—melted butter)

beurre manié: (French—manipulated butter) Kneaded blend of butter and flour used in thickening sauces because it will not lump.

beurre noir: (French—black butter) Browned butter sauce seasoned with finely chopped parsley and wine vinegar.

beurre salé: (French—salt butter)

beverage: Liquid refreshment other than water: ale, beer, cider, coffee, fruit juice, liqueur, liquor, milk, tea, soft drink, vegetable juice, etc.

białystok roll: Round sourdough roll topped with thin slices of onion, first made in Polish province of Białystok.

b-i-b: Abbreviation for bottled in bond.

biborate of soda: Borax.

bicarb: Slang for bicarbonate of soda.

bicarbonate of soda: Baking soda.

biddies on a raft: Slang for poached eggs on toast.

biefstuk: (Dutch—beeksteak)

bien cuit: (French—well-cooked; well-done)

bier: (Dutch—beer)

Bier: (German—beer)

bière: (French—beer)

Bierstube: (German—tap room)

biffstek: (Swedish—beefsteak)

biftec: (Spanish—beefsteak)

biftec a la pobre: (Spanish—beefsteak of the poor) Beefsteak served with two fried eggs, onion rings, and fried potatoes —a Chilean specialty.

bifteck: (French—beefsteak)

bigarade: (French—Seville orange) Roast duck served with a sour-orange sauce.

bigarreau: (French—variegated kind of *cerise,* or cherry)

bigarreau cherry: Sweet, firm-fleshed cherry.

bigeye bass: California food fish of the perch family.

big-eyed herring: Alewife.

big-eyed mackerel: Chub mackerel.

big-necked clam: Gaper clam of the Pacific coast.

bilberry: Whortleberry.

bill of fare: Menu.

billot: (French—chopping block)

billy: Australian for a metal can with a lid, used chiefly for boiling water for tea.

billy goat: Slang for mutton.

biltong: (Afrikaans—beef jerky)

bind: To make a mixture hold together by adding cheese, cream, eggs, gelatin, etc.

birch beer: Carbonated soft drink flavored with oil of birch; old-fashioned birch beer was home-made from fermented birch ex-tracts and was mildly alcoholic.

bird-grape wine: Wine made from fermented juice of bird grapes found in the Bahamas and along the east coast of Florida and Georgia.

bird pepper: Most pungent of all capsicum peppers.

bird's-nest soup: Soup made from the mucilaginous lining of the nests of Asiatic swifts; a sea-soned gelatin is sometimes used to simulate the true basis of this soup.

birlie: British slang for a loaf of bread.

birne: (German—pear)

birra: (Italian—beer)

birthday cake: Cake baked in honor of someone's birthday, and often decorated with tiny candles and the person's name or the words "Happy Birthday."

biscotin: (French—sweet biscuit)

biscotto: (Italian—cooky)

biscuit: (French—cooky; medici-nal wafer)

biscuit: In the U.S., an unsweet-ened breadlike muffin, usually served hot; in England, a cooky.

biscuit cutter: Sharp-edged uten-sil for cutting biscuits or cookies from dough; many have decora-tive shapes such as a circle, crescent, or star.

biscuit tortoni: Frozen ice-cream dessert topped with macaroon crumbs.

biscuitware: Unglazed porcelain or pottery cups, mugs, plates, and platters.

bisky: British slang for biscuit.

bismarck: Mixture of champagne and stout popular with many Britons; the term is also used in the American Midwest to mean a jelly doughnut.

bismarck herring: Boned salt her-ring preserved in spices and wine vinegar, named in honor of the 19th-century statesman Prince Otto von Bismarck.

bisque: Thick creamy soup con-taining shellfish or meat; the term is also used for an ice-cream mixture such as a tor-toni containing grated nuts and crushed macaroons.

Bisquit: Better brand of cham-pagne cognac.

bistecca: (Italian—beefsteak)

bistik: (Malay—beefsteak)

bistro: Barroom, and lunchroom, or tavern.

bitochky: (Russian—meatballs; meatcakes)

bitok: Russian-style hamburgers made of ground meat, tiny bits of bread, and onions.

bitter chocolate: Unsweetened chocolate for cooking.

bitter cress: Winter cress.

bitter herbs: Horseradish eaten during Passover services by Jews to remind them of their slavery under the Egyptians be-fore their exodus from Egypt.

bitter melon: Warty East Indian cucumberlike vegetable, popu-lar with Chinese cooks who use it in soups and stews.

bitter orange: Species of orange resembling sweet orange but possessing a very bitter and acidy pulp; the essential oil of bitter orange is used in cooking and in making marmalade.

bitters: Aromatic or astringent liquids of high alcoholic content; used chiefly in cocktails.

bittersweet: Chocolate confection containing comparatively little sweetening; bittersweet chocolate is occasionally used in baking.

bivalve: Edible two-shelled mollusk such as the clam, mussel, oyster, or scallop.

bizcochos: (Spanish—biscuits) Hardtacks.

bizcochuelo: (Spanish—spongecake)

bkt: Abbreviation for basket.

blåbærsuppe: (Danish—bilberry soup)

black: Cup of coffee without cream.

black abalone: Small species of dark-shelled abalone found in Pacific Coast waters.

black-and-white: Chocolate soda with vanilla ice cream.

black apricot: Hybrid fruit tree with purplish foliage bearing dark-colored apricots.

black bass: Freshwater game fish found in many parts of eastern North America; Kentucky, large-mouthed, and small-mouthed species are favored by fishermen and fish eaters.

black bean soup: Soup made of black beans, celery, hard-boiled eggs, salt pork or bacon, and seasonings.

black beauty: Wisconsin cheddar cheese preserved in a cylindrical black wax coating.

blackberry: Any of several black or dark-purple edible berries from various prickly brambles comprising the genus *Rubus;* blackberries may be used in fruit desserts, in preserves, for

native wines, etc.; in England the blackberry is called the bramble.

blackberry cordial: Alcoholic beverage made from blackberries.

blackberry dumpling: Fruit dumpling filled with blackberries.

blackberry mousse: Mixture of blackberries, whipped cream, sugar, and egg whites.

blackberry pancakes: Pancakes whose batter is made with canned, fresh, or preserved blackberries.

blackberry shortcake: Shortcake covered with blackberries and blackberry juice.

blackberry wine: Beverage made from fermented blackberry juice.

black bread: Dark coarse bread made from barley, cornmeal, and rye flours; the term is often used to describe any dark-brown bread.

black caraway: European herb unrelated to the true caraway but used similarly in baking, cooking, and salad making; sometimes called black cumin.

black cod: North Pacific food fish not related to the true cod; it is also known as beshow or sablefish.

black crab: Edible land crab found in Florida and many of the West Indies.

black crappie: Calico bass.

black cumin: Black caraway.

black currant cordial: Alcoholic beverage made of black currants, brandy, and sugar.

black-eyed pea: Edible seed of either of two tropical leguminous vines; it is one of the most popular of all legumes because of its nourishing qualities.

blackfish: Any dark-colored fish such as the tautog found along the Atlantic Coast; blackfish is also the name of the pilot whale.

black grouper: Medium-sized grouper found along the Atlantic coast as far north as Massachusetts, an excellent food fish esteemed by many.

Black Horse: Canadian ale.

blackjack: Caramel coloring used in cake batter; licorice-flavored candy or chewing gum; whitefish taken in Michigan lakes.

black mustard: Species of mustard plant very similar to the white mustard; the leaves are used for pickling and cooking; the seeds are ground and made into condiments.

black pepper: Pepper.

black pudding: Sausage made of pig's blood, oatmeal, and suet.

black salmon: King salmon or any dark-colored salmon.

black sapote: Mexican variety of persimmon containing dark-fleshed, practically seedless fruit.

black sea bass: Common sea bass, an important food fish found along the Atlantic Coast.

black sloe: Wild plum used in flavoring sloe gin.

blackstrap: Dark-brown molasses or a molasses-and-rum drink; blackstrap is the final residue of sugar-cane processing and is used as an additive in cattle-feeds and as raw material for making industrial alcohol.

black stripe: Mixture of molasses and rum served with chopped ice and nutmeg.

black sugar: Licorice juice.

black-tailed shrimp: Shallow-water shrimp found from Alaska to California, caten in salads, stews, and many other dishes.

black tea: Fully fermented teas such as congou and orange pekoe.

black velvet: Cocktail concocted of champagne and stout in equal proportions.

black walnut: Edible nut of a native American timber tree; the nuts are used in flavoring ice creams and many confections.

blade rib roast: Roast of beef cut from upper ribs.

blade roast: Roast of beef cut from upper portion of chuck.

blade steak: Veal cut from the upper portion of the shoulder.

blanc: (French—white) Broth made of white meat, vegetables, flour, and water.

blanc de blanc: (French—white of white) Champagne made from white grapes.

blanc de chine: (French—chinese white) White porcelain dinnerware sometimes embossed slightly.

blanc d'oeuf: (French—egg white)

blanch: To remove skins of fruits, nuts, and vegetables by boiling from 1 to 5 minutes before draining and peeling; the term also means to precook briefly to remove pungency or to parboil.

blanchi: (French—blanched; parboiled)

blanc mange: (French—white food) Molded white pudding dessert made of flour and milk or milky gelatin.

bland: Buttermilk-and-water beverage originating in the Orkneys.

blanquette: French-style stew covered with white sauce: chicken blanquette, crab blanquette, etc.

blanquillo: Perchlike ocean food fishes such as whitefish and tilefish.

Blatz: American beer brewed in Milwaukee, Wisconsin.

blaze: To pour warmed brandy, rum, or whiskey over food and then set it afire just before serving.

bleach: To whiten by parboiling or scalding; the term also means to whiten celery by banking earth around the stalks so the sun will not turn them green.

blend: To combine and mix ingredients until they are smooth.

blended whiskey: Whiskey blended from straight bourbon and straight rye or from a straight whiskey and grain neutral spirits.

blender: Electrical device for blending foods and drinks, consisting of rapidly revolving blades set in the bottom of a mixing jar; blenders are used in preparing batters, dressings, frappés, purées, and any other dish that requires intensive mixing.

blintz: Fried pancake roll with cheese or fruit filling.

bliny: (Russian—buckwheat cake)

bliny s syrom: (Russian—cheese blintz)

bloater: Half-cured herring often served at English breakfasts.

blødkogt æg: (Danish—soft-boiled egg)

blomkål: (Swedish—cauliflower)

blomkål gratin: (Danish—cauliflower au gratin)

blood orange: Red-pulped sweet orange.

blood pudding: Sausage made of pig's blood and suet.

blood sausage: Sausage containing dried blood as a major ingredient.

bloody mary: Cocktail made of vodka, tomato juice, and seasoning.

b-l-t: Slang abbreviation for bacon, lettuce, and tomato sandwich.

blueberry: Small blue berry found on certain shrubs; blueberries are served as a fruit course or made into pies or tarts or in making country wine.

blue blazer: Hot drink made of boiling water, honey, rock candy, and whiskey.

blue cheese: Blue-veined cheese similar to that produced in Roquefort, France.

blue crab: Common American crab taken in coastal waters from Delaware to Texas, called soft-shelled crab when found molting.

blue dorset: Aged white cheese originating in Dorsetshire, England, and also known as blue vinny.

bluefish: Atlantic food fish also known as skipjack or skip mackerel because it sometimes leaps above the surface of the sea.

blue gage: Blue plum.

bluegill: Bluegill bream or bluegill sunfish, a popular freshwater pan fish in much of the United States.

blue john: Bluish-tinged milk low in butterfat, or milk starting to sour.

blue lake: Stringless string bean.

blue-mountain tea: Goldenrod from which a medicinal tea is sometimes brewed.

blue plate: Compartmented plate for serving a meat course with side orders of sauces and vegetables all on the same dish; the original blue plate had a blue design, but today such plates appear in other colors.

blue point: Small oyster dredged from the south shore of Long Island.

blue vinny: Blue dorset.

Blumenkohl: (German—cauliflower)

blushing bunny: Slang for welsh rabbit colored with tomato soup.

Blutwurst: (German—blood sausage)

boar: Male peccary, pig, razorback, or other swine.

boat: receptacle for holding gravy, melted butter, or seasoned sauce.

boca chica: (Spanish—small mouth) Petite sandwich and other light snack.

bock beer: Heavy-bodied beer brewed in the spring, usually advertised with a picture of an old goat atop a beer barrel.

Bockwurst: (German—buck sausage) Heavy-bodied frankfurter.

bodega: (Spanish—grocery store; warehouse, wine cellar)

boels: Mild Danish cheese.

boereworst: (Dutch—farmer sausage)

boeuf: (French—beef)

boeuf à la flamande: (French—beef in Flemish style)

boeuf à la mode en gelée: (French—cold braised beef in aspic)

boeuf bourguignon: (French—beef in the Burgundian manner)

boeuf braisé: (French—braised beef)

boeuf épicé: (French—spiced beef)

boeuf fumé: (French—smoked beef)

boeuf rôti: (French—roast beef)

boeuf salé: (French—corned beef)

bøf: (Danish—beefsteak)

bøf tatar: (Danish—tartar steak) Raw scraped beef mixed with capers and raw egg yolk.

bogavante: (Spanish—large-clawed lobster)

bogberry: Dwarf American raspberry or small European cranberry.

bog bilberry: Scandinavian berry used in cooking.

Bohne: (German—bean)

boil: To cook in hot water of 100 degrees centigrade or 212 degrees Fahrenheit.

boiled coffee: Coffee made by pouring boiling water over coarse-ground coffee in a scalded pot and allowing mixture to simmer until desired strength is reached; egg shells are sometimes tossed in to clarify the brew.

boiled dinner: Meal consisting of corned beef, other meat, or fowl boiled with vegetables; boiled dinners are popular in New England, Pennsylvania, and such places as the British Isles.

boiled peanuts: Green peanuts boiled in their shells in salt water seasoned with tabasco sauce and black pepper, a favorite dish in some parts of the South where they are eaten while hot and moist.

boiler: Kitchen utensil for boiling food or water; boiler also means a chicken one year old or older whose flesh must be made tender by boiling.

boilermaker: Glass of fortified wine followed by a bottle of beer—powerful intoxicant combination.

boiling point: Temperature at which water boils, 212 degrees Fahrenheit or 100 degrees centigrade.

boisson: (French—beverage; drink)

bok choy: (Chinese—chinese cabbage)

bokser: (Hebrew—St. John's bread) Carob seed pods.

bolacha: (Portuguese—sea biscuit)

bolillo: (Spanish—bobbin) Hard roll.

bolita: (Spanish—small ball) Fritter.

bollito: (Italian—boiled)

bologna: Baloney.

bombay duck: Bummalo, an Asiatic lizard fish in India, often dried and curried and served as a relish.

bombay gelatin: Agar.

bombe: (French—bombshell) Molded ice cream, custard, or sherbet, called bombshell because of the bulging shape of the mold.

bombe glacé: (French—iced bombshell) Frozen dessert containing two or more mixtures served from a *bombe-* or cone-shaped mold.

bombe **mold:** Utensil for shaping a *bombe.*

bon appetit: (French—good appetite)

bonbon: (French—candy; sweetmeat)

bonbonnière: (French—candy box or dish)

bonbon **spoon:** Spoon for serving *bonbons,* candies, and nuts.

bonded: Kept in bonded warehouses under government supervision, said of whiskey, especially 100-proof whiskey at least four years of age.

bone: To remove the bones from fish, meat, or fowl.

bone china: Translucent white chinaware made in England from a formula including white bone ash.

bone glass: Milk-white glassware (cups and dishes as well as glasses) made from a formula including white bone ash.

boneless: Served without bones, said of fish, flesh, or fowl.

boneless neck: Beef cut from upper corner of chuck where body meets the neck and hence is muscular rather than bony.

bonensoep: (Dutch—bean soup)

bone porcelain: Bone china.

bon femme: (French—good woman; good wife) Cooked in a casserole, usually applied to fowl.

bon goût: (French—good taste) Menu term indicating something is properly seasoned.

boning knife: Short narrow-bladed knife used for removing bones from fish, poultry, and meat.

bonito: (Spanish—pretty) Tunny fish or tuna.

bonnekamp: Belgian bitters.

bonnet pepper: Tropical American capsicum pepper plant cultivated as a source for paprika and pimiento.

bonnyclabber: Thick sour milk in which whey has not separated from the curd, used in baking and as a beverage.

bon vivant: Person who enjoys eating and drinking, especially on festive occasions.

boova shenkel: (Pennsylvania-German—boys' legs) Filled dumplings or hollow noodles well stuffed.

booyaw: Meat and vegetable stew favored by Michiganites and others—cubed chicken or pork with chopped vegetables and some seasoning.

booze: Slang for hard liquor—brandy, gin, rum, whiskey, etc.

bor: (Hungarian—wine)

borage: Hairy-leafed herb similar to spinach greens.

borax: Sodium tetraborate, used as a cleaning agent and water softener.

bordeaux: Red or white wines first produced around Bordeaux in southwestern France; bordeaux, like burgundy, is not the name of a wine but of a family of wines, including clarets, sauternes, graves, barsacs, etc.

bordeaux red: Claret wine.

bordelais: (French—in the manner of Bordeaux)

bordure: (French—border) Edging of rice or mashed potatoes around an entrée dish.

borecole: Kale.

börek: (Turkish—pastry) Thin dough filled with white cheese, egg, and parsley.

borscht: (Russian—cabbage and beet soup) made of red beets and/or cabbage, onions, parsnips, and potatoes; usually colored with red beet juice and served with thick sour cream.

Bosc: Taper-necked yellow-russet pear.

Bosco: Brand name for a vitaminized chocolate-flavored syrup.

boston baked beans: Baked beans.

boston brown bread: Steam-cooked hotbread made with buttermilk, cornmeal, rye and wheat flour, molasses, and some raisins, usually served with baked beans.

boston butt: Upper portion of lean shoulder of pork.

boston cracker: Thick hard round unsalted cracker served with chowders, seafood dishes, and shore dinners.

boston cream pie: Two-layer cake filled with thick cream or custard and topped with chocolate icing.

boston strawberries: Slang for baked beans.

boter: (Dutch—butter)

bottled gas: Butane or natural gas compressed into steel tanks for use in cooking where gas lines are not installed.

bottled-gas stove: Any range adapted to use butane or other bottled gas.

bottled in bond: Aged in a bonded warehouse for at least four years; said of whiskey usually 100 proof.

bottle opener: Utensil for prying force-fit metal tops from bottles.

bottle party: Entertainment where guests bring their own alcoholic refreshments.

bottle rack: Metal or wooden storage rack for holding bottles of wine at the correct angle.

bottoms: Dregs or lees resulting from sedimentation of bottled wines.

botulism: Food poisoning due to botulin spores present in spoiled food.

bouchée: (French—a mouthful) Small puff pastry filled with various foods.

boudanne: Cow's-milk cheese of type originally imported from France.

boudin: (French—pudding)

bouillabaisse à la marseillaise: (French—fish soup in the style of Marseilles). Fish soup made with various fishes, seafoods, spices, vegetables, and white wine.

bouilli: (French—boiled; braised; stewed)

bouillir: (French—to boil)

bouillon: Clear soup made by boiling beef or other meat in water.

bouillon cubes: Tiny cubes containing salt plus compressed essence of beef, chicken, or fish; immersed in hot water, they turn into bouillon.

boulanger: (French—baker)

boulangerie: (French—bakery)

boulette: (French—small ball) Small meatball dipped in egg-and-bread-crumb mixture and fried.

bouquet: Aroma of a wine; the bouquet of the very best wines is without trace of decay, mold, or vinegar.

bouquet garni: (French—nosegay trimming). Cheesecloth bag containing herbs used in garnishing braised dishes, sauces, soups, and stews; the herbs are tied in a bag while being cooked with a main dish and later removed.

bourbon: Whiskey of a type originating in Bourbon County, Kentucky; modern bourbon is distilled from a fermented mash chiefly of corn.

Bourbon Red: Medium-size reddish-brown type of domestic turkey, originating in Kentucky.

boureka: (Spanish-Ladino—blintz

or knish) Pastry of paper-thin dough filled with three kinds of cheese, or sometimes with meat or spinach, and baked.

bourgueil: Tart red wine originating near town of Bourgueil in east central France.

bourguignonne: (French—Burgundian)

bourlghour: (Armenian—cracked wheat)

bourlghourlama: (Armenian) Stew made of lamb, cracked wheat, and several vegetables.

bovine extract: Slang for milk.

Bovril: Brand name for a beef essence used in making beef tea, gravy, and soup.

bowieware: Scots woodenware such as bowls, breadboards, buckets, plates.

boxberry: Wintergreen.

box lunch: Picnic-style lunch served usually in a cardboard or plastic box, often consisting of a sandwich, a piece of fried chicken, some crackers, and a piece of fruit.

boysenberry: Hybrid berry resembling a giant raspberry, named for 20th-century botanist Rudolph Boysen who developed it.

b/p: Abbreviation for baking powder.

braaivleis: (Afrikaans—meat roasted on a spit) South African barbecue.

brabançonne: (French—Brabant style)

brace: Pair of game animals or birds such as a brace of squirrels or a brace of ducks.

bra cheese: Creamy soft cheese of mild-flavored type developed in Italian town of Bra near Austrian border.

brachetto: Italian-type of red table wine originating in Piedmont area.

braciuola: (Italian—chop) *braciuola alla Milanese:* (Italian —Milan-style chop) Veal chop.

bragget: Spiced and honeyed ale.

Brahma: Large domestic poultry of Asiatic origin, characterized by pea combs and feathered legs.

brains: Delicacies prepared from the brains of calves, other beef cattle, pigs, and sheep; brains require careful preparation and must be very fresh.

braise: To brown or to cook by first searing and then simmering in a small amount of liquid.

braiser: Dutch-oven type of cooking pot fitted with a tight cover and used for braising.

bramble: Blackberry.

brambleberry: English term for blackberry.

bramble jelly: Blackberry jelly.

bramborovénudle: (Czech—potato noodles)

bran: Seed coat of a cereal such as rye or wheat.

brander: To broil on a brander, a Scots grill.

brandied: Candy, dessert, preserves, or other food flavored or doused with brandy.

brandied fruits: Apricots, dates, figs, and pears preserved in brandy-flavored syrup.

Brandkäse: (German—brand cheese) Sour-milk curd cheese flavored with beer.

brandy: Spirits distilled from wine; the finest brandies are believed to be those produced in the Armagnac and Cognac regions of France.

brandy butter: Hard sauce flavored with brandy.

brandy-glass warmer: Wire cradle shaped to support an uptilted brandy glass above an alcohol lamp or candle whose flame is enough to warm the glass just before use.

brandy inhalers: Brandy glasses holding 4 to 12 ounces or more; large-size inhalers are often used as flower vases.

branja de brailia: Romanian-style cheese similar to Greek teleme.

bran muffin: Muffin made with bran, flour, eggs, molasses, and raisins.

Branntwein: (German—brandy)

brans: Slang for bran muffins.

brasenose ale: Punch made of heated ale and powdered sugar with roasted apples floating in it, named for Brasenose College, Oxford, where it was drunk on Shrove Tuesdays.

Brassica: Genus of the cabbage group which includes broccoli, brussels sprouts, cabbages, cauliflowers, radishes, and turnips.

Bratapfel: (German—baked apple)

braten: (German—to roast)

Brathuhn: (German—roast chicken)

Bratkartoffel: (German—fried potato)

Bratwurst: (German—fried sausage) Mild-flavored frying sausage sold in links and kept cold until cooked.

Braunschweiger: (German— Brunswick style) Smoked liver sausage of a type first made in Braunschweig (Brunswick), Germany.

brawn: Pork headcheese made of feet, heads, and legs.

brazier: Pan for holding burning coals, over which open-flame cooking is done; there are many types, including a tripod-supported metal bowl fitted with cast-iron or wire grill, the Japanese hibachi, and others; some braziers have spits for turning meat above the coals; others have a barbecue oven over the turning spit.

Brazilian tea: Maté from southern Brazil near border of Uruguay.

brazil nut: Brown-shelled wedge-shaped creamy-white nut from the brazil-nut tree; it is also called the pará nut, as many are imported from the Brazilian state of Pará.

brazil water: Slang for coffee.

bread: Food made of flour, a leavening agent such as baking soda or yeast, and some milk or water; breads are made of many kinds of flour and are baked in many shapes.

bread: To cover with bread crumbs.

bread-and-butter pickles: Spiced relish made of thinly sliced cucumbers and onions.

bread-and-butter plate: Small plate used for serving bread and butter.

breadbasket: Woven basket for carrying and serving bread; breadbasket is also a slang term for stomach.

breadboard: Wooden board for cutting bread, making sandwiches, slicing rolls, and so forth.

breadbox: Ventilated box made of metal, plastic, or wood and used for storing bread, rolls, cake, and the like.

bread crumbs: Crumbs of bread, crackers, and rolls used in many recipes, particularly for coating foods to be fried.

bread flour: Flour high in gluten so it rises well; true bread flour is not easily available to retail shoppers in the U.S.

bread knife: Long-bladed knife with scalloped or serrated edge used for slicing bread or rolls, cutting cake, etc.

breadmaker: Electrically-operated utensil of stainless steel, consisting of a beater and a bowl and used for mixing dough for bread, pastry, rolls, and so forth; it is available in home-kitchen and big-bakery models.

bread pudding: Pudding made of leftover bread, eggs, milk, sugar, and flavoring.

breadsauce: Butter-and-milk sauce thickened with plain or toasted bread crumbs.

bread stick: Long crisp stick-shaped roll served with soups or appetizers.

bread tray: Ceramic, glass, or metal dish for serving bread, cake, rolls, or muffins.

breakfast: Morning meal so named because it breaks the fast imposed by sleeping.

breakfast cereal: Cooked or prepared cereal such as oatmeal, cornflakes, puffed rice, shredded wheat, and similar food.

breakfast cheese: Small round spreadable cheese with a pungent flavor; popular in Germany.

breakfast food: Breakfast cereal.

breakfast knife: Medium-size spreading knife.

breakfast plate: Medium-size plate used for serving breakfast.

breast: Tender white chest meat of chicken, duck, or other fowl; or the breast meat of beef, lamb, pork, and so forth.

breast of lamb: Cut of lamb served braised or stewed.

Brennevin 60 percent: Probably most potent of all alcoholic drinks as this aquavit contains 60 percent of alcohol by volume.

Brennsuppe: (German—burned soup) Brown soup characteristic of Austrian cooking.

Bretonne: (French—Breton)

Bretzel: (German—pretzel)

brew: Ale, beer, or beerlike beverage.

brew: To prepare a beerlike beverage from hops and malt or other fermentables.

brewer's yeast: Yeast suitable for brewing ale and beer; this by-product of beer brewing is often eaten as a food because of its high protein and vitamin B content.

brickbat: Rennet cheese of type developed in England during the 1700's.

brick cheese: Cheese shaped like a brick, like the many American cheeses which are marketed in this form; some cheeses are weighted with bricks while ripening and are also called brick cheeses.

brick ice cream: Commercially packaged ice cream sold in brick form.

brick sugar: Brick-shaped lumps of sugar.

brie: Creamy cheese of much pungency; first made in the old province of Brie east of Paris.

Brillat-Savarin, Jean Anthelme (1755–1826): Famous French gastronome, author of *La Physiologie du goût*, "The Physiology of Taste"; his name is applied to a method of preparing small pieces of lamb and mutton.

brindza: Hungarian-style rennet cheese made from goat's milk and sheep's milk, popular throughout Hungary and the Balkans.

brine: Water solution supersaturated with salt used in pickling and preserving perishables.

brinjaul: Anglo-Indian name for eggplant.

Brinsen: (German—brindza cheese)

brioche: (French—blunder; mistake) Light roll of yeast dough rich in butter and eggs, often made in the shape of a large ball with a smaller one topping it.

brisket: Lower chest or breast of an edible animal, usually sold boned; briskets are prepared in many ways.

brisling: Norwegian herringlike fish often canned like sardines.

britannia: Alloy of antimony, copper, and tin used in making many kitchen utensils.

britanniaware: Utensils made from britannia metal.

brittle: Crisp nut-filled candy such as almond brittle, peanut brittle, etc.

broad bean: String bean and wax bean, both eaten in their shells; the term also applies to fava or horse beans although they are shell beans.

broadbill: Edible swordfish.

broasted: California slang for broiled and roasted, foods first broiled and then roasted.

broccio: (Italian—twiggy) Corsican cheese made from sour sheep's or goat's milk.

broccoli: Variety of cauliflower perfected to yield tender sprouts.

broccoli rab: Cabbage plant grown for its tender shoots, also called flowering turnip, italian turnip, and turnip broccoli although it is neither a turnip nor a true broccoli.

brochan: Scots porridge.

brochette: (French—skewer) Utensil used for broiling chunks of beef, lamb, or veal *en brochette.*

brocsea casserole: Casserole containing broccoli and seafood.

brød: (Danish and Norwegian—bread)

bröd: (Swedish—bread)

Brödchen: (German—small loaf)

brodo: (Italian—broth; consommé)

broil: To cook by direct heat over live coals or under electric coils or gas flames.

broiler: Young chicken, 2½ pounds or less, tender enough to be broiled; the term is also used for that part of a range especially made for open-flame cooking.

bronx: Cocktail made of gin, dry or sweet vermouth, and orange juice.

brood: (Dutch—bread)

broodkaas: (Dutch—bread cheese) Hard flat nutty cheese.

brook trout: Favored fresh-water food and game fish, also known as speckled trout.

Brot: (German—bread)

Brötchen: (German—roll)

broth: Liquid wherein any food is boiled or steamed; broth is used in making sauces, soups, and gravies.

brouillé: (French—mingled; mixed)

brown: To seal in the juices of fish or meat by scorching or searing the surface; or to finish off (usually a roast) by letting its outer surface cook to an even brownish color.

brown betty: Baked dessert made by layering buttered crumbs, apples, spices, and sugar; if cranberries are substituted for apples, it is called cranberry betty, and so on.

brown bread: Dark-colored bread; *see* black bread and boston brown bread.

brown gravy: Gravy wherein flour and drippings are browned before liquid is added.

brownie: Heavy, moist chocolate cake containing chopped nuts and served in small rectangles; in Australia the term refers to bread made of currants and brown sugar or molasses.

brown mustard: Black or indian mustard, darker colored than white mustard.

brown rice: Unpolished rice retaining some of the bran layer.

brown sauce: Flour sauce containing browned fats or gravies, sometimes called sauce espagnole.

brown stock: Beef stock.

brown sugar: Half-refined sugar whose crystals are covered with a moist brown syrup.

brown trout: Freshwater fish native to Europe but introduced to American streams; the name is also applied to the smallmouth black bass.

bruingebrande suiker: (Dutch— burned sugar; caramel)

brunch: Breakfast + lunch—late morning meal.

bruncheon: Breakfast + luncheon.

brunkaalssuppe: (Danish—green cabbage soup)

brunswick stew: Meat and vegetable stew; or a stew made of game meat, chicken, okra, and tomatoes—a hunter's stew.

brush: To coat thinly with butter, oil, or egg.

brussels biscuit: Belgian-type zwieback.

brussels cheese: Skimmed-milk cheese of soft fermented type originating in Brussels, Belgium.

brussels sprout: Tiny cabbage heads growing on the stem of the brussels sprout plant related to the true cabbage.

Bruststück: (German—breast piece) Brisket.

brut: (French—dry, crude, raw) Tart or very dry champagne or wine.

bruxelles: Brussels cheese.

bruxelloise: (French—Brussels style)

bu: Abbreviation for bushel.

bubble gum: Children's chewing gum so formulated that it can be blown into big bubbles.

buccan: Caribbean word for a rack for roasting, smoking, and drying meat, also the meat itself; buccan supplied local pirates as a sea ration and earned them the name "buccaneers."

buck: Male antelope, deer, hare, goat, or rabbit.

buckling: Austrian smoked herring.

buckwheat: European herb related to docks and sorrels and not a true wheat; its triangular seed is ground into flour or boiled whole.

buckwheat cake: Pancake made of buckwheat flour.

buckwheat groats: Whole or ground roasted buckwheat used in casseroles, cereals, pancakes, soups, stuffings, and many kosher-style dishes.

buckwheat honey: Dark honey made from buckwheat.

budding: (Danish—pudding)

budín: (Spanish—pudding)

budino: (Italian—pudding)

Budweiser: American beer brewed in St. Louis, Missouri.

buffalo fish: Large coarse food fish of the sucker family, found in the Mississippi Valley.

buffet: Term with a number of meanings: refreshment or sandwich counter; sideboard; counter and shelf arrangement for storing and serving food; type of meal where guests serve themselves from dishes prepared and set out on counters or tables.

buffet-galley: Compact compartment aboard an airplane or a place where beverages and foods are prepared before serving.

buffware: Buff- or tan-colored earthenware often designed for table service.

buisson: (French—bush) Mound-shaped pyramid of food, particularly crayfish or lobster, which is said to be served *en buisson*.

buko: Ham-, lobster-, mushroom-, and shrimp-flavored Danish cheese.

bulgarian milk: Fermented milk such as yogurt.

buljong: (Swedish—broth; consommé)

bull: Male cattle, elk, or moose.

bullace: Wild plum related to the damson.

bullace gin: Gin flavored with bullace instead of the usual juniper berries.

bull cook: Lumber-camp term for the man assigned to hauling water, cutting firewood, cleaning quarters, and performing other camp-keeping chores.

bullhead: Large-headed catfish; an important fresh-water food fish.

bullock: Castrated bull, steer, or young bull.

bull's-eye: Candy striped brown, black and white and flavored with peppermint.

bull's eye: Highball of hard cider and brandy.

bully beef: English slang for canned beef; the term is thought to be a corruption of *boeuf bouilli* (French—boiled beef).

bumbu: (Malay—spice)

bun: Any small, raised, sweet cake or roll, usually spiced and glazed, such as a butter bun, a cinnamon bun, a hot-cross bun.

Bündnerfleisch: (German—meat prepared in the style of Graubünden) Swiss-style air-dried meat sliced paper thin.

bung: Cork or wooden stopper fitted into the bunghole of a barrel or cask.

bunny: Pet name for a baby rabbit or a bar girl attired to resemble one; also a nickname for welsh rabbit.

buntop: Frankfurter or hotdog on a roll.

buñuelo: (Spanish—fritter)

buñuelos de espinaca: (Spanish—spinach fritters) Uruguayan specialty.

bun warmer: Metallic vessel with tight-fitting cover for keeping buns and muffins warm while they are being served.

buon' appetito: (Italian—good appetite)

Burbank: Name of many varieties of fruits and vegetables developed in California by the turn-of-the-century horticulturist Luther Burbank.

burette: Oil-and-vinegar cruet.

burger: Slang for hamburger.

Burgie: Burgermeister beer, a brand name for an American beer.

burgoo: Kentucky stew of meat and vegetables; also an oatmeal porridge served to sailors.

burgundy: Red or white table wines of a type originating in Burgundian region of France: chablis, pommard, savigny, etc.; burgundy can also mean a large thin-skinned pink-fleshed grapefruit.

burgundy cheese: French-style soft white cheese of a type originating in Burgundy.

burnet: Cucumber-flavored leaves plucked from a small shrub of the rose family for use in salads, sauces, and soups.

burnt almond: Roasted almond.

burro: (Italian—butter; Spanish —jackass)

busboy: Waiter's assistant.

Busch: Bavarian-type beer brewed in St. Louis, Missouri.

busgirl: Waitress' assistant.

bushel: Dry measure containing 4 pecks or 32 quarts.

butcher knife: Medium-length knife, heavy-bladed for heavy duty, used for chopping and cutting.

butler's pantry: Serving pantry between dining room and kitchen; *see also* pantry.

butler's tray: Serving tray made to be rested on cross-legged tray stand for waiter's convenience in serving a meal.

butt: Ham shoulder or the thick end of a ham.

butter: Emulsified food made from churned cream, usually salted and lightly colored.

Butter: (German—butter)

butter-and-honey cream: Mixture of equal parts of butter and honey.

butterbean: Baby lima bean; the term is also applied loosely to shell beans and snap beans.

butterboat: Small gravy boat used for serving melted butter.

butter brown: Slang for buttered toast.

buttercake: Layer cake made from recipe rich in butter.

butter chip: Tiny dish for holding a pat of butter.

butter clam: Finely flavored Pacific Coast clam.

butter cream: Cake filling or fondant made by creaming butter and powdered sugar.

buttercup squash: Turban (winter) squash with a sweet-potato flavor.

butterdish: Small covered dish for serving butter, usually in the shape of a quarter-pound stick of butter.

butterfat: Fat content in dairy products such as cheese, milk, and ice cream.

butterfish: Small circular food fish of the harvestfish family found along the Atlantic Coast.

butterhead: Small, close-leafed variety of lettuce.

butterie: Scots butter biscuit or roll.

butterine: Artificial butter such as margarine.

butter knife: Dull, broad-bladed knife for cutting, serving, and spreading butter.

buttermilk: Thick milky liquid left after butter has been churned out.

buttermilk biscuits: Baking-powder biscuits made with buttermilk instead of sweet milk.

butternut: American tree of the walnut family.

butter pat: Ball or small rectangle of butter, often embossed with a design.

Butterreis: (German—buttered rice)

butter sauce: Flour-and-water sauce enriched with broth, seasoning, and butter.

butterscotch: Candy consisting of boiled brown sugar, butter, and corn syrup; butterscotch is also used as a flavoring extract in puddings, cakes, and other desserts.

butter spreader: Butter knife.

buttery: Pantry for serving beverages and sandwiches or a storeroom for beverages and food.

button onion: Small pickled onion.

buzzard: Military slang for chicken or turkey.

byob: Slang abbreviation for bring your own beer.

Byrrh: Brand of French apéritif flavored with bitter herbs and fortified with brandy.

byscute: Top-quality bran.

byzantine sauce: Sauce containing bitter almonds plus a dash of rose honey and candied rose petals.

c: Abbreviation for cup.

C: Celsius or centigrade, temperature scale on which water freezes at 0 degrees and boils at 100, named Celsius in honor of Anders Celsius, 18th-century Swedish astronomer, who devised the centigrade scale.

caballa: (Spanish—mackerel)

cabaret: If pronounced *cab-are-ray:* a restaurant serving liquor and featuring nightclub entertainment; if pronounced *cab-are-ett:* a serving table or tray complete with coffee or tea service.

cabbage: Leafy vegetable of mustard family with green or reddish-purple leaves on a short stem; cabbage is usually shredded, quartered, and used in soups and salads or served with meats.

cabbagehead: Compact head or edible portion of this vegetable.

cabbage lettuce: Cabbage-shaped head lettuce.

cabbage palm: A palm with edible buds which are used in salads or cooked as vegetables.

cabernet: Red wine grape grown chiefly in Bordeaux region but also produced in California.

cabillaud: (French—codfish)

cabinet cherry: Black cherry.

cabinet pudding: Egg-and-cake pudding made in a mold and served hot with a sauce; sometimes cabinet pudding is made with cookies or bread instead of cake.

cabinet wine: Any top-quality Rhine wine good enough for the vintner's own cabinet or private stock.

cabob: Shish kebab.

cabrales: Spanish-type goat's-milk cheese.

cabrito: (Portuguese and Spanish —kid)

cabs: Slang for cabbages.

cacao: (French and Spanish— cocoa)

cacao: South American tree yielding a bean from which chocolate is derived.

cacao butter: Cocoa butter.

cacau: (Portuguese—cocoa)

cacciatore: (Italian—hunter)

cachaça: Crude Brazilian rum.

cachar tea: Any of several Indian teas, named for the Cachar district of Assam, India.

cachou: (French—cateclin) Term for a perfumed bonbon, violet-scented or coated with licorice, used to sweeten the breath.

caciocavallo: (Italian—horse cheese) Rennet cheese made from cow's milk; the cheeses are dried in pairs, one on each side of a pole, like a rider astride a horse.

cactus: Plant of the genus *Cactus,* famous for its ability to survive in the desert; cacti are stripped of their spines and eaten pickled, preserved, or raw.

cactus candy: Confection containing prickly-pear leaves with the skin and spines removed.

cactus salad: Prickly-pear leaves peeled of their needles and green skin and served as a salad.

caddy: Small container for holding cookies, crackers, or tea leaves.

cadelinha: (Portuguese—clam)

cadger: Hard British biscuit.

'cado: Slang contraction for avocado.

caerphilly: Hard rennet cheese originating in Caerphilly, Wales.

caesar salad: Salad of romaine lettuce, olive oil, raw egg, grated cheese, bread croutons, and seasonings.

caf: Slang for café, cafeteria or caffeine.

café (French and Spanish—coffee) Small restaurant where coffee and light refreshments are served.

café au kirsch: (French—coffee with *Kirschwasser*) Coffee drink made with egg whites, *Kirschwasser,* sugar, and cracked ice.

café au lait: (French—coffee with milk) Hot coffee and hot milk poured simultaneously; in Louisiana and in many parts of France, some chicory is added for flavor.

café brûlot: (French—firebrand coffee) Black coffee served with flaming brandy or cognac; *café brûlot* is often seasoned with cinnamon, cloves, or lemon peel and may be sweetened with brown sugar, and topped with whipped cream.

café car: Railroad car containing beverage and sandwich bar.

café chantant: (French—singing restaurant) Nightclub.

café com leite: (Portuguese—coffee with milk) Hot coffee with hot milk poured at the same time.

café complet: (French—perfect coffee) Term for a continental breakfast—coffee with hot milk, rolls, butter, and jam.

café con leche: (Spanish—coffee with milk) Beverages usually prepared by pouring hot black coffee and hot milk into the cup at the same time.

café crème: (French—coffee with cream)

café doublé: (French—double coffee) Double-strength coffee.

café frappé: (French—iced coffee)

café liégeois: (French—coffee in the manner of Liége) Ice cream dessert flavored with coffee.

café listo: (Spanish—ready coffee) Latin American instant coffee produced from some of the world's best grown in the highlands of El Salvador.

café noir: (French—black coffee) Coffee served without milk or cream.

café royale: (French—royal coffee) Black coffee and cognac with sugar.

café salvador: (Spanish—Salvador [Saviour] coffee) Espresso-type instant coffee produced in El Salvador.

cafetal: (Spanish—coffee plantation)

cafeteria: Self-service restaurant.

cafetorium: (Cafeteria + auditorium—combination popular in industrial plants and military establishments.

café turc: (French—Turkish coffee)

café vierge: (French—virgin coffee) Coffee made with whole-roasted coffee beans instead of grounds or powder.

cafèzinho: Brazilian-style extra-strong coffee.

caffè: (Italian—coffee)

caffè espresso: (Italian—expressed coffee) Dark beverage expressed from pulverized coffee subjected to live steam.

caffè freddo: (Italian—chilled coffee)

caffelatte: (Italian—milk coffee) Hot coffee and hot milk poured simultaneously.

caguama: (Spanish—sea turtle)

CAI: Abbreviation for Culinary Arts Institute.

cajú: (Portuguese—cashew)

cake: Typically American dessert made by combining three basic sets of ingredients—rich (eggs, butter, sugar, flavorings), dry (flour, baking powder or soda, salt), and wet (milk, sour milk, or water).

cakebox: Breadbox.

cakebread: Bread of sweetened, cakelike quality bread baked in the shape of cakes.

cake cooler: Wire rack for holding freshly baked cakes, cookies, tarts, etc., to cool them before frosting.

cake cover: Cake-shaped cover of metal or plastic, used to protect a cake and keep it fresh.

cake decorator: Device for extruding icing in various shapes and designs, used in decorating a special-occasion cake.

cake flour: Soft-wheat flour used in making cakes, waffles, and other baked goods that require a light, fine texture.

cake mix: Packaged dessert mix usually requiring only the addition of eggs and liquids.

cake pan: Pan for baking cake, usually of aluminum or coated sheet metal; some pans are provided with spring-form sides and removable bottoms; most are circular, loaf, oblong, or rectangular, but many fancy-shaped pans are also available.

cake spice: Prepared blend of spices for mincemeat, pies, fruit cakes, spice cakes.

cal: Abbreviation for calorie.

cala: Picnic ham—short for "California ham."

calamansi: Philippine citrus fruit tasting somewhat like a sweetened lemon or lime.

calamar: (Spanish—cuttlefish or squid)

calamar en su tinta: (Spanish—squid in its own ink) Squid served in its own dark-purple ink, usually on a mound of rice.

calamaro: (Italian—cuttlefish or squid)

calamus: Sweet flag and its aromatic root.

calas: Fritter-like creole confection of eggs, flour, rice, sugar, and yeast, served very hot with a sprinkling of finely powdered sugar; calas are sold by street vendors in the coastal parishes of Louisiana.

calavo: Brand name for an avocado cultivated in California, the mainstay of many salads and seafood combinations.

caldo: (Italian—hot or warm; Portuguese and Spanish—soup) Soup usually featuring potato and leek stock plus bits of boiled beef, chick peas and seasoning.

caldo asturiano: (Spanish—Asturian-style soup)

caldo de congrio: (Spanish—conger-eel soup)

caldo de gallina: (Spanish—chicken soup)

caldo gallego: (Spanish—Gallegan-style soup)

caldo verde: (Portuguese—green soup) Soup made of thinly-sliced cabbage and mashed potatoes.

calf: Young of a bovine animal; female calves are called heifers, males are bull calves; calf is also the name for the young of many other quadruped herbivores such as elk, elephant, and hippopotamus.

calf liver: Liver from a calf, tenderer than beef liver.

calf meat: Veal usually supplied from a young beef animal.

calf's-foot jelly: Gelatin made by boiling the feet of calves.

calibogus: Rum-and-spruce-beer drink popular in Newfoundland, Nova Scotia, and parts of coastal Maine.

calico bass: Freshwater food fish of the Great Lakes and Mississippi River, named for its mottled coloring; a Pacific Coast sea bass is also called calico bass.

calico bean: Kidney bean or sieva bean.

calico corn: Indian corn of mottled and varicoated kernels, ranging in color from golden yellow, pink, and red to deep purple and black.

calico crab: Shallow-water crab of the Atlantic Coast, brightly spotted with red; calico crab is also a term for the lady crab, a swimming crab of the same region, also spotted.

california dip: Dry onion-soup mix blended with sour cream and eaten as a dip with potato chips, tortilla chips, etc.

california halibut: Important Pacific Ocean food fish of the flounder family, taken from San Francisco to Baja California in Mexico.

California Long White: Large irregular oval baking potato.

California orange: Any orange grown in California, particularly the navel orange.

california pea beans: Small nearly round variety of bean favored for use in making baked beans.

california pompano: Common Pacific Ocean food fish related to the butterfish of the Atlantic, not a true pompano.

california sardine: Tiny food fish of the herring family, also known as pilchard on many parts of its range along the Pacific Coast.

California tokay: Hungarian-type tokay wine produced in California.

California wines: Domestic wines are grown in California from vines originally brought from Europe.

Calimyrna: California + Smyrna —trademarked name for a variety of fine figs developed to combine the best qualities of figs from California and Smyrna (Izmir, Turkey).

calipash: Turtle meat adhering to the upper shell.

calipee: Turtle meat adhering to the under shell.

calisaya: Probably bitterest of all bitters used in spicing cocktails, made from chinchona bark and full of its bitter quinine taste.

callalu: Guyana-style soup made with crab, ham, shrimp, and vegetables.

caloric punsch: Sweet Scandinavian liqueur made of rum and syrup.

calorie: Unit of energy—or heat-producing value of food; calorie is defined as the amount of heat needed, at a pressure of one atmosphere, to raise the temperature of one gram of water 1°C.

caluso: Italian sweet wine from the Piedmont.

calvados: Dark-brown apple brandy of type made in Calvados Department in northern France.

camarão: (Portuguese—shrimp)

camarão frito: (Portuguese—fried shrimp)

camarón: (Spanish–prawn)

cambric tea: Mixture of milk, sugar, tea, and hot water—a mild beverage enjoyed by children and many others.

cambridge cheese: English soft rennet cheese first made in Cambridge, England.

camembert: Strongly pungent soft cheese first made in northern French town of Camembert.

cameriere: (Italian—waiter)

camote: (Spanish—a kind of sweet potato) Valuable vegetable discovered by early Spanish explorers in Mexico, Peru, and other parts of the New World.

Campari: Brand of bitter Italian vermouth characteristic of the Piedmont.

campfish: Slang for illegal fish.

campmeat: Slang for illegal venison or other game meat taken out of season or outside the bounds of game laws.

can: Cylindrical container in which beverages and foods are preserved and sold; commercial cans are made of aluminum or sheet steel lined with tin, and are available in standard sizes: 8 ounce; No. 1 (11 ounces or 1⅓ cups); No. 300 (14 ounces or 1¾ cups); No. 1½ or 303 (16 ounces or 2 cups); No. 2 (20 ounces or 2½ cups); No.

2½ (28 ounces or 3½ cups);
No. 3 (32 ounces or 4 cups);
No. 10 (106 ounces or 13¼
cups).

canada goose: Wild goose of
North America.

canada potato: Jerusalem artichoke.

canada tea: Wintergreen.

canadian bacon: Bacon cut from
boned loins and backs of hogs,
often hickory smoked.

Canadian whiskey: Light-bodied
blend of barley, corn, and rye
whiskey, distilled in Canada,
delicately colored and flavored.

canapé: Appetizer composed of
bread or crackers topped with
one of a variety of decorative
spreads; canapés are served at
cocktail parties or as an *hors
d'oeuvre* before dinner.

canapé butters: Canapé spreads
made by mixing creamed butter
with anchovies, chives, egg,
horseradish, or any of dozens of
other substances.

canard: (French—duck)

canard à la Montmorency: (French
—duck in Montmorency style)
Roast duck with cherries.

canard à la pressé: (French—
pressed duck)

canard rôti: (French—roast duck)

canard sauvage: (French—wild
duck)

canary banana: Dwarf banana.

candelabrum: Branched candle-
stand; the plural is candelabra.

candied: Cooked in sugar or syrup
until translucent; or crystallized.

candied angelica: Stalks of angelica herb candied with syrup.

candied apple: Apple on a stick—
apple coated with red-colored
sugar candy and served on a
stick.

candied peel: Grapefruit, lemon,
lime, orange, tangerine, or other
citrus-fruit peel prepared by
cooking in sugar and syrup.

candle: To examine an egg by
holding it between the eye and
a light (originally a candle) to
see if it is blood clotted, cracked,
fertile, or stale; large egg producers candle eggs electroni-
cally and sort them accordingly.

candlefish: Small food fish of the
North Pacific related to the
smelt; candlefish are so oily that,
when dried and threaded on a
wick, they can be burned like
candles.

candy: Confection containing sugar or other sweet-tasting substance, and cooked or molded to
a solid or semisolid consistency.

cane: Sugarcane.

canela: (Spanish—cinnamon)

cane sugar: Sugar extracted from
sugarcane.

caneton: (French—duckling)

caneware: Buff-yellow stoneware
of a type first developed by
Wedgewood; it is popular in
kitchenware utensils such as
nests of matching bowls.

cangrejo: (Spanish—crab)

canisté: (Cuban-Spanish—
canistel)

canistel: Bland yellow-orange eggfruit related to the sapote.

canister: Small container, usually
of metal or plastic, for holding
such staples as coffee, flour, salt,
sugar, or tea; canisters usually
come in matched sets decorated
for display on kitchen shelves.

canja: Thick soup or stew served
com arroz (with rice) or *de
galinha* (with chicken).

canneberge: (French—cranberry)

canned cow: Military slang for condensed milk.

canned food: Food hermetically sealed in cans or similar containers to preserve its freshness indefinitely.

canned heat: Solidified alcohol vacuum packed in a can; when the can is opened and the alcohol lighted, it burns with a flame hot enough to boil water, to warm foods in a chafing dish, or to make coffee or tea.

cannelé: (French—fluted) Pastry crust formed into a wavy edging or vegetables cut into decorative designs and shapes.

cannelle: (French—cinnamon)

cannelloni: (Italian—large macaroni) Tubular soup noodles.

cannelon: (French—pipelet) Puff pastry or roll usually stuffed with forcemeat.

canonaus: Sweet red Sardinian wine.

cant: Slang for cantaloupe.

cantal: French-style rennet cheese also known as auvergne, auvergne bleu, and fourme.

cantaloup: (French—cantaloupe)

cantaloupe: Muskmelon with hard rough rind and sweet orange-colored flesh, named for Cantaloupe in central Italy where the fruit was first grown in Europe.

cantaloupe à la mode: Cantaloupe served with ice cream.

canteen: Metal or plastic container for holding water or some other liquid while hiking or cycling; canteen is also a bar, cafeteria, or informal restaurant maintained for military servicemen.

cantina: (Portuguese—canteen; Spanish—wine cellar; saloon)

canton ginger: Fine grade of ginger crystallized while still green.

cantonware: Blue-and-white porcelain china of a type imported from Canton, China during the last two centuries.

canvasback: North American wild duck esteemed as delicacy by many hunters.

cape cod: Largest hard-shell clam found along the Atlantic Coast.

cape cod turkey: Sailor's slang for codfish.

cape crayfish: Spiny rock lobster imported from South Africa's west coast.

cape grape: Native grape of South Africa used in wine making.

capelin: Small marine fish of the smelt family found in arctic waters; it is used both as food and as bait for cod.

capellini d'angelo: (Italian—angel's hair) Longest and thinnest pasta produced.

cape lobster: Spiny rock lobster usually imported in frozen form from southwest South Africa.

capers: Berries or flower buds of caper plant found around Mediterranean coast of Europe and North Africa; used as condiments in dressings and sauces and in packing many salted and smoked fishes.

cape smoke: Bantu beverage drunk in South Africa where it is made from fermented corn.

cape wine: South African wine vinted from native cape grapes.

capirotada: Mexican bread pudding flavored with cinnamon, and pine nuts, and made with day-old bread and cottage cheese.

caplin: Capelin.

capoletti: Triangular ravioli.

capon: Castrated male chicken or rabbit raised for meat-production purposes.

capon chicken: Desexed male chicken 7 to 10 months old and weighing more than 4 pounds.

caponette: Chemically castrated chicken or other fowl.

cappelletti: Italian-style small raviolilike cases of dough filled with cheese, minced meat, or chopped vegetables.

capper: Wrenchlike device for opening screw caps on bottles, jars, and other food containers.

Cappuccino: (Italian—Capuchin) Coffee-and-milk mixture forced through an espresso device.

câpre: (French—caper [the plant])

capretto: (Italian—kid; young goat)

capri: Delicate red wine originally produced on the isle of Capri near Italy; Capri wines were said to have been favorites of the Emperor Tiberius.

caprino: Argentinian goat's-milk cheese.

Capsicum: Genus of tropical herbs of the potato family, yielding a many-seeded berry called a chili or a pepper; red pepper, paprika, and bird pepper belong to this genus.

caracol: (Spanish—snail)

carafe: (French—decanter; water bottle)

caramel: Substance obtained by cooking sugar until it thickens into a porous mass; caramel is used as a flavoring and coloring agent in soups, gravies, puddings, and whiskey, and is made into confections of various kinds.

caramel fruit: Sugar-glazed fruit.

caramelize: To cook sugar slowly until it turns brown and sticky.

caramelvla: (Dutch—caramel custard)

carapace: Upper shell of crabs, crayfishes, lobsters, and turtles.

caraway: Pungent herb of the carrot family whose seeds are used to flavor baked goods and many other dishes.

caraway loaf: American-type caraway cheese.

caraway oil: Essential oil obtained from caraway seeds, and used in flavoring liqueurs and salad dressings.

caraway-seed biscuits: Baking-powder biscuits sprinkled with caraway seeds.

caraway-seed bread: Rye bread flavored with caraway seeds.

caraway-seed cakes: Hard-baked coffee rolls flavored with caraway seeds.

carbonada: (Spanish—charred meat) Uruguayan term for a stew of meat, fruit, and rice.

carbonada criolla: (Spanish—Creole charred meat) Argentine term for beef stew baked in a pumpkin shell.

carbonado: Meat scored before broiling or grilling.

carbonated water: Water charged with carbon dioxide; also called soda water and sparkling water.

carbonated wine: Wine charged with soda water.

carbon dioxide: Heavy, colorless gas, CO_2, used in preparing carbonated beverages.

carbonnade: (French—broiled meat) Belgian-style spareribs cooked in beer.

carborundum stone: Abrasive for sharpening cleavers, knives, and other sharp-edged kitchen utensils.

carcavelos: Sweet white Portuguese wine.

carciofi: (Italian—artichokes)

cardamom: Aromatic East Indian herb used as a condiment and flavoring agent in many different dishes.

cardamom oil: Pale-colored essential oil distilled from cardamom seeds and used for flavoring.

cardinal of the sea: Boiled lobster, so called because of its cardinal red.

Cardinals: Large dark-red grapes created by crossing Ribier and tokay varieties.

cardoon: Celerylike stalk blanched and used as a vegetable or as a cheese-making agent.

Carême, Antonin (1784-1833): Cook of kings and king of cooks, founder of French cookery in the classic sense—*la grande cuisine*. Carême died poor although he had served royalty and written more than ten volumes about his culinary art.

cari: (French—curry)

carimañolas: Panamanian pork fritters.

Carling: Canadian ale and beer brewed in Toronto, Ontario.

Carlsberg: Danish beer brewed in Copenhagen.

carne: (Italian and Spanish—meat)

carne asado: (Spanish—roast meat)

carne assada à Portuguesa: (Portuguese—roast meat in Portuguese style) Portuguese pot roast.

carne fredda assortita: (Italian—cold assorted meat) Cold cuts.

carne fría: (Spanish—cold meat) Cold cuts.

carob: Evergreen tree of the Mediterranean area where it yields pulp-filled pods often called St. John's bread; carob pods are used as cattle feed and often eaten by children; they are also known as bokser.

carob flour: Flour ground from dried carob seeds, used as a food stabilizer and thickener.

carob powder: Fine-ground carob pods used in baking cakes, candies, cookies, icings; carob powder is high in calcium and low in starch.

Carolina tea: Indian tea.

carota: (Italian—carrot)

carotte: (French—carrot)

carottes à la Flamande: (French—carrots in Flemish style) Carrots cooked in sugar and cream.

carp: Large and long-lived freshwater food fish; some carp tagged by Napoleon in the early 1800's are still swimming in protected ponds near Paris; the decorative first cousin of the carp is the goldfish; carp is cooked in many ways, particularly stuffed.

carpe: (French—carp)

carrageen: Purplish seaweed found off coasts of Europe and North America; called irish moss when dried and bleached, it is used in making jellies and blanc manges.

carre: (French—back and shoulder cuts of meat)

carrelet: (French—flounder; fluke [the fish])

carrot: Orange-red-to-yellow root vegetable eaten boiled, pickled, or raw; carrots are attractive in salads, soups, and stews because of their brilliant color.

carrot cake: Cake made of carrots, eggs, nuts, and raisins.

carrot-seed oil: Essential oil derived from seeds of the carrot plant; it is used in flavoring and in preparation of liqueurs; the term carrot-seed oil is also applied to a fatty oil obtained from the same source and used in coloring butter and margarine.

Carta Blanca: Mexican beer brewed in Monterrey.

carte de vins: (French—wine list)

carte du jour: (French—menu of the day)

carvie: Scots for caraway seeds.

carvie cake: Scots oatmeal cake made with caraway seeds.

carving set: Utensils for carving a roast: carving fork, usually two tined; carving knife, often provided with a finger guard; and sharpening steel for honing the knife.

casaba: Sweet winter muskmelon having pale-yellow flesh and golden-yellow rind; casabas are named for the Turkish town of Kasaba where they were first grown.

casanova: Celery-and-truffles salad.

caseralla: Soft creamy Greek cheese.

casere: Brittle Greek sheep's-milk cheese celebrated for its biting quality.

cashew: Tropical American tree cultivated for its crescent-shaped nuts; cashews are roasted to eliminate their caustic oils.

cassata: (Italian—cream tart) Fruit-and-ice-cream confection.

cassava: Tropical plant of the spurge family, whose roots yield a nutritious starch; also called manioc, cassava is cultivated throughout the tropics where it is an important dietary staple; tapioca comes from cassava, as do local forms of bread, beer, and hard liquor.

casserole: (French—saucepan) Covered dish made of earthenware, glass, or metal commonly used for baking one-dish meals; *casserole* can also mean the food itself, in France: a dish with rice arranged on a platter in *casserole* shape; in America: a combination of meat with rice, spaghetti, macaroni, or noodles cooked together in a sauce.

Cassia: Genus of tropical plants yielding drugs and medicinal juices of various kinds.

cassia bark: Chinese cinnamon.

cassia bud: Dried flower of chinese cinnamon—not to be confused with the true cassia, a mild laxative.

cassolette: Small casserole for individual portions.

cassoulet: (French—bean stew) Casserole dish made with shell beans and meat.

castagna: (Italian—chestnut)

castagnola: (Italian—fire cracker) Macaroon flavored with chocolate and cinnamon.

castanha do Brasil: (Portuguese—brazil nut)

castrato: (Italian—mutton)

catawba: Light-red native American grape used in making sparkling white wine; the best such wines are vinted in western

New York, western Pennsylvania, and northern Ohio.

catchup: Catsup.

catfish: Freshwater and saltwater fish with whiskerlike barbels that give them a catlike look; freshwater catfish are often placed in tubs of clear water after they are captured so they can purge themselves of mud and sand before they are cooked.

catfishburger: Hamburger made of catfish.

catsup: Spiced tomato-sauce seasoning; the name is a corruption of Malay *kechap*—spiced sauce for fish; catsups are also made of cranberries, cucumbers, and grapes.

cattalo: Cattle + buffalo crossbreed developed to produce best features of beef cattle and the American bison or buffalo.

cattley guava: Strawberry guava used in making guava jams, jellies, and pastes.

caudle: Beverage made of warm ale or wine strengthened with eggs, spices, and sugar; in Scotland oatmeal or gruel is often added.

cauli: Slang for cauliflower.

cauliflower: Plant of the cabbage family whose compact white flower head is an important vegetable; cauliflower is usually boiled in salted water and served with some kind of sauce.

caustic soda: Sodium hydroxide; powerful cleansing agent used in dissolving fats and greases, particularly on stoves and in ovens where they may have hardened with heat.

cavendish: Dwarf banana also known as the chinese banana;

cultivated extensively in Jamaica, and many parts of tropical Central and South America.

caviar: Salted and seasoned roe, usually of the sturgeon; caviar is a long-standing favorite as a cocktail canapé spread, served in any of a number of different ways; the finest caviar is reputed to be that processed in Russia from the roe of Caspian Sea sturgeon, particularly the sterlet.

cavolfiore: (Italian—cauliflower)

cavolo: (Italian—cabbage)

cayenne pepper: Pungent powder derived from capsicum fruits such as chili and guinea pepper; cayenne is used in cheese dishes, egg, fish, and meat courses, many sauces, etc.

cazuela: (Spanish—earthenware stewing pan) Vegetable mixture prepared in a cazuela.

cc: Abbreviation for cubic centimeter.

C.E.: French abbreviation for *cuvée extra* (French—special sort), an indication of quality.

cebolla: (Spanish—onion)

cece: (Italian—chick) Chick pea.

ceci all' olio: (Italian—chick peas with olive oil)

cédrat: (French—citron)

cel: Slang for celery.

céleri: (French—celery)

celeriac: Variety of celery with a large, edible turniplike root.

celery: Herbaceous vegetable of the carrot family, whose crisp stalks are eaten raw or boiled; celery is blanched during growth by having dirt mounded around it to keep the stalk white.

celery-and-olive dish: Compartmented dish of ceramic, glass, or metal for serving celery and olives.

celery cabbage: White-stalked vegetable with light green leaves, tender enough to be used in salads; it is also called chinese celery cabbage.

celery knob: Celeriac.

celery oil: Oil extracted from celery seeds, and used in flavoring.

celery root: Celeriac.

celery salt: Ground celery seed mixed with salt and used to season bouillon, eggs, fish, salad dressings, and so forth.

celery seed: Flavoring seed of the celery plant usually imported from France, Holland, and India, used for flavoring fish courses, salads, and vegetable dishes.

celery tonic: Carbonated beverage flavored with celery extract.

celestine: Mineral water of a type first bottled and served at Vichy, France.

cellaret: Compartment for storing bottles of wine.

cellophane: Transparent cellulose wrapping used to protect many foods displayed in markets and stores; cellophane has been largely superseded by superior plastic wraps offering greater strength as well as protection against bacteria and moisture.

Celsius: see centigrade.

celtuce: Celery + lettuce—vegetable derived from lettuce but having an edible stalk tasting like a combination of celery and lettuce.

cena: (Italian and Spanish— supper)

centigrade: Temperature scale invented by Anders Celsius and now called Celsius by international agreement on which water boils at 100 degrees and freezes at 0 degrees.

ceramic: Pottery material such as chinaware, earthenware, plaster, vitreous enamel, etc.

cerdo: (Spanish—pork; pig)

cerdo asado: (Spanish—roast pork)

cereal: Seeds of such grasses as corn, rice, and wheat prepared in breakfast-food form.

cereza: (Spanish—cherry)

cerf: (French—stag)

cerise: (French—cherry)

certified milk: Milk produced by dairies operating under health regulations imposed by a medical or public-health service; such milk may be pasteurized or unpasteurized.

certosino: (Italian—Carthusian) Honey cake filled with almonds and citron peel.

cerveja: (Portuguese—beer)

cervelas: (French—saveloy)

cervelat: Saveloy.

cervelle: (French—brains)

cerveza: (Spanish—beer)

cetriuolo: (Italian—cucumber)

cevabçiçi: (Yugoslav—beef and veal sausages)

ceylon cinnamon: Bark of the cinnamon tree and source of the spice used in cooking; ceylon cinnamon is of a higher grade than chinese cinnamon or cassia bark.

ceylon tea: Tea of a type originally produced on island of Ceylon; see pekoe.

chablis: Dry white burgundy wine first made near Chablis, France.

chafing dish: Utensil for cooking or warming food at the table; modern chafing dishes are usually decorated and stand on a tripod over an alcohol lamp or electric heating element.

chain mixer: Short length of stainless-steel chain dropped into a cocktail mixer before it is shaken; agitation of the chain tends to emulsify the contents.

chair blanche: (French—white meat)

chair noir: (French—dark meat)

challah: Braided egg bread sometimes topped with sesame seeds, baked for the Jewish sabbath and for other holidays.

chalota (or *xalota*): (Portuguese —shallot; scallion)

chamomile: Bitter medicinal tea prepared from an herb of the genus *Antehmis.*

champagne: Effervescent double-fermented wine, originating in the Champagne district east of Paris; the first stage of fermentation takes place in the cask where the grape juice turns to wine; the second stage takes place in the bottle where the wine changes from still to sparkling; champagnes are graded *brut* (driest), *extra sec* (extra dry), *sec* (dry), *demi-sec* (middling dry), *demi-doux* (middling sweet), and *doux* (sweet.)

champagne cider: Double-fermented cider; the first stage turns apple juice into cider; the second stage turns still cider into a sparkling beverage.

champagne cocktail: Cocktail made of champagne, angostura, sugar, and lemon twist.

champagne glass: Stemmed glass holding 4 to 6 ounces of liquid; sometimes the stem is hollow.

champagne jelly: Champagne jellied with fruit acid, pectin, and sugar.

champagnization: Process of turning still wines into sparkling.

champignon: (French—mushroom)

champignons au gratin: (French —mushrooms with a crust) Baked mushrooms.

channel bass: Sea bass found in the Gulf of Mexico and in southern coastal rivers, also called red drum; channel bass is an important food and game fish.

channel cat: Catfish caught and eaten throughout much of the southern United States.

chanterelle: (French—decoy bird) Small yellow mushroom with a faint apricot aroma.

chantilly: Flavored and sweetened whipped cream used in mouselines, or in other dishes and pastries served *à la Chantilly* (French—in the style of a town north of Paris).

chapatty: Pancake or tortilla of India and Ceylon, made of wheat flour and baked on a griddle over an open fire.

chapon: (French—capon) Crust of bread boiled in soup or a crust of bread rubbed with garlic and put into a salad.

chaponneau: (French—young capon)

charcuterie: (French—pork butcher's shop) Assortment of sausages.

chard: Leafstalks of the artichoke, not to be confused with Swiss chard, a kind of beet.

chardonnay: White wine grape originating in Burgundy region of eastern France.

charged water: Water charged with carbon dioxide, also called soda water or sparkling water.

charger: Big serving platter.

charlotte: Molded dessert made of gelatin, custard, fruits, or whipped cream poured into a lining of spongecake, ladyfingers, or bread.

charlotte martinique: (French— Martinique-style charlotte) Mold of strawberry ice cream and ladyfingers crowned with whipped cream.

charlotte russe: (French—Russian charlotte) Charlotte made of bavarian cream or whipped cream and ladyfingers.

chartreuse: Greenish-yellow liqueur of kind developed by Carthusian monks at La Grande Chartreuse, their mother house near Grenoble, France; chartreuse also means a mold of fruit or vegetables with rice.

chasseur: (French—hunter; cavalryman) Sauce made with mushrooms, parsley, white wine, and shallots; dishes served with this sauce are said to be à la chasseur.

châtaigne: (French—chestnut)

chateaubriand: Method of preparing fillet of beef, named after Vicomte François René de Chateaubriand, 19th-century French statesman whose chef invented it; the term also refers to a cut of meat yielding a chateaubriand steak.

château potatoes: White potatoes parboiled and braised.

chatter water: British slang for weak tea.

chaud: (French—hot)

chaudière: (French—soup kettle; caldron)

chausson: (French—puff pastry)

chawan-mushi: (Japanese— chicken and shrimp) Chicken, shrimp, and vegetables steamed with egg custard and flavored with ginko nut.

chayote: Squash popular in Mexico and the West Indies.

checks (or chex): Poultry eggs with cracked shells but intact membranes or eggs with imperfect shells selling for less than regular graded eggs.

cheddar: Whole-milk process cheese originally made in the village of Cheddar in Somersetshire, England; cheddar varies from sharp to bland and from orange-yellow to white.

cheddar cheese soup: Canadian specialty featuring cheddar cheese cooked with consommé, grated onions, butter, flour, milk, and seasoning.

cheese: Milk product consisting of the curd separated from the whey, flavored, compressed or molded into various shapes, and ripened; usually either rennet or (less often) pepsin is used to coagulate the curd, although sometimes a vegetable substance is substituted; hard cheeses like cheddar and emmenthaler are formed by pressure, while brie, camembert, and other soft cheeses are merely turned into molds to ripen.

cheese biscuit: Baking-powder biscuit made with grated cheese.

cheese board: Small cutting board, often made with a vitreous tile insert, for cutting cheese and arranging it for serving.

cheese bread: Cheese-flavored bread.

cheeseburger: Hamburger fried with a coating of melted cheese.

cheese butter: Butter-and-cream-cheese mixture or butter mixed with a creamy cheese of the camembert type.

cheesecake: Sweet-sour confection made of cottage or cream cheese, eggs, sugar, and other ingredients baked in a springform pan lined with graham-cracker or zwieback crumbs, or in a pastry shell.

cheese cutter: Cheese slicer.

cheese dream: Cheese, milk, and egg mixture spread on bread and toasted, or cheese-filled french toast, or toasted-cheese sandwich.

cheese fondue: Semiliquid preparation of cheese, butter, eggs and seasoning; fondue is usually served hot in a chafing dish; guests eat it by dipping into the mixture with bread sticks or toast spears.

cheese hoop: Broad metal or wooden hoop into which curd is pressed when the cheese is being made.

cheese knife: Broad-bladed knife for cutting or spreading cheese.

cheesemonger: Old English term for a person dealing in and selling cheese.

cheese press: Utensil for pressing the curd in a hoop or mold as cheese is being made.

cheese scoop: Spoonlike table implement for scooping out contents of a ball- or pineapple-shaped cheese.

cheese server: Decorative wooden platter for holding and serving cheese, crackers, *hors d'oeuvres,* and other appetizers.

cheese slicer: Bladed utensil or small saw frame with wire blade for slicing cheese; cheese slicers are also useful for slicing beets, butter, hard-boiled eggs, potatoes, and other foods.

cheese soufflé: Puffy baked cheese-and-egg dish consisting of shredded cheese, eggs, flour, milk, and other ingredients.

cheese spread: Cheese processed soft enough to be spread; any of several commercial sandwich spreads made of mild cheese flavored with chili, chives, onion, etc.

cheese starter: Lactic-acid bacterial culture used in fermenting milk, the first step in cheese making; rennet is the usual agent.

cheese stick: Crisp cheese-flavored bread stick.

cheese wafer: Cheese-flavored cracker.

cheesewich: Cheese sandwich.

chef: (French—chief) Skilled male cook who manages a large kitchen or galley.

chef de cuisine: (French—kitchen chief) Top-ranking chef who is often assisted by other chefs such as the baker, the pastry chef, the poultry chef, etc.

chef de rang: (French—chief of rank) Perfect waiter, one who can serve alone, having completed his apprenticeship, and having served as a *commis de rang* (French—clerk of rank).

chela: Large claw of a lobster or crab.

chelo: (Persian—golden rice)

cherimoya: Sweet custardlike tropical fruit widely cultivated in tropical and subtropical parts of the Americas, including Hawaii and the West Indies.

cherry: Tree of the almond family yielding juicy red fruit; many wild and cultivated varieties grow in Europe and America; cherries are eaten raw or are made into compotes, jams, jellies, liqueurs, pies, and many other dishes.

cherry bounce: Cherry-flavored liqueur made of cider, rum, or whiskey; or diluted cherry brandy.

cherry brandy: Distilled from fermented cherry juice, or brandy flavored with cherries.

cherry gin: Cherry-flavored gin.

Cherry Heering: Danish cherry liqueur of exceptional quality.

cherry liqueur: Alcohol or brandy flavored with black cherries.

cherry olive: Pickled cherry served as an appetizer.

cherry phosphate: Carbonated soft drink flavored with cherry.

cherry pie: Pie made from cherries and long a favorite in many places; cherry pie recipes are so numerous their very numbers indicate the popularity of this pie.

cherry rum: Cherry-and-rum mixture in which the cherries are well steeped in the liquor.

cherrystone: Intermediate-size hard-shell clam found along the Atlantic Coast.

cherry tomato: Small-sized tomato.

cherry whiskey: Cherry-flavored whiskey liqueur.

cherry wine: Ferment made from cherry juice.

chervil: Aromatic garden herb of the carrot family used as flavoring in soups and salads.

cheshire: Old English cheddar cheese first made in Cheshire County, available in red or white or white with an irregular blue-mold stripe; Cheshire is also a breed of medium-sized white swine.

chesky: Cherry-and-whiskey drink.

Chester White: Large white swine bred from stock developed in Chester County, Pennsylvania.

chestnut: Tree of the beech family whose edible nuts are eaten boiled, mashed, and roasted; roasted chestnuts were sold to or traded with early Dutch settlers by the Indians.

chestnut bean: Chick pea.

chestnut stuffing: Poultry filling made of mashed boiled chestnuts, bread crumbs, cream, and minced onions.

chevreuil: (French—roebuck venison)

chewing gum: Chewy confection offered in many flavors: fruits, licorice, mints such as wintergreen, etc.; chewiness comes from chicle or plastic.

Chex: Brand of breakfast cereal; *see* checks.

chianti: Italian-type red table wine originally vinted in the Chianti district of Tuscany in central Italy.

chiavari: Italian rennet-type sourmilk cheese also known as *cacio romano* or Roman cheese; the cheese bears the name of a town in northwestern Italy.

chicago: Cocktail made of brandy, sugar, angostura, champagne, curaçao, and lemon twist; chicago is also a pineapple soda or sundae.

chicha: Ecuadorean-type wine sauce.

chiche: (French—chick peas)

chick: Newly hatched chicken; chicks are sometimes substituted for small game birds in roasts and stews as their tender flesh can be seasoned to resemble quail and other wild birds.

chicken: Domestic poultry, one of the most popular of all fowls because of its high egg production, and the digestibility of its meat.

chicken à la king: Diced and creamed chicken, cooked with mushrooms and pimientos and served in patty shells or on toast.

chickenburger: Fried-meat patty made with chicken.

chicken cacciatore: Italian-style chicken fried in olive oil and simmered in a sauce made of herbs, stewed tomatoes, and wine.

chicken gumbo: Creole soup of chicken or beef broth with okra, garlic, celery, onions, tomatoes, and spices.

chicken halibut: Small halibut under 10 pounds.

chicken lobster: Tender young lobster.

chicken steak: Boneless chuck steak.

chicken tetrazzini: Creamed chicken and mushrooms with cheese and spaghetti browned in the oven, named for early-20th-century operatic soprano Luisa Tetrazzini.

chick pea: Asiatic member of the pea family whose pods contain one or two nutlike legumes, also called chestnut bean, dwarf pea, and garavance; chick peas are cultivated in many parts of the world and are prepared in many ways.

chicle: Rubbery gum obtained from the tropical American tree called the sapodilla; chicle is used as the chewy base of chewing gum; it was discovered in Yucatan by early Spanish explorers who found Indians chewing it as a pastime.

chicorée: (French—endive)

chicory: European herb related to endive used in salads; chicory roots are roasted and ground for use in adulterating or flavoring coffee; many people enjoy chicory as a coffee substitute; its leaves are sometimes used in salads.

chief steward: Four-striped ship's officer in charge of cooking and domestic services for a vessel's crew and passengers and of ship's stores.

chiffonade: (French—something shredded)

chiffon cake: Very light cake made with vegetable oil instead of solid shortening such as butter, margarine, etc.

chiffon pie: Fluffy custard pie containing gelatin, eggs, whipped cream, plus some distinctive color and flavor; the ingredients are poured into a baked pie shell and chilled.

chihuahua cheese: Milky-white cheese made in border state of the same name in northern Mexico, produced from goat's milk.

Chilean wines: Wines produced in Chile.

chiliburger: Mexicanburger.

chili: Capsicum pepper raised in many parts of tropical America for its fruit, a source of cayenne or red pepper.

chili con carne: (Spanish—chili-pepper sauce with meat) Popular dish served with or without beans.

chili powder: Ground chili peppers used in preparing *chili con carne* and other spicy dishes.

chili relleno: (Spanish—stuffed chili pepper) Chili filled with ground meat, grated cheese, or saffron-colored rice.

chili sauce: Tomato sauce flavored with red chili peppers, plus onions, sugar, vinegar, and a variety of spices.

chili vinegar: Sauce made with chili peppers and vinegar.

chill: To cool without freezing; food is usually chilled by being placed in a refrigerator or icebox, or out of doors in cold weather.

china bean: Cowpea or black-eyed pea.

chinaware: Tableware of a type first imported from China in the 17th century when most European pottery was rather crude and coarse.

chinese banana: Dwarf banana.

chinese bean oil: Soybean oil.

chineseburger: Hamburger patty containing rice.

chinese cabbage: White-stalked vegetable resembling celery, sold in many oriental markets as *bok choy;* chinese cabbage is used in many Chinese stir-fry dishes, but is not to be confused with another vegetable, chinese celery cabbage.

chinese cinnamon: Cassia bark somewhat coarser than ceylon cinnamon, also used in flavoring, pickling, and preserving.

chinese gelatin: Agar.

chinese goose: Brown or white goose of a type domesticated from a variety native to China.

chinese lemon: Citron.

chinese mustard: Indian mustard.

chinese nut: Litchi.

chinese watermelon: Wax gourd about the size of a pumpkin; the white pulp of this Asiatic fruit is used in soups and stews.

chinook salmon: Largest and commercially most important of Pacific Ocean salmon, also called king salmon or guinnat; chinooks swim upstream to spawn in all Pacific Coast rivers from Bering Strait to Monterey Bay and attract fishing vessels from as far as Japan and Russia.

chip: Thinly cut and crisply fried slice of potato, banana, carrot, parsnip, plantain, and other fruits and vegetables treated the same way.

chip dip: Cocktail dip flavored with bacon, cheddar cheese, garlic, horseradish, onion, and other popular flavors.

chipolata: Cocktail sausage.

chipped beef: Dried salted beef sliced very thin.

chip potato: French-fried potato.

chit: Signed voucher attesting that possessor is entitled to receive food or drink; the word comes from *chitty* (Hindi—marked).

chive: Onion-flavored member of the lily family; finely chopped chives are added to such dishes as omelets, salads, soups, and stews as well as cocktail dips.

chlodnik: Polish-style cold vegetable and yogurt soup, a popular summer dish with Poles and Russians who make it with buttermilk and serve it during harvesting; chlodnik tastes somewhat like vichyssoise.

chlorination: Introduction of very small amounts of chlorine into water to disinfect and purify it for drinking.

choc: Slang for chocolate.

choclo: (Spanish—ear of corn)

chocolade taart: (Dutch—chocolate cake)

chocolate: Flavoring substance obtained from cacao beans taken from cacao tree found throughout the American tropics; roasted cacao beans are ground and heated to produce unsweetened chocolate liquor sold in cake form; sweet chocolate is made by adding sugar to the liquor before it is molded and cooled.

chocolate chip: Small morsel of semisweetened chocolate sold commercially for use in cakes, cookies, and many other desserts.

chocolate-covered insect: Exotic cocktail confection.

chocolate cream: *Fondant*-centered candy coated with sweet or semisweet chocolate.

chocolate shaving: Thin sliver of bitter or semisweet chocolate shaved from hard bars and used in decorating cakes, pastries, and pies.

chocolate soufflé: Puffy dessert made of chocolate, eggs, cream, and other ingredients.

chocolate syrup: Sweet syrup made with chocolate or cocoa, corn syrup, sugar, salt, and vanilla, a popular flavoring agent in many desserts and

often poured over puddings and sundaes.

chocólatl: (Nahuatl—chocolate) Mexican-Indian word (sometimes spelled *xocoatl*) meaning a bitter foaming beverage; Spaniards altered chocólatl to suit the European palate, adding ground almonds, cinnamon, and brown sugar.

choctaw beer: Slang for bootleg beer made in the South during Prohibition.

choesels à la Bruxelloise: (Belgian French—kidney stew in Brussels style)

choice beef: Second-best grade of beef, by the U.S. Department of Agriculture grading.

choisi: (French—select) Term applied to many menu items, although they may not be as choice as the adjective would imply.

choke apple: Crabapple.

chokecherry: Astringent cherry native to North America, used in jams and jellies and sometimes eaten raw.

choke pear: Astringent pear used in cooking or preserving.

chop: Small cut of meat usually attached to a rib; chop also means a Chinese or Indian customhouse seal indicating the quality of the item for sale—finest grade was first chop, next grade was second chop, etc.

chop: To cut to pieces with sharp, hard, downward strokes.

chophouse: English-style restaurant featuring chops, steaks, and other meat dishes.

chopine: (French—chopin) Old liquid measure equaling 1.8 pints.

chopped meat: Ground meat, such as used for hamburger, meat loaf, etc.

chopping block: Butcher's solid hardwood block for chopping fish, meat, or poultry.

chopping board: Hardwood kitchen board used when chopping or mincing meats and vegetables.

chopping bowl: Hardwood bowl used for chopping or mincing food with a curve-bladed chopping device.

chopping knife: Mincing device with one or two crescent-shaped blades set beneath a yoke handle, the utensil most often used with a chopping bowl.

chopsticks: Oriental eating utensils composed of two slender rattan sticks held between thumb and fingers.

chop suey: (Cantonese Chinese— odds and ends) American-Chinese stew of chicken, fish, meat, seafood, and/or such vegetables as sautéed bean sprouts, mushrooms, onions, water chestnuts, and soybean seasoning; chop suey is usually served with steamed rice and hot tea in small cups.

chorizo: (Spanish—sausage)

chou: (French—cabbage)

chou au lard: (French—cabbage with bacon)

choucroute: (French—sauerkraut)

chou de mer: (French—sea cabbage; sea kale)

chou-fleur: (French—cauliflower)

chou-palmiste: (Haitian-French —palmetto cabbage) Heart of palm.

choux de Bruxelles: (French— brussels sprouts)

chowchow: Pickle-and-vegetable relish in a sauce of mustard, sugar, and vinegar; chowchow is also the name of a Chinese sweet preserve of ginger and fruit.

chowder: Thick soup or stew of corn, clams, codfish, crabs, oysters, or other seafood or vegetable combination.

chowder beer: Boiled alcoholic mixture of black spruce bark, molasses, and water.

chow mein: Chinese-style stir-fried dish with a meat or seafood base served atop fried noodles.

christalinna: Hard tangy rennet cheese produced in Switzerland from cow's milk.

chromeware: Chrome-plated kitchen utensils such as bread and cake boxes, nested canister sets, coffee makers, tea kettles, flatware, etc.

chub: Carplike fish used as food or bait.

chub mackerel: Small mackerel taken from the North Atlantic.

chuck: Meat cut from around the neck and shoulder blade, including the first three upper ribs.

chuck wagon: Horse- or mule-drawn kitchen most commonly used on Western cattle drives; modern Western-style eating places are sometimes called chuck wagons.

chufa: A sedge, native to Europe, with small edible nutlike tubers; also called earth almond.

chuleta: (Spanish—chop)

chum: Dog salmon.

chunk honey: Honey in its wax comb.

chupe de locos: (Spanish—hotch-potch of madmen) Chilean-style abalone soup.

chupe de mariscos: (Spanish—hotchpotch of shellfish) Chilean-style shrimp-and-scallop stew.

churn: Device for making butter and buttermilk by agitating milk and causing butterfat to separate from the liquid.

churn milk: Buttermilk.

churrusco: (Spanish—roasted meat) Beef, pork, and sausages barbecued over an open fire, a pampas-style barbecue popular in southern South America.

churro: (Mexican—cruller)

chutney: Spicy relish originating in Ceylon or India; chutneys are made of pickled ginger, mango, raisins, tamarind, etc.; American and British chutneys are made of apples, bananas, and peaches.

cider: Apple juice allowed to ripen and take on a sweet cidery flavor; if fermented, this sweet cider becomes alcoholic and is called hard cider; if allowed to sour, it turns into vinegar and is called cider vinegar.

cider apple: Any apple of a grade suitable for yielding apple juice.

cider oil: Mixture of cider and honey, also called cider royal.

cider press: Device for pressing apples to extract their juice.

cider royal: Mixture of cider and honey.

cider vinegar: Vinegar made from fermented apple juice.

cider wine: Hard cider sugared and spiced, or a sweetened intoxicant made from spiced cider.

cidre: (French—cider)

ciervo: (Spanish—deer)

ciliegia: (Italian—cherry)

cincinnati oysters: Waiters' slang for pork products; Cincinnati was once Ohio River center for shipment of pork and processing of pork products.

cinder toffee: Crunchy toffee.

cinnamon: Aromatic bark of a tropical laurel tree; the best grades are from Ceylon and Viet Nam, coarser varieties from China; cinnamon is widely used in flavoring baked goods and in the preparation of many beverages.

cinnamon-bark oil: Light-colored essential oil extracted from cinnamon bark for use in flavoring.

cinnamon biscuit: Baking-powder biscuit made with ground cinnamon and other ingredients.

cinnamon bun: Cinnamon-and-sugar-filled bun made from raised coffee-cake dough.

cinnamon snail: Cinnamon bun baked in a coil.

cinnamon toast: White or raisin toast flavored with sugar and cinnamon.

Cinzano: Brand of fine Italian vermouth.

cioppino: Italian-style fish or shellfish stew resembling bouillabaisse.

cipolla: (Italian—onion)

circassian walnut: English walnut.

ciruela: (Spanish—plum)

ciruela pasa: (Spanish—dried plum; prune)

cisco: Variety of whitefish, an important food fish of the Great Lakes region.

citrange: Tart-flavored fruit produced by crossing sweet orange and trifoliate orange.

citric acid: Mild acid extracted from citrus fruits and used for flavoring and preserving.

citroen: (Dutch—lemon)

citron: Fragrant greenish-yellow citrus fruit whose rind is usually dried and preserved, and used in fruitcakes and in crystallized sugar confections.

citronnat: (French—candied lemon peel)

citronné: (French—lemon-juice flavored)

citrus fruit: Subtropical and tropical trees of the rue family, valued for their juices and as flavoring agents: citron, grapefruit, lemon, lime, orange, kumquat, shaddock, tangerine, etc.

civet: (French—furred game stew) Hare or rabbit stew made with red wine and blood.

clabar: (Gaelic—mud) clabber.

clabber: Milk soured and thickened by natural fermentation action of lactic-acid bacteria.

clabber cheese: Cottage cheese curds.

clabbered milk: Curdled sour milk often eaten plain or with jam, jelly, or other sweetening.

claggum: Chewy molasses candy.

clair: (French—bright; clear)

clairet: (French—light-red) Light table wine.

clam: Bivalve mollusk found on many North American sea beaches and mudflats, both hard-shelled and soft-shelled varieties; many of the smaller specimens of the hard-shelled variety are eaten on the half shell; most of the soft-shelled varieties are eaten fried or steamed.

clambake: Outdoor social gathering usually featuring steamed soft-shelled clams or clams covered with wet seaweed while being baked on hot rocks.

clam bar: Counter or restaurant where clams and other seafoods are served.

clam chowder: Souplike stew of clams quick-cooked in milk; Manhattan-style clam chowder substitutes tomatoes for milk.

clam dip: Clam spread.

clam juice: Broth remaining in the pot after clams are steamed.

clam spread: Mixture of minced clams, cream cheese, chopped onion, and worcestershire sauce prepared as a sandwich spread or a cocktail dip.

clam steamer: Double-boiler steaming pot for cooking clams and other seafoods, used also for corn, chicken, and many other foods.

claret: Bordeaux-type red table wine.

claret cup: Iced claret flavored with grapefruit, lemon, lime, or orange.

clarete: (Spanish—claret)

clarifier: Substance used to clarify a liquid, such as eggshells in coffee.

clarify: To make a liquid clear by ridding it of all suspended matter; coffee is clarified by adding egg shells or egg whites; fruit juices are clarified by straining.

clary: Strong-scented sage of the mint family, used in England as a potherb.

clary sage: Clary.

clayware: Kiln-fired pottery bowls, cups, and plates.

clear soup: Consommé.

cleaver: Broad-bladed chopping knife used by butchers for cleaving bones and hard cuts of meat; small-size cleavers are available for household use.

clementine: Hybrid produced by crossing the orange with the tangerine.

clingstone: Peach or plum whose flesh clings to the stone.

clotted cream: Heavy clotted substance obtained by alternately scalding and cooling cream; clotted cream is served chilled as a dessert or as a spread for bread or cake; *see* devonshire cream.

cloves: Dried flower buds of East Indian myrtle tree, used as a spice throughout the world in flavoring baked goods, hams, soups, stews, etc.; clove also means a segment of a root bulb, as a clove of garlic, etc.

clovisse: (French—a variety of *palourde* or clam)

club cheese: Cheese made from ripened cheddar or a mixture of cheeses with the addition of wine and spices.

club sandwich: Three-decker sandwich consisting of three pieces of toast separated by two layers of filling; a club sandwich is held together with toothpicks and topped with a pitted olive.

club soda: Carbonated water.

club steak: Small steak cut from the short loin.

coachman's cooler: Mixed fruit juices served in a tall glass.

coagulate: To cause a creamy or liquid food to change into a curdlike mass.

coalfish: Dark-backed marine food fish related to the cod, also known as pollock.

coal-oil stove: Cooking range fueled by coal oil.

coalport: English porcelain produced at Coalport in Shropshire.

coaster: Small pad or plate for protecting a table surface from wet glasses.

coating-spoon stage: Stage in cooking when the mixture forms a film on a spoon.

cob: Ear of corn.

cobbler: Deep-dish fruit pie made with a thick upper crust; cobbler also refers to an iced drink made of fruit, sugar, and wine.

coche-comedor: (Spanish—dining car)

cochon de lait: (French—milk pig; suckling pig)

cocido: (Spanish—cooked; a stew)

cock: Mature male of the domestic fowl or other birds.

cock-a-leekie: Scots dish consisting of a capon boiled with white leeks, then simmered in broth with more leeks, pepper, prunes, raisins, and salt.

cockerel: Young cock.

cock's comb: Rooster's comb.

cocktail: Iced alcoholic drink composed of a distilled liquor with fruit juice, wine, or other flavors, served as an appetizer or apéritif; the term is also used of cold seafood appetizers: clam cocktail, shrimp cocktail, mixed seafood cocktail, etc.

cocktail frank: Tiny frankfurter suitable for cocktail snacks.

cocktail glass: Stemmed glass holding 2 to 4 ounces of liquid.

cocktail hour: Predinner period when cocktails are usually served, 4 to 6 P.M.

cocktail napkin: Small cloth or paper napkin, usually decorative, used when serving cocktails.

cocktail olive: Small olive served at cocktail parties on a plastic pick or a wooden toothpick.

cocktail onion: Tiny pickled onion used as flavoring agent in certain cocktails.

cocktail strainer: Strainer made to fit the top of a cocktail shaker to separate ice, pulp, seeds, etc., from drink being poured.

cocoa: Powdered chocolate reduced in fat content; high-fat type contains more than 22 percent, medium-fat less than 22 percent.

cocoa butter: Fat extracted from cacao beans smelling and tasting of chocolate and used in candy making.

cocoa shell: Husk of cacao bean; boiled cocoa shells produce a weak chocolate-flavored beverage.

coconut: Tropical palm yielding a large fruit whose outer husk conceals a coconut-milk reservoir encased in coconut meat; coconut palms are found throughout the tropics and have been carried by warm ocean currents as far north as Bantry Bay in Ireland; shredded coconut meat is used in baking, candy making, and cooking.

coconut milk: Clear fluid obtained from the center of a fresh coconut.

coconut water: Coconut milk.

cocotte: (French—stewpan) Casserolelike stewing pan used for cooking and serving; food served this way is said to be *en cocotte.*

cocui: (Venezuelan-Spanish—agave) Cactus brandy.

cod: Soft-finned food fish of the North Atlantic, eaten baked, boiled, broiled, flaked, smoked, and in many other ways; the cod, of great economic importance, has long been a food staple in many countries.

coddled egg: Egg cooked slowly in water just below the boiling point.

codling: Small codfish.

cod sounds: Cod air bladders, often served for breakfast in New England homes and on many ships where they are cooked in a caper-flavored white sauce.

coenatio: (Latin—dining room)

coeur: (French—heart)

coeur à la crème: (French—heart in cream style) Heart-shaped cream cheese served with cream and jam.

coffee: Berries of a tropical shrub of the madder family, roasted, ground, and brewed into a beverage; coffee is cultivated in most tropical countries; milder coffees originate in the highlands of Colombia and El Salvador; roasting methods vary from country to country as does blending.

coffee and: Slang for coffee and cake, and crullers, and doughnuts, and rolls, etc.

coffee bread: Coffee cake.

coffee cake: Cake made of yeast dough enriched with eggs, ground nuts, and sugar; coffee cakes are often baked in a twist or braid; many have fruit fillings and most are covered with a sweet glaze or icing.

coffee cocktail: Coffee-colored cocktail made of brandy, port, and sweetening; a raw egg is sometimes mixed in this concoction.

coffee cone: Drip-filter coffee maker whose central funnel is shaped like a perforated cone for holding a filter paper and ground coffee.

coffee cream: Cream containing between 18 and 36 percent butterfat.

coffee cup: Drinking cup designed to hold coffee, larger than a teacup.

coffee grinder: Adjustable device for grinding or pulverizing coffee beans, also called a coffee mill.

coffee klatsch: Meeting where coffee is served and gossip is exchanged.

coffee mill: Coffee grinder.

coffee ring: Ring-shaped coffee cake.

coffee roll: Sweet roll.

coffee royale: Coffee flavored with rum, cinnamon, and whipped cream.

coffee service: Ceramic or metal serving set consisting of coffeepot, creamer, sugarbowl, and serving tray.

coffee set: Coffee service plus cups and saucers.

coffee shop: Small lunchroom or restaurant, usually associated with a hotel or motel.

coffee spoon: Small spoon for stirring an after-dinner coffee or demitasse.

cognac: Brandy distilled from local wine in the district around Cognac in west-central France; there are many cognac-type

brandies but the real one is considered by many to be the world's finest.

coho: Small salmon of the North Pacific taken extensively in British Columbian waters.

coil pottery: Pottery built up out of successive rolls of clay instead of by the action of the potter's wheel; most American-Indian pottery is of coil design.

coing: (French—quince)

coinguarde: Quince liqueur imported from France.

coin silver: Silverware containing as little as 50 percent silver or as much as 92.5 percent silver with the balance consisting of copper and other metals.

Cointreau: Orange-flavored liqueur made in France and named for the family who first produced it.

Coke: Cola drink.

cola: Carbonated soft drink made of kola-nut extract, vegetable coloring, coca leaves, and some sweetener.

colander: Perforated metal basket for straining macaroni, noodles, rice, spaghetti, and other water-filled foods.

colazione: (Italian—collation) Meal; *prima colazione* is breakfast; *colazione di mezzogiorno* (midday meal) is lunch.

colby: American cheese similar to cheddar.

colcannon: Irish dish of cabbage and potatoes served hot with a lump of butter.

cold cellar: cold-storage area of a basement used for perishables.

cold cuts: Assorted cheeses and meats thinly sliced.

cold flour: Slang for pulverized sugared corn.

cold-meat fork: Flat-tined serving fork.

cold slaw: Cole slaw.

cole: Cabbage or sea kale.

cole slaw: Raw shredded cabbage leaves served with a thin dressing.

col fermentada: (Spanish—fermented cabbage)

coliflor: (Spanish—cauliflower)

coll: Hobo slang for a stew composed of odds and ends.

collard: Smooth-leaf variety of cabbage.

collard greens: Leaves of the collard boiled and served like spinach.

collation: Light meal or refreshment.

collins: Summer cocktail.

collins glass: Tumbler holding 10 to 14 ounces.

collop: Small piece or slice of boneless meat.

cologneware: Mottled brown-and-gray glazed stoneware of type made into jugs and tankards as well as cookie and cracker jars.

Colombian coffee: High-grade coffee grown in Colombia, used in enriching blended coffees.

colonial goose; Australian slang for a leg of mutton stuffed with herbs and seasoned with various condiments.

Columbia River salmon: Chinook or king salmon.

comb honey: Honey in the comb.

combine: To bring ingredients together.

combo: Slang for combination sandwich such as a ham and cheese.

combo beverage: Slang for a combination beverage such as rum and Coke.

combo salad: Slang for a combination salad such as egg and potato.

comedor: (Spanish—dining room)

comestible: Food.

comfit: Dried fruit, root, or seed preserved with sugar or an old-fashioned-style candy, jam, or jelly.

Comice: Large round-shaped yellowish variety of pear.

comida: (Spanish—meal; food)

commercial beef: Fifth-grade beef, according to U.S. Department of Agriculture standards.

commis de rang: French—assistant waiter) One who has served his apprenticeship but is not yet a perfect waiter *(chef de rang)* and able to serve by himself.

compote: Stewed fruit, usually served from a compote bowl.

compote bowl: Stemmed decorative vessel of glass, metal, or porcelain for serving fruit compote.

compote de fruits: (French— stewed fruits)

compote glass: Tall-stemmed glass used for serving compote or ice cream.

compotier: Centerpiece dish on a raised base for serving fruits, compotes, or other cold desserts.

compressed yeast: Cake yeast combined under pressure with flour and starch.

con: (Spanish—with)

coñac: (Spanish—brandy; cognac)

concentrated milk: Evaporated milk not subjected to high pressure or temperature.

conch: Large gastropod mollusk with a spiral shell; clamlike conch meat is used in appetizers, chowders, soups, and stews; horse conchs, king conchs, or queen conchs are all edible.

concombre: (French—cucumber)

condensed milk: Canned milk evaporated and sweetened.

condiment: Pungent seasoning for enhancing the flavor of food; catsup, mustard, pepper, salt, spice, seasonings, etc., are all condiments.

condiment of condiments: Common salt.

condimento Italiano: (Italian—Italian condiment) Combination of marjoram, oregano, rosemary, sage, savory, sweet basil, and thyme, used in preparing Italian dishes.

condiment set: Matched containers and cruets for mustard, pepper, salt, olive oil, and vinegar, sometimes arranged on a rack or special tray.

conejo: (Spanish—rabbit)

confection: Candy or sweetmeat.

confectioner's sugar: Cane sugar finely pulverized and highly-refined for use in making candy and icings.

confiserie: (French—confectionery)

confit de dinde: (French—preserve of turkey; canned turkey)

confit d'oie: (French—preserve of goose; canned goose)

confiture: (French—preserved fruit)

congou: Black tea from China.

congre: (French—conger eel)

congrio: (Spanish—conger eel)

conserve: Berries, fruits, or vegetables preserved in sugar; conserve also means a preserve prepared from a mixture of fruits.

consommé: (French—consumed) Clear soup such as bouillon or meat broth.

consommé célestine: (French—celestine consommé) Chicken consommé garnished with small round slices of rolled pancakes stuffed with finely chopped chicken and chervil leaves.

consommeé madrilène: (French—consommé Madrid style) Clear broth with tomato juice and seasoning.

conta: (Portuguese—account; bill; check)

continental breakfast: Coffee and hot rolls.

conto: (Italian—bill; check)

coo-coo: Barbados-style cornmeal pudding.

cook: One who prepares food.

cook: To prepare food by baking, boiling, broiling, frying, roasting, steaming, or by any other method.

cookbook: Reference work containing directions and recipes for preparing food.

cooked cheese: Cheese made from cooking clabbered curd and adding flour.

cooker: Pressure cooker.

cookery: Art of fine cooking.

cookie: Small flat cake baked on a traylike pan, usually made of eggs, flavoring, flour, shortening, and sugar; countless recipes describe their preparation with spices, chocolate, nuts, fruit, jelly, etc.

cookie cutter: Metal device for cutting cookies out of dough before baking; cutters come in many different geometrical and fancy shapes.

cookie jar: Large covered jar of crockery or glass for holding cookies.

cookie pan: Aluminum pan of shallow design for baking cookies.

cookie press: Utensil for expressing cookie dough in a special shape onto a baking pan.

cookie sheet: Cookie pan without rim, usually just a flat rectangular metal plate.

cookstove: Kitchen stove.

cooler: Room or compartment of the refrigerator for cooling food.

cooper: Basket designed to hold wine bottles.

Coors: American beer brewed in Golden, Colorado.

Coosa Valley: Select sweet potato strain developed in Alabama's fertile Coosa Valley.

copper sponge: Copper-wire scouring pad for cleaning pots and pans.

copperware: Utensils, often ornamental, made of copper; because of copper's high degree of heat transmission; many modern stainless-steel pans and pots have copper bottoms.

copracake: Coconut cake.

copra kana: (Hindi—spiced coconut rice)

coq: (French—cock; rooster)

coq au vin: (French—chicken with wine) Chicken sautéed in butter and then simmered in wine.

coq au vin rouge: (French— chicken in red-wine style) Chicken cooked in red-wine sauce.

coquille: (French—shell) pastry shell molded and baked to re-semble a scallop shell; it is usually served filled with creamed chicken, crab, or fish flakes, etc.

coral: Lobster ovary; cooked it turns a lovely coral shade and this is used in coloring seafood sauces.

cordero: (Spanish—lamb)

cordial: Fruit-flavored drink of heavy consistency; liqueurs are of the same heavy consistency but their flavoring comes from herbs or spices.

cordial glass: Liqueur glass holding ¾ to 2 ounces of liquid.

Cordon Bleu: (French—Blue Ribbon) Famous school of cooking in Paris; colloquially, a cordon bleu is a good chef or cook.

core: Seed-filled center of such pomaceous fruits as the apple, pear, and quince, or the hard central section of the pineapple or the tough central stems of leafy plants such as the cabbage.

corer: Curve-bladed utensil for removing fruit and vegetable cores.

coriander: Aromatic herb of the carrot family whose seeds are used for flavoring candies, curries, liqueurs, pickles, and preserves.

coring knife: Corer.

corkage: Charge for opening and serving wine.

cork extractor: Wire-pronged device for removing corks from bottle necks.

corkscrew: Pointed spiral metal device for removing corks from bottles.

corn: Native American cereal grass also known as Indian corn or maize; sweet corn is for cooking, field corn for animal fodder; hundreds of valuable food products are derived from corn.

corn: To cure in brine, especially cuts of fresh beef such as rump, brisket, and plate (frozen meat does not corn well as the meat softens after defrosting); corn is an old term meaning grain or small particle, and refers to the time when corning was done with granular salt instead of with brine.

cornball: Candied popcorn ball.

corn beef: Corned beef.

cornbread: Bread products made with cornmeal and raised with baking powder.

corncake: Cornmeal bread baked in a frying pan or on a griddle; sometimes called johnnycake or hoecake.

corndab: Cornbread.

corn dodger: Crusty corncake.

corned beef: Beef preserved in brine with appropriate spices.

corn flour: White or yellow corn finely ground, used for baking breads, muffins, pancakes, waffles, etc.

corn fritter: Fritter made with cooked corn kernels.

corn grit: Hominy grits.

corn holder: Two-tined short-handled fork; stuck in at either end of a hot cob, they provide handles for easier eating.

corn husk: Leaves covering ear of corn.

cornhusker: Midwestern cheddar cheese of the moister variety.

corniehon: (French—gherkin)

Corningware: Heat-resistant brand of glassware.

Cornish: Domestic poultry produced for meat, originally bred in Cornwall, England.

cornish hen: Small-size hen usually cooked by broiling.

cornish pastry: Ground meat and vegetables stuffed into dough pockets or pastry shells and baked.

corn juice: Slang for corn whiskey.

corn liquor: Corn whiskey.

cornmeal: White or yellow corn coarsely ground.

corn mule: Slang for corn whiskey, so called because it is reputed to have the kick of a mule.

corn on the cob: Sweet corn cooked and eaten on the cob.

corn oyster: Corn fritter made with green corn.

corn pone: Oval stick of cornbread often made without milk or eggs.

corn popper: Deep, closed, sievelike utensil for popping corn.

corn pudding: Dessert made of kernel corn, eggs, and milk.

corn salad: European herb of the valerian family.

cornstarch: Starch derived from corn, used in thickening gravies and puddings; cornstarch thickening is used in many Chinese dishes.

cornstick: Cornbread baked in a mold to resemble a small ear of corn.

corn sugar: Dextrose derived from cornstarch.

corn syrup: Sweet syrup derived from corn, used in baking, candy making, and brewing; many people pour corn syrup on bread, hotcakes, or waffles.

cornucopia: Conical metal form for making pastry cones, or coneshaped paper containers for nuts and sweetmeats shaped like traditional horn of plenty.

coronado: (Spanish—crowned) Baked meringue filled with custard or pudding and topped with ice cream, whipped cream, and maraschino cherries.

coronata: White wine first made in Coronata, small town near the north Italian port of Genoa.

cos: Lettuce with long crisp leaves, also known as romaine lettuce.

cos lettuce: Romaine lettuce.

costermonger: English term for a person who sells fruits and vegetables.

costmary: Tansy-scented herb of the thistle family whose leaves are used to flavor meats and salads, and sometimes ale and beer.

costoletta alla Bolognese: (Italian —cutlet in Bologna style) Veal cutlet with melted cheese.

costoletta alla Milanese: (Italian —cutlet in Milan style) Breaded veal cutlet.

cot: Slang for apricot.

côte: (French—rib)

côté-à-côté: (French—side by side) Dining side by side as when seated with another on one side of a table or counter.

côte de boeuf: (French—beef rib)

côtelette: (French—chop)

côtelette au naturel: (French— natural-style chop) Simply cooked chop.

côtelette d'agneau: (French— lamb chop)

côtelette de mouton: (French— mutton chop)

côtelette de porc frais: (French— fresh pork chop)

côtelette de veau: (French—veal cutlet)

cotherstone: Rennet cheese of stilton type originating in Yorkshire, England.

cottage cheese: Sour-milk curds processed for creamy or dry presentation, sold fresh and uncured; cottage cheese is used in baking, cooking, and salad making, as well as eaten plain.

cottage-fried potatoes: Home-fried potatoes.

cottage loaf: Loaf of bread containing a smaller round part atop the larger bottom.

cottage pie: Shepherd's pie.

cottage pudding: Plain cake covered with hot sweet sauce.

cotton candy: Candy made from spun sugar, a carnival or amusement-park specialty.

cottonseed oil: Oil extracted from cottonseed and other grains, used for cooking or in salads.

coulis: (French—strained-jelly gravy)

country sausage: Farm-style sausage usually pork links or bulk sausage made of pork.

coupe glacée: (French—iced cup) Ice cream or sherbet combined with fruit or other ingredients; *coupe* is always served in a rimless bowl or cup.

coupette: (French—cuplet) Small *coupe* for serving fruit salad or seafood cocktail.

court bouillon: (French—short broth) Aromatic liquid in which fish, meat, or vegetables are cooked; usually water, oil, or butter is added, or lemon or vinegar plus some seasoning; the broth is usually preboiled before the main items (fish, meat, or vegetables) are added.

Courvoisier: Cognac brand name of a type supposedly drunk by Napoleon.

couscous: Arab dish of farina sometimes flavored with steamed meat and vegetables.

couvert: (French—cover charge) Restaurant charge which covers bread, butter, and place setting.

cowboy coffee: Slang for black coffee without sugar.

cow creamer: Cream jug shaped like a cow.

cowcress: Wild watercress.

cowfish: Horned trunkfish of the Atlantic Coast taken as a food fish from Cape Hatteras to Cape Cod.

cow juice: Slang for milk.

cowpea: Edible seed of a tropical leguminous vine, sometimes called black-eyed pea; cowpeas are popular legumes because they are very nourishing and can be made quite tasty when cooked correctly.

cow tureen: Cow-shaped soup tureen made of white porcelain.

crab: Aquatic crustacean with a broad carapace and pincerlike claw feet; crabmeat is served boiled, broiled, deviled, fried, in salads, and in seafood-cocktail combinations.

crabapple: Native American wild apple yielding small red fruit with a somewhat sour taste, used chiefly in jellies and for decorating fruit bowls and displays.

crabe: (French—crab)

crab foo yung: Chinese omelet containing flaked crab, bean sprouts, eggs, onions, and spices.

crab louie: Seafood salad containing bits of cooked crab and fresh green vegetables mixed with louie dressing, garnished with slices of hard-boiled egg and to-mato; it was named by Enrico Caruso in honor of a chef in a Seattle club.

cracked cocoa: Cacao nibs—roasted or dried cacao beans, shelled and freed from the germ or sprouting portion.

cracked ice: Ice hammered into small pieces for use in drinks, particularly those which must be shaken up before pouring and serving.

cracker: Thin, crisp bakery product made of flour and water plus some characteristic flavor; many kinds of crackers are popular, including arrowroot crackers, graham wafers, cheese niblets, oysterettes, pilot biscuits, soda crackers, etc.

Cracker Jack: Brand name for a molasses-coated popcorn.

crackermeal: Dry unsweetened crackers crushed and sifted into fine meal used in coating, stuffing, and topping.

crackleware: Ceramic ware with a crackled and crazed finish.

crackling: Residue left after fat or lard is rendered from beef, pork, or poultry.

crackling bread: Cornbread made with cracklings.

cracknel: Hard and brittle biscuit.

crack stage: Point in candy making when a driblet of syrup dropped into a cup of cold water is so brittle it cracks; this occurs when the temperature of the syrup being cooked is between 290 and 310 degrees Fahrenheit.

cran: Slang for cranberry.

cranberry: Bright red berry of a low shrub of the blueberry family; cranberries are usually found in boggy places and were originally called crane berry, because they were a favorite food of marsh cranes; cranberries are used in jellies, juices, sauces, and wines.

cranberry butter: Cranberries boiled and sieved or puréed and combined with sugar, grated orange rind, and lemon juice; cranberry butter is used as a spread or condiment.

cranberry cocktail: Chilled cranberry juice.

cranberry jam: Cranberry sauce.

cranberry jelly: Jelly made from cranberries, popular as a side dish with cold cuts, poultry, and seafood.

cranberry sauce: Relish made of seeded cranberries, traditional with turkey on Thanksgiving.

cranberry wine: Wine made from fermented cranberries.

crappie: Freshwater sunfish of the Mississippi River Valley and the Great Lakes, usually pan fried.

craquelin: (French—cracknel)

crawfish: Crayfish.

crayfish: Freshwater crustacean resembling a small lobster (spiny rock lobster is sometimes called a sea crayfish); crayfish are served in salads, soups, and stews or boiled and served alone with tabasco sauce.

cream: Yellow top part of unhomogenized milk; coffee cream has between 18 and 36 percent butterfat; cream containing more than 36 percent is called whipping cream, and anything with less than 18 percent is regarded as milk.

cream: To soften ingredients by beating until they are creamy, soft, and well blended.

creamed butter: Whipped butter.

creamer: Cream pitcher or small jug for serving cream.

cream filling: Custard or other creamy sauce used for filling cakes, cream puffs, eclairs, tarts, etc.

cream nut: Brazil nut.

cream of tartar: Purified tartar, a grape-juice derivative used in baking powders or as a smoother in cooked icings.

cream-of-tartar tree: Australian silk-cotton tree yielding an acid fruit, also called the Australian baobob.

cream pie: Thick cream or custard filling in prebaked pie shell.

cream puff: Round shell of puff pastry filled with cream custard or ice cream.

cream sauce: White sauce.

cream sherry: Commercial term for a sweet brown sherry.

cream soda: Carbonated soft drink flavored with sugar and vanilla.

cream soup: Thick puréed broth or soup thickened with agar, barley, cornstarch, rice, or vegetables.

cream-soup cup: Double-handled broad-mouthed cup for serving cream soups.

creamware: Cream-colored pottery.

credenza: (Italian—credence; faith) Buffet or serving sideboard of type once used by a servant who pretasted his master's food and wine to make sure it did not contain poison.

crème: (French—cream)

crème au beurre: (French—cream with butter; butter cream)

crème bavoroise: (French—Bavarian cream)

crème brûlé: (French—burned cream) Frozen dessert containing heavy whipped cream, cornstarch, egg yolks, milk, and sugar.

crème chantilly: (French—Chantilly cream) Vanilla-flavored whipped cream.

crème d'ananas: (French—cream of pineapple) Pineapple-flavored liqucur.

crème de banane: (French—cream of banana) Banana-flavored liqueur.

crème de cacao: (French—cream of cacao) Chocolate flavored liqueur.

crème de café: (French—cream of coffee) Coffee-flavored liqueur.

crème de cassis: (French—cream of black currant) Black-currant liqueur.

crème de mandarine: (French—cream of tangerine) Brandy and tangerine-peel liqueur.

crème de menthe: (French—cream of mint)—Greenish mint-flavored liqeuur.

crème de moka: (French—cream of mocha) Chocolate-and-coffee-flavored liqueur.

crème de noix: (French—cream of walnut) Walnut-flavored liqueur.

crème de noyau: (French—cream of fruit pit) A liqueur containing crushed-cherrystone flavoring.

crème de rose: (French—cream of rose) Pink liqueur distinguished by its rose aroma.

crème de thé: (French—cream of tea) Tea-flavored liqueur.

créme de violette: (French—cream of violet) Violet-flavored liqueur with the characteristic perfume of the flowers.

crème d'orange: (French—cream of orange) Cherry and orange flame-colored liqueur containing brandy.

crème faussée: (French—fake cream) Substitute for cream—cream made of vegetable oil and used as a whipped-cream substitute.

crème fourettée: (French—whipped cream)

créme moulée à la vanille: (French molded cream with vanilla; vanilla custard)

crème moulée au caramel: (French—molded cream with caramel) Egg-custard pudding in caramel sauce.

crémeux: (French—creamy)

crème vichyssoise: (French—Vichy-style cream) Vichyssoise cream soup containing leeks and potatoes and served cold.

Crème Yvette: Domestic brand of violet-flavored liqueur.

creole: Prepared with okra, peppers, rice, tomatoes, and seasoning.

creole sauce: Hot and spicy sauce served with fish, meat, omelets, etc.

crêpe: (French—crepe; veil) Thin pancake made of egg batter poured sparingly into a frying pan; after cooking, *crêpes* are usually filled with some mixture and rolled up, then served from a chafing dish.

crêpe aux champignons: (French—pancake with mushrooms)

crêpe suzette: Thin pancake made with orange-flavored batter and filled with an orange-flavored cream; just before serving they are drenched with liqueur and set ablaze.

crèpinette: (French—flat sausage)
crescent: Crescent-shaped bun, cookie, or roll.

cress: Pungent-leafed plant of the mustard family, of which there are several varieties; garden cress and watercress are used chiefly in salads.

cresson: (French—cress)

cresson de fontaine: (French—watercress)

creuse: Rennet-type skim-milk cheese of type first made in Creuse, a department in central France.

crevallé: Food fish of the pompano family common in Florida and California waters.

crevette: (French—shrimp)

criado: (Portuguese—waiter)

crimp: To decorate a piecrust edge by crimping it between the thumb and forefinger or pressing it with the tines of a fork; crimp also means to gash a freshly caught fish so its muscles will contract.

criollo: (Spanish—creole)

crisphead: Head lettuce.

croaker: Food fish found along Atlantic and Gulf coasts of the United States, so-called for the croaking noises they make.

crock: Thick earthenware jar or pot.

crockery: Articles made of thick earthenware.

crocus cloth: Abrasive-surface cloth for the fine polishing of metal utensils.

croissant: (French—crescent) Crescent-shaped roll of very light consistency; *croissants* are considered more pastry than bread.

crookneck squash: Yellow summer squash with a curved neck.

croquette: (French—crunchy little ball) Ball of minced chicken, fish, meat, seafood, or vegetables coated with egg and bread crumbs and fried.

crosscut shank: Beef crosscut from the fore shank.

croustade: (French—crust dish) Bread or pastry shell brushed with butter and fried in deep fat, or a bread or pastry shell used for holding a creamed filling or ragout.

croûte: (French—crust)

croûte au pot: (French—crust for the pot) Clear soup with toasted bread crusts set afloat on its surface.

crouton: (French—crustlet) Stale bread diced, fried, and used in garnishing soups.

crow garlic: Wild onion, so-called because Indians believed crows scattered the seeds.

crown roast: Lamb or pork loin skewered into a circle so the rib bones protrude to form a crown.

crudités: (French—crudity; rawness) Raw vegetables such as carrots, celery stalks, cucumbers, radishes, and so on served as appetizers.

cruet: Stoppered glass bottle for serving olive oil, vinegar, and other condiments at the table.

cruller: Fried cake made in oval or oval-twist shapes from doughnut dough and served with a sprinkling of confectioner's sugar.

crumber: Miniature carpet sweeper for removing crumbs from the table.

crumpet: Unsweetened leavened bread cooked on a griddle; crumpets are similar to english muffins but of porous consistency with surface holes; the name comes from a Middle English word meaning wafer.

crunch candy: Any crisp and crunchy confection.

crushed ice: Crumb-size ice used in cooling drinks served.

crusher: Utensil for crushing food or ice.

crust: Somewhat hard and usually brown external part of anything baked or roasted; crust also means the tartarous encrustation inside a wine bottle.

crusta: Cocktail served from a glass lined with lemon peel and with rim crusted with sugar frosting.

crustacean: Shelled aquatic invertebrate such as a barnacle, crab, crayfish, lobster, shrimp, etc.

crystal: Clear lead glass of the highest quality, used in the production of most fine ornamental glassware.

crystal vinegar: Vinegar rendered colorless by distillation or filtration.

cuba libre: (Spanish—free Cuba) Mixed drink of rum and lime juice; the name dates back to an era before the Spanish-American War.

cuban sandwich: Cuban variation of poor-boy sandwich served in New Orleans.

cuban spinach: Herb related to portulaca and also called indian lettuce.

cube: To cut into cubes.

cube soup: Broth made from beef, chicken, or vegetable bouillon cubes dissolved in hot water; if the water is drawn from a spigot without boiling, the result is called sink soup.

cube steak: Tough cut of beef sliced thin and tenderized by pounding with a steak hammer.

cube sugar: Compressed cubes of granulated sugar.

cucumber: Succulent gourd eaten raw or pickled; the French frequently cook cucumbers and eat them hot.

cucumber vinaigrette: Appetizer or relish of very thinly sliced cucumbers and onions drenched in sour cream and vinegar.

cuenta: (Spanish—account; bill; check)

cuisine: (French—kitchen; cookery) A general term applied to cooking and also used to indicate a national style of cooking, such as Italian cuisine, German cuisine, etc.

cuisson: (French cooking; cooking time; stock or liquid used in cooking something)

cuke: Slang for cucumber.

cultured milk: Skim milk soured with a lactic-acid bacteria to produce a smoothly emulsified mixture.

cumin: Aromatic seed of an herb of the carrot family, used in spicing cheeses, drinks, salads, and sauces.

cup: Hollow vessel for holding liquids, usually furnished with a handle; in cooking a cup is a liquid measure containing ½ pint or a dry measure containing 8 ounces or 16 tablespoons.

cup cake: Small sweet cake baked in a muffin tin, usually topped with sugar frosting.

cuppa': English slang for a nice cup of tea.

curaçao: Orange-flavored cordial produced from the skins of bitter oranges cultivated on island of Curaçao in the Netherlands Antilles.

curaimir: Irish-style venison cutlets marinated in wine.

curd: Coagulated milk particle created by souring; the watery part remaining is called the whey.

curd cheese: Cottage cheese.

curd knife: Cheese slicer.

cured: Preserved with salt or by drying.

currant: Small red or white acid berry used in jams and jellies; currant also refers to a small seedless raisin grown in the Levant and used in confectionery.

currant wine: Cordial produced from fermented raisin currants.

curried: Prepared with strong spices such as cardamom, pepper, tumeric, and ginger, and colored with saffron.

curry: Hot Indian condiment compounded of many spices, used in cooking many fish, meat, seafood, and vegetable dishes.

cush: Bread or crackers cooked in broth.

cusk: Edible saltwater fish of a species related to the cod.

custard: Smooth-textured egg-yolk pudding baked in a slow oven.

custard apple: Fruit of any of the various trees of the genus Annona.

custard cup: Cooking cup of heat-resistant porcelain or pyrex for baking individual custards.

custard pie: Cream pie.

cutlery: Sharp-edged cutting utensils such as cleavers, knives, parers, scissors, shears, especially those used in preparing and eating food.

cutlet: Small slice of meat, usually carved from the leg or rib.

cutlings: Barley or oatmeal grits.

cutter beef: Second lowest grade of beef, according to U.S. Department of Agriculture designation, used for making sausage.

cutting block: Hardwood block, oil-finished and two inches thick, for cutting bread or mincing meat and vegetables.

cuttlefish: Small cephalopod mollusk, similar to the squid, containing an internal shell called a cuttlebone; cuttlefish are usually served boiled atop steamed rice or as part of a seafood stew; the purplish juice of this marine invertebrate is responsible for much of its flavor.

cuvée extra: (French—special quality) Term applied to wines, often shown on labels in abbreviated form: C.E.

cygnet: Young swan.

cymling: Scalloped variety of summer squash.

dab: Small and tasty flounder fished off the American and European coasts of the North Atlantic.

dace: Small carplike freshwater food fish related to the minnow and common in American and European streams and rivers.

dad: Scots for big portion or large slice.

dagang babi: (Malay—pork)

dagang goreng: (Malay—fried meat) Marinated beef strips.

dagang sapi: (Malay—beef)

Dagger ale: Ale of type sold at the Dagger tavern in Holborn, London, in Elizabethan times.

dagwood: Slang for a gigantic sandwich.

daikon: Huge Japanese radishes with roots up to a yard long, eaten raw or cooked like turnips.

daiquiri: Cocktail made of white rum, lime juice, and sugar, and named after the mining town in southeastern Cuba where American troops landed during the Spanish-American War.

dairy: Farm building where cream and milk are stored or a retail store making a specialty of selling dairy products.

dairy butter: Freshly prepared unsalted butter.

dairy cattle: Milk-producing breeds such as Brown Swiss, Dutch Belted, Guernsey, Holstein-Friesian, Jersey, etc.

dairy cream: Unadulterated cream.

dairy farm: Farm devoted to the production of milk.

dairy products: Milk products.

dairy restaurant: Place specializing in serving dairy products to the exclusion of fish, meat, and seafood dishes.

daisy: Cocktail made of brandy, gin, rum, or whiskey with grenadine, lemon juice, and sugar.

dallop: Dollop.

dalmation cherry: Marasca.

damasco: (Portuguese—apricot)

damascus plum: Damson plum.

damascusware: Highly colored Turkish pottery often used to decorate dining tables.

damask: Patterned napkins and tablecloths or other napery woven of reversible cotton or linen damask cloth.

Damen: (German—ladies) Hungarian rennet cheese made from cow's milk.

damson: Small dark purple plum originally from Asia Minor.

damson gin: Damson-flavored gin.

dandelion: Bright yellow wild-flower of the chicory family whose leaves are used in making salads and wine; dandelion roots are sometimes dried and ground to make a native coffee.

dandelion spinach: Chopped and boiled dandelion leaves, often creamed with egg whites and butter.

dandelion wine: Wine made from fermented dandelion flowers.

dandy funk: Sailor's slang for hardtack biscuits baked in molasses.

danish: Danish pastry.

danish blue: Pungent roquefort-type cheese made with cow's milk instead of sheep's.

danish pastry: Layered pastry famous for its flaky texture and rich filling.

Danoise: (French—Danish) Sauce made of white wine flavored with grated cheese and lobster butter; the term is also applied to various canapés, salads, etc., supposedly made in the Danish manner and described as *à la Danoise*.

dansk kage: (Danish—Danish cake; Danish pastry)

danzig brandy: *Danziger Goldwasser.*

Danziger Goldwasser: (German— Danzig gold water) Citrus-peel-and-herb-flavored liqueur containing tiny flecks of gold leaf; mixture is well shaken before serving so flecks of gold appear to swim in the clear liqueur.

dapur: (Malay—kitchen)

daragaluska: (Hungarian—dumpling)

darjeeling: Orange pekoe black tea grown in mountains of northern India.

darne: (French—slice) Thick slab of fish flesh.

dash: Informal measurement consisting of 3 to 5 drops or a pinch (less than $\frac{1}{8}$ teaspoon).

dasheen: Taro.

date: Sugary fruit of the North African and Asiatic date palm introduced into California; dates are dried and eaten raw, cooked in cakes, pastries, and puddings, or are homogenized and served in malted milks and ice cream sodas.

date fig: Variety of fig commonly dried.

date plum: Persimmon.

date sugar: Sugar made from date-palm sap.

datte: (French—date) Fruit of the date palm.

daube: (French—a kind of stew)

daurade: (French—gilded) Gilt-head fish.

decant: To pour liquid from one vessel to another—gently so not to disturb the sediment.

decanter: Stoppered bottle of ceramic, glass, plastic, or metal for holding liqueurs, liquors, and wines to be served at table; most fine decanters are made of crystal.

decker: Layered sandwich containing three or more tiers of bread separated by filling; double decker is a sandwich with two layers of filling whereas a triple decker has three.

deep-dish: Baked in a deep dish: deep-dish custard, deep-dish pie, etc.

deep-dish pie: Fruit pie with top crust only, baked in a deep baking dish.

deep fat: Hot fat used in deep-fat frying.

deep-fat fryer: Deep pan or utensil with a wire-mesh basket for holding food to be fried by immersion in deep fat; once cooked the basket is raised so the food can drain excess fat back into the pan or pot.

deep freezer: Kitchen appliance for storing food at below-freezing temperatures.

deep fry: To fry in fat deep enough to cover whatever is being fried.

deep fryer: Deep-fat fryer.

deg: Abbreviation for degree.

déglacer: (French—to deglaze) Diluting pan juices with alcohol, soup stock, or wine to remove particles gathered during cooking.

deglet nur: Near Eastern date prized for its sweetness and keeping qualities, now cultivated extensively in southern California.

dehydrated food: Anhydrated food.

déjeuner: (French—lunch)

déjeuner à la fourchette: (French —luncheon with fork) Late heavy breakfast or luncheon where meat is served.

déjeuner de noce: (French—wedding breakfast)

Delaware: Native American wine made from red Delaware grapes.

Delaware punch: Punch made of brandy, orange juice, and chilled sauterne, also known as fishhouse cooler.

delftware: Blue-on-white porcelain pottery originally made in Delft, Holland, for dining room and kitchen use.

delicacy: Food or drink considered rare or luxurious.

delicatessen: (corrupt German—delicate eating) Ready-to-eat foods such as dairy dishes, baked goods, cold meats, roast fowl and roast beef, pickled and smoked fish, pickles, olives, and all such related foods; nowadays the term usually means a store where such prepared delicacies are sold.

delicia: Celery stalk stuffed with blue cheese.

Delicious: Variety of light-red American apple, having a distinctive shape and aromatic scent.

Delikatessaufschnitt: (German— cold cuts)

delly: Slang for delicatessen.

delmonico potatoes: Scalloped potatoes baked in a cheese sauce, named in honor of New York restaurateur Lorenzo Delmonico.

delmonico steak: Club steak.

demerara rum: Rum of type distilled in the Demerara district of Guyana formerly known as British Guiana.

demijohn: Narrow-necked glass or earthenware container enclosed in wicker and used for storing cooking oil, liquors, and wines; demijohns hold from 1 to 10 gallons, and usually are provided with wicker handles; they are named after Dame-Jeanne, French term for a large wicker-covered container.

demitasse: Small after-dinner cup of coffee.

dent-de-lion: (French—tooth-of-lion or dandelion)

derby: Rennet cheese of type made from cow's milk in Darbyshire County, England.

desayuno: (Spanish—breakfast)

dinner chimes: Small set of metal bars or hollow tubes mounted over a resonator box and struck with a soft-padded hammer to announce a meal is ready.

dinner fork: Large round-tined fork used with the dinner knife.

dinner knife: Largest-size eating knife used with dinner fork.

dinner music: Music played during a meal.

dinner plate: Large-size plate for serving the main course, 10 to 12 inches in diameter.

dinnerware: Dining service of china, glass, glazed pottery, plastic, or other suitable material.

dip: Flavored cream mixture for dipping crackers, potato chips, tortilla chips, etc.; dips are made of cream cheese or sour cream flavored with bacon bits, seafoods, onions, pickles, and other flavoring agents.

diplomate: (French—diplomatic) Sauce flavored with lobster butter, truffles, and brandy.

dish: Ceramic or glass dinnerware; dish can also mean food prepared in a particular fashion.

dishcloth: Cloth for washing dishes; dishcloths should be thoroughly washed and dried after each meal to prevent their becoming a source of bacterial contamination.

dish mop: Short-handled small mop.

dish rack: Drainboard rack for holding dishes and glasses after they are washed.

dishrag: Dishcloth.

dish towel: Towel for drying dishes.

dishwasher: Electrical appliance for washing and drying dishes.

dishwashing brush: Long-handled bristle brush used in washing dishes.

disposer: Electrically operated garbage-disposal appliance connected to the waste line of many modern kitchen sinks.

dissolve: To break up and liquefy, to melt.

distilled vinegar: Colorless vinegar made by distilling ordinary vinegar.

distilled water: Water obtained by condensing steam; this is a way of obtaining fresh water from salt water and is used aboard ocean-going ships as well as in many coastal installations where good freshwater is scarce.

dittany: Name applied to three different herbs: cretan dittany, an herb native to Crete; fraxinella, a Eurasian herb; and bastard dittany, a European mint.

divinity: Fudge made with egg whites, corn syrup, and sometimes added flavoring such as cherry, coconut, mint, pineapple, etc.

doce: (Portuguese—sweet; dessert)

dock: Sorrel.

dodger: Corn dodger.

doe: Adult female antelope, deer, goat, rabbit, etc.

dog salmon: Large species of edible salmon taken along the Pacific Coast; smaller than the chinook salmon, it is also called chum.

dog snapper: Member of a large family of edible fish found chiefly in Florida and West Indies waters.

dolce: (Italian—sweet; dessert)

dolce-piccante: (Italian—bitter-sweet)

dolce verde: (Italian—sweet green) Rich type of sweet Italian cheese veined with blue despite its name, served with dessert courses at the end of a meal.

dollop: Blob or lump of some semiliquid such as butter, sour cream, ice cream, peanut butter, etc.

dolly varden: Char trout taken in northwestern streams from Alaska to northern California.

dolma: (Arabic—stuffed) Dish popular from Afghanistan to Morocco, containing mixture of chopped meat, onions, rice, and seasoning, wrapped in cabbage leaves and baked.

dolmadakia: (Greek—stuffed leaves) *Dolmades*.

dolmades: (Greek—stuffed) Greek form of *dolma* with grape leaves substituted for the cabbage leaves of the Arab dish.

domaci beli sir: Yugoslavian sheep's-milk cheese cured in a sheepskin.

domestic beer: American-brewed beer.

domestic science: Study of housekeeping, cooking, and sewing.

domestic wine: American-vinted wine; California leads all states in the quantity and variety of its wines, but New York, Ohio, and other states also have valuable wine industries.

dooar: Black tea grown in Dooar district of Bengal, India.

dop: (Dutch shell; husk) Grapeskin brandy.

Dos XX: Mexican beer.

dot: To cover the surface of food with small pieces of butter, cheese, etc.

Dotter: (German—egg yolk) Cheese made of skimmed milk and egg yolks plus seasoning.

double boiler: Cooking utensil consisting of double saucepans one resting above the other; the bottom pan is filled with boiling water, which heats the top and its contents without danger of burning.

doubleburger: Two hamburgers on one bun.

double cheese: Cheese made entirely from cream or to which cream has been added instead of milk.

double consommé: Concentrated consommé produced by prolonged cooking or by adding bouillon cubes.

double cream: Heavy cream skimmed from milk after a full day (24 hours).

double-crème: (French—double cream) Soft cream cheese.

double-decker: Two-layer sandwich; *see also* decker, club sandwich.

double old-fashioned glass: Tumbler holding 8 to 10 ounces of liquid.

double saucepan: Double boiler.

doucette: (French—corn salad [the herb])

dough: Soft mass of moistened flour or meal firm enough to knead; thinner mixtures suitable for pouring are called batters.

doughnut: Ring-shaped sweet cake fried in deep fat and someitmes served with a sprinkling of confectioner's sugar.

doughnut joint: Cheap lunchroom.

doux: (French—sweet)

doz.: Dozen.

dozen: Twelve of anything.

dragée: (French—sugar plum) Almond coated with sugar and flavored.

Drambuie: Brand name for an aromatic liqueur made from Scotch whiskey.

draw: To eviscerate; to remove entrails.

drawer divider: Shallow tray set inside a drawer to divide it into handy sections for storing utensils.

drawn butter: Melted butter, sometimes seasoned with herbs.

draw one, draw two, etc.: Restaurant slang for pouring one or two or more cups of coffee.

dredge: To coat or sprinkle with crumbs, flour, salt, or seasoning.

Dresdener Bierkäse: (German— Dresden-style beer cheese) Sourmilk hand cheese flavored with beer and first developed in this city in the south of Germany.

Dresdener Kuhkäse: (German— Dresden-style cow cheese)

dressing: Stuffing.

dried beef: Beef dried, salted, and smoked.

dried fruit: Fruit dehydrated by evaporation: dried apples, apricots, figs, peaches, pears, prunes, raisins, etc.

dried milk: Milk dehydrated by evaporation; also called milk powder or powdered milk.

dried vegetables: Vegetables concentrated and evaporated.

drikkevand: (Danish—drinking water)

drip coffee: Coffee brewed in a dripolator; boiling water is poured over the coffee grounds,

drips through tiny orifices, and steeps in the pot below.

dripolator: Three-part coffee maker consisting of a lower steeping pot, a sievelike middle section holding finely ground coffee, and a top section with a perforated base so hot water poured into it will drip down through the coffee grounds and into the lower pot.

dripping pan: Pan for catching drippings as from roasting meats.

drippings: Fats and juices drawn from foods, particularly meats, during cooking.

drive-in: Restaurant serving beverages and food to motorists who drive in and eat at a counter or from portable trays clamped to the car window.

drop cookie: Cookie baked from dough dropped by teaspoonfuls 2 or 3 inches apart on a baking sheet.

drumstick: Poultry leg between the ankle and thigh.

drupe: Hard-stoned pulpy fruit of the almond family: almond, apricot, cherry, peach, plum, etc.

dry: Comparative lack of sweetness, usually applied to champagnes and still wines.

dry cheese: Hard dry German cheese such as *Sperrkäse* or *Trockenkäse*.

dry curd: Uncreamed and unsalted cottage cheese used for baking; dry-curd cheese may be creamed and used in salads and sandwiches.

dry ice: Frozen carbon-dioxide gas used for refrigerating perishables; dry ice freezes at −109 degrees Fahrenheit, whereas ordinary ice freezes at only 32 degrees F.

dry manhattan: Cocktail made of blended whiskey, dry vermouth, angostura bitters, and a maraschino cherry.

dry martini: Cocktail made of gin and dry vermouth and served with a lemon twist or a small green olive.

dry-pack soup: Dehydrated soup.

dubbelsmörgas: (Swedish—Double buttered bread) Sandwich.

Dubonnet: Brand name of a French apéritif characterized by its somewhat bitter medicinal flavor.

duchesse: (French—duchess) Purée of potato and egg yolk used as a border or garnish for foods served *à la duchesse; a duchesse* is also a *petit-four* made of nuts, sugar, and egg whites.

duck: Domestic waterfowl served pressed, roasted, and in various other ways.

duckling: Young duck.

duck press: Aluminum and stainless-steel device for pressing boned duck and other poultry.

duckwheat: Tartarian buckwheat, a sturdy variety that will grow in a cold climate and poor soil.

duel cheese: Rennet cheese of Austrian origin made from cow's milk.

dugléré: Fish prepared in a poaching liquid of onions, tomatoes, seasoning, and wine, and named for its inventor, the chef of the Café Anglais.

du jour: (French—of the day; today's) Food of the day.

dulce: (Spanish—sweet) Sweetmeat or other confection.

dulce de leche: (Spanish—milk candy) Dessert popular in River Plate countries: Argentina, Paraguay, Uruguay.

dull: Term indicating that a liquor or tea is cloudy.

dulse: Edible red seaweed dried for use as a natural candy, popular along both coasts of the North Atlantic.

Dumas, Alexandre (1802-1870): Novelist and author of the *Dictionnaire de Cuisine*—humorous and informative compendium of culinary matters.

dumpling: Leavened dough cooked by boiling or steaming, usually in a stew; dumpling can also mean a fruit dessert made of apples, berries, cherries, or other fruits wrapped in pastry dough and baked.

dumpling cutter: Gear-toothed-wheel utensil for cutting dumpling dough and leaving a serrated edge.

Duncan: Large pale-yellow grapefruit prized for its thin skin and flavorsome yellow flesh.

dundee cake: Light Scots fruitcake served at tea.

dundee shortbread: Cookies made of butter, eggs, wheat flour, and sugar, and molded in a design originated in Dundee, Scotland.

dunderfunk: Broken ship's biscuits mixed with molasses and baked in flat cookie form.

dungeness crab: Large fine-flavored crab taken along the North Pacific coast, first caught near the town of Dungeness, Washington.

dunking tray: Party platter or tray holding an assortment of dips and dunks.

durazno: (Spanish—peach)

duraznos en crema: (Spanish—peaches in cream)

Durham: Shorthorn beef cattle developed in Durham County, England.

Duroc-Jersey: Large swine developed in America to produce red lard.

durra: Variety of sorghum grass, grown throughout the world as a food crop.

durum: Variety of hard wheat high in gluten producing proteins and therefore used chiefly in making macaroni, noodles, spaghetti, and similar alimentary pastes.

dust: To sprinkle lightly with cinnamon, flour, or sugar.

Dutch Belted: Breed of cattle developed in the Netherlands, black with a broad white band about their middle.

Dutch cattle: Dairy cattle of Holstein-Friesian breed especially developed for milk production.

dutch cheese: Cottage cheese or small round hard cheese like edam or gouda.

dutch cupboard: Buffet with open upper shelving.

dutch gin: Hollands; see gin.

dutch gold: Imitation goldleafing sometimes applied decoratively to tableware.

dutch lunch: Single serving of cold cheeses and sliced meats.

dutch oven: Heavy kettle with tightly fitting lid for braising or steaming foods; dutch ovens can be used for baking over camp fires.

dutch-process cocoa: Cocoa nibs treated with alkalies to enrich the color, flavor, and aroma of the cocoa, a process developed by Dutch settlers in Surinam and the Netherlands Antilles.

dutch sauce: Hollandaise sauce.

dutch settle: Seat with a hinged back which can be lowered onto the arms to make a table.

dutch treat: Meal or outing where everyone pays for his own portion of the bill.

dutchware blue: Delft pottery.

duxelles: (French—mushroom hash) Finely chopped mushrooms, sautéed, and used for garnishing fish and poultry dishes.

D/W: Abbreviation for Der Wienerschnitzel, a chain of hot-dog stands selling frankfurters with chili, kraut, or mustard.

dwarf banana: Small chinese banana cultivated in Central America and the West Indies.

dwarf pea: Chick pea.

dzo: Hybrid produced by crossing the domestic cow with the Tibetan yak.

earth apple: Old name for Jerusalem artichoke or a cucumber; the French call a potato an earth apple (*pomme de terre*).

earth ball: Truffle.

earth chestnut: Earthnut.

earthenware: Dishware made of porous clay fired at low heat; earthenware usually implies the coarser varieties of dishware although some modern designs take advantage of this quality to bring out new and interesting ceramic textures.

earthnut: Name applied to any of several tubers, roots, or subterranean pods such as the chufa and the peanut; earthnut is also another name for truffle.

easter egg: Decorated, candied, or colored egg, or an egg-shaped confection, prepared for Easter; the egg is a pre-Christian symbol of fertility, and its use at Easter is thought to symbolize the resurrection of Jesus after his crucifixion and entombment.

East Indian arrowroot: Indian arrowroot.

eats: Slang for food.

eau: (French—water)

eau de selz: (French—seltzer water; soda water)

eau de vie de Dantzig: (French —Danzig whiskey) *Danziger Goldwasser*.

eau de vie de grain: (French— spirits of grain) Whiskey.

eau de vie de vin: (French—spirits of wine) Brandy.

ECCAA: Abbreviation for Executive Chefs de Cuisine Association of America.

eccles cake: Small round currant-filled cooky.

échalote: (French—shallot)

éclair: (French—lightning; gleam) Finger-shaped pastry filled with cream or custard.

écrevisse: (French—crayfish)

écumante: (French—foaming) Pudding sauce.

edam: Cannonball-shaped hard yellow cheese made in Edam in northeastern Holland; it is protected by a red wax covering.

edammer kaas: (Dutch—edam cheese)

eddike: (Danish—vinegar)

edelweiss camembert: Pungent and creamy Swiss-German cheese used as a spread on cocktail crackers or as a dessert.

edger: Utensil for impressing a design around the edge of pastry or pie dough.

edible plant: One of more than 70,000 species of plants in the world today which can be eaten in some form.

edible spun protein: Engineered food.

eel: Snakelike bony fish found in streams of Europe and North America and in all warm seas; eels have a sweet-flavored flesh high in vitamins A and D, and are eaten baked, fried, pickled, and smoked; most eel dishes are regarded as delicacies.

ees eeghian: (Modern Greek—to your health) A toast.

eetzaal: (Dutch dining room)

egg albumen: Egg white.

egg apple: Eggplant.

eggbeater: Rotating beater operated by an electric motor or by hand, used in beating eggs, whipping cream, etc.

eggbread: Golden-yellow batter bread or spoonbread; eggbread is also the name of a golden-yellow bread often sold as egg *challah.*

egg cheese: Semihard cheese made by adding eggs to the curds, a Finnish specialty.

egg cooler: Cup-shaped wire basket for boiling eggs so they may be easily and quickly removed and cooled in cold water.

eggcup: Small cup just big enough to hold a boiled egg.

egg foo yung: Chinese omelet made of eggs, bamboo shoots, chinese cabbage, and some chopped chicken, meat, seafood, or vegetable plus seasoning.

eggfruit: Bland yellow-orange fruit of a tropical tree native to Florida and the West Indies; sometimes called canistel or *canisté,* its Cuban-Spanish name; eggfruit is also another name for eggplant.

egghot: Hot beverage concocted of beer, cinnamon, raw eggs, and sugar.

eggnog: Beverage made of eggs, cream or milk, sugar, and flavoring; eggnog is sometimes fortified with brandy, rum, whiskey, or wine, and is usually served with a dash of cinnamon or nutmeg, or with a cinnamon stick.

egg noodles: Commercial noodles containing at least 5.5 percent egg solids.

eggplant. Oval-shaped fruit ranging in color from purplish-black to off white to pale yellow; served baked, boiled, or fried.

egg poacher: Small saucepan with inserts for holding whole raw eggs while they are being poached over boiling water.

egg pop: Eggnog.

egg powder: Dried eggs, used when fresh eggs are not available and also by many commercial bakeries, because it is easy to store and to handle.

egg roll: Chinese specialty consisting of an egg-dough casing filled with chopped chicken, meat, seafood, or vegetables, then fried.

egg sauce: Any sauce containing eggs, usually a cream sauce containing chopped hard-boiled eggs.

eggs, shirred: Eggs baked gently in some kind of garnish: cream, bread crumbs, egg white, tomato sauce, etc.

eggs benedict: Buttered muffin or toast rounds covered with thin slices of ham and topped with poached eggs; they are served with cheese, hollandaise, or white sauce.

eggs florentine: Eggs garnished with spinach, or eggs served atop spinach.

egg shears: Scissorslike utensil for shearing off the tops of soft-boiled eggs.

egg slicer: Aluminum or plastic utensil provided with fine steel wires for slicing a hard-boiled egg with one motion.

eggs parmentier: Scrambled eggs served with potatoes.

egg timer: Hour-glass-shaped device for timing the boiling of eggs, usually made so that the sand runs from the top to the bottom in three minutes.

egg white: White or albumen portion of an egg, used in frostings, as an omelet leavener, for making pie meringues, and in baking many kinds of light cake.

eggwich: Slang for egg sandwich.

egg yolk: Yellow nutritive heart of an egg, used in making custards, hollandaise, mayonnaise, and other sauces, and as a salad garnish when hard boiled, or raw as in caesar salads.

égoutture: (French—drippings)

Ei: (German—egg)

Eier in Schale: (German—eggs in the shell) Boiled eggs.

eier kichel: (Yiddish—egg cookie)

eight-ounce can: Commercial container holding one cup of liquid or semisolid beverage or food.

eighty-one: Lunchroom slang for a glass of water.

eighty-two: Lunchroom slang for two glasses of water.

eighty-six: Lunchroom argot meaning "Don't serve her," "Don't serve him," or "Nothing is left (of dish or drink ordered)."

ein Dunkles: (German—one dark) Beer.

ein Helles: (German—one light) Beer.

ein Prosit: (German—a toast)

Eis: (German—ice; ice cream)

Eisbein in Gelee: (German—jellied pig's knuckles)

elbing: Hard sharp rennet cheese made of cow's milk, originally made in the Elbe River Valley of northern Germany.

elbow macaroni: Elbow-shaped tubes of macaroni.

elderberry: Berry fruit of a member of the honeysuckle family, used in making jams, jellies, and native wines.

elderberry wine: Cordial produced from fermented elderberries.

electric knife: Electrically vibrated knife blade used for cutting bread, slicing cheese, or carving meat.

electric mixer: Utensil for beating, blending, and mixing, sometimes with attachments for juicing and grinding.

electric range: Electrically operated stove.

electric smoker: Electrically operated device for smoking fish or meat in 10 to 12 hours.

electronic cooking: Method of cooking in which foods are subjected to high-frequency radio-wave radiant energy; molecular activity generates heat within the foods, and they cook from inside out, browning and crusting occurring last; cooking is rapid and complete.

Elijah's cup: Cup of wine which is placed on the table at Passover for the prophet Elijah.

elite prim: (Norwegian—choice whey cheese) Savory spread made of caramel, *gjætost*, and cow's milk.

elixir: Alcohol and sweetening agent used as an aromatic flavor.

el presidente: Cocktail made of dark rum, dry vermouth, cointreau, and grenadine.

elver: Young eel, often canned and served as cocktail canapé.

ematur: (Albanian—almond puff pastry)

embalmed beef: Soldier's slang for canned meat of any kind.

emery stone: Knife-sharpening stone or grinding wheel

émincé: (French—minced) Cold sliced meat served in a hot sauce.

emmenthaler: True name for the real Swiss cheese with the holes, as first developed in the Ems Valley of Switzerland.

empanada: (Spanish—meat pie) Turnover filled with cheese, cooked fish, ground meat, or stewed vegetables.

empanada de almejas: (Spanish —clam turnover)

empanada de carne: (Spanish— meat turnover)

empanada de langosta: (Spanish —crayfish turnover)

empanada de legumbres: (Spanish—vegetable turnover)

empanada de pescado: (Spanish —fish turnover)

empanada de queso: (Spanish— cheese turnover)

empanado: (Spanish—breaded)

Emperor: Large light-red or purplish-red grape with few seeds.

empire wine: Any wine produced in the British Commonwealth.

emulsion: Intimate mixture of two or more liquid ingredients such as milk and water, oil and wine, or a suspension of a resinous substance in a liquid.

enamelware: Camping and kitchenware covered with a

vitreous enamel coating to prevent acid reactions and rusting of the base metal; many eating and kitchen utensils come in enamelware.

en chemise: (French—in shirt) With the skin on, said of potatoes boiled thus.

enchilada: Mexican scroll-rolled tortilla, filled with chicken, fish, meat, seafood, or vegetable combinations and served with a chili sauce and grated cheese.

enchiladas de gallina: (Spanish— chicken enchiladas)

enchiladas de pescado: (Spanish —fish enchiladas)

enchiladas de carne: (Spanish— meat enchiladas)

enchiladas de legumbres: (Spanish—vegetable enchiladas)

en croûte: (French—in a crust)

endive: Salad herb, also called escarole, favored for its somewhat sharp and biting flavor; endive is also chicory leaf, another salad green with a sharp flavor.

en fête: (French—on holiday) Table set festively.

engadine: Whole-milk rennet cheese originating in this valley of the Inn River in Switzerland.

engineered food: Meatless meat substitutes made of soy-protein fibers and certain color and flavor additives; some engineered foods look and taste like hamburgers, others like hotdogs, ham, or sausage.

english breakfast tea: Black Formosan tea of Keemun type yielding a dark brew favored by the English.

english china: Bone china of a type originally made in England.

english chop: Boned lamb or mutton chop sometimes filled with a kidney where the bone is removed.

english dairy cheese: English-style hard cheddarlike cheese used in baking and cooking.

english herring: Common herring taken from the North Atlantic.

english monkey: Cheese and tomatoes baked on bread or served on toast.

english muffin: Unsweetened breakfast cake made of rolled bread dough baked on a griddle.

English service: Form of dinner service in which the host fills heated soup plates from tureen placed before him; the butler or maid serves guests in the order indicated by the host, who later serves the entree himself, while the hostess serves vegetables.

english sole: Snout-nosed flatfish taken along the Pacific Coast.

english walnut: Large hard-shelled eating walnut, fruit of a Eurasian tree also called circassian, european, french, and persian walnut; as it was carried to many parts of the world in English ships, it gained the name of english walnut.

enguinar otourtma: (Armenian—artichokes stuffed with spiced ground meat)

en papillote: (French—in paper) Food wrapped in foil or paper to hold its shape and retain its juices while cooking.

ensalada: (Spanish—salad)

ensalada de apio: (Spanish—celery salad)

ensalada de arroz: (Spanish—rice salad)

ensalada de guacamole: (Spanish—guacamole salad)

Ente: (German—duck)

entrecôte: (French—between the ribs) Beef from between the ribs.

entrée: (French—entrance) In the United States, the main dish; in England, any dish served before the roast; in France, the third course, usually served with brown or white sauce.

entremés: (Spanish—relish; side dish)

entremets: (French—interposed) Dessert course served in France after the cheese course.

Enzian: (German—gentian) Herb brandy.

épaule de mouton: (French—shoulder of mutton)

epergne: Decorative centerpiece consisting of several group receptacles supported by a main stem, usually made of crystal, porcelain, or silver, and used to hold hors d'oevres, olives, and salted nuts, or flowers.

epicure: Person with a sensitive appreciation of fine foods and fine wines.

épigramme: (French—epigram) Dish of two kinds of fish, meat, or vegetables, or one kind of food cooked in two different ways.

épinard: (French—spinach)

Erbse: (German—pea)

Erbsensuppe: (German—pea soup)

eriwani: (Russian—sheep's-milk cheese)

Ersatz: (German—imitation; substitute) Artificially compounded beverage or food engineered to imitate the original: ersatz bread, ersatz milk, etc.

erwtensoep: (Dutch—pea soup)

escallop: To bake food in a sauce topped with crumbs.

escalope: (French—collop) Thin slice of fish or meat.

escargot: (French—snail)

escarole: Endive.

Escoffier, Auguste (1847-1935): Famous French chef called the Emperor of Chefs by Kaiser Wilhelm II; Escoffier established kitchens in the Carlton and Savoy hotels of London, and in 1920 was made a Chevalier of the Legion of Honor because of his contribution to the culinary art.

Eskimo Pie: Trademark name of a confection consisting of ice cream coated with chocolate.

espagnole: (French—Spanish) Cooked in a brown sauce made of meat, roux, bacon, tomatoes, and other vegetables, and sometimes seasoned with sherry wine.

espinaca: (Spanish—spinach)

Essig: (German—vinegar)

estaminet: (French—smoking room in a coffee house)

esterhazi rostelyos: (Hungarian—Esterhazy steak) Steak served in sour-cream sauce named in honor of a princely Magyar family which did much to encourage the preparation of fine food.

estragon: (French—tarragon)

esturgeon: (French—sturgeon)

etiquette: Social forms established by courteous people to insure pleasant and polite behavior at all times, including while dining and drinking.

étouffée: (French—smothered) Cooked in a closed pot so the food is braised and smothered in its own juices.

étuvée: (French—same as *étouffée*)

eupeptic: Enjoying good digestion, the opposite of dyspeptic.

European plan: Board without meals.

european walnut: English walnut.

evaporated milk: Unsweetened milk evaporated to less than half its original bulk before it is canned.

evian: Bottled alkaline mineral water first found at Evian-les-Bains in France.

eviscerate: To degut, to remove the entrails of an animal.

ewe: Mature female goat or sheep.

ewe cheese: Cheese made from ewe's milk.

ewer: Vase-shaped pitcher provided with a carrying handle and a pouring lip.

exhaust fan: Fan for driving out smoke-laden air from the kitchen or the range itself.

extract: Essential oil dissolved in alcohol to produce flavors such as anise, almond, lemon, licorice, maple, peppermint, vanilla, etc.; flavoring extracts are widely used in baking and candy making.

extractor: Utensil for squeezing juice from fruits, meats, and vegetables, or a device for removing corks from bottles.

extra fin: (French—top quality)

extrait: (French—extract)

extra sec: (French—very dry) With less than two percent sugar, usually applied to champagne.

F: Abbreviation for Fahrenheit—
(temperature scale where water
freezes at 32 degrees and boils
at 212), named Fahrenheit in
honor of Gabriel Fahrenheit,
18-century German physicist,
who devised it.

faba: Fava bean.

fadge: Barley pancake.

fagiolino: (Italian—string bean)

fagiuolo: (Italian—bean)

fagottino: (Italian—little bundle)
Type of Venetian pastry)

faience: Highly colored glazed
earthenware or pottery.

fairy shrimp: Freshwater shrimp,
so called because of its delicate
coloring.

faisan: (French—pheasant)

faisán: (Spanish—pheasant)

falernian: Wine produced in the
Campania of ancient Italy, a
favorite of the Roman poet
Horace.

Falstaff: American beer brewed in
St. Louis, Missouri.

family flour: All-purpose flour.

family style: Self-service, with
food set on the table in serving
bowls so diners may help themselves.

fan: (Chinese—rice)

fanche: (Chinese—dining car)

fannie daddies: Coastal New England name for fried clams.

fannings: Coarse siftings of tea.

fantail mullet: Food fish popular
in Florida and throughout the
West Indies.

fantail shrimp: Large shrimp split
lengthwise and fried.

fanting: (Chinese—dining room)

FAO: Abbreviation for the Food
and Agriculture Organization of
the United Nations, founded in
1945 to carry on the work of the
International Institute of Agriculture of the League of Nations; the FAO is charged with
feeding vast masses of people
threatened by food shortages
and population explosion.

farce: (French—stuffing) Forcemeat or other filling.

farci: (French—filled; stuffed)

farfalla: (Italian—butterfly) Egg-
noodle bow.

farfel: (Yiddish—noodle) Kosher-
style dumplings made of egg
barley, often served in consommé or soup.

faar i kaal: Scandinavian-style
braised lamb and cabbage.

far i kal: (Norwegian—lamb and cabbage)

farina: Meal made of cereal grains and used in preparing puddings, soups, and breakfast cereals; farina is also the name for purified wheat middlings.

farinaceous: Mealy.

farmer cheese: Pressed cheese made of skimmed or whole milk and of type made on farms.

farmhouse loaf: Homemade bread or a loaf baked to look homemade and so advertised.

farm-style ice cream: Rich homemade ice cream containing heavy cream, eggs, sugar, and flavoring.

faro: Sour-tasting Belgian beer.

farsangi fank: (Hungarian—carnival doughnuts)

farstufning: (Swedish—lamb stew)

fastnacht kucka: (Pennsylvania-German — fast night cakes; Shrove Tuesday cakes) Rectangular or round doughnuts.

fat: Any edible shortening such as butter, vegetable oil, olive oil, renderings of fish, flesh, and fowl, nut or fruit oils, etc.

fatback: Pork cut from along the top back over the mid-spine.

fattoush: Arabian mixed salad.

fava bean: Large shell bean resembling the lima bean.

FDA: Abbreviation for the Food and Drug Administration of the U.S. Department of Health, Education, and Welfare.

feaberry: Gooseberry.

feather fowlie: Scots chicken-and-ham soup fortified with sweet cream and egg yolk.

Feige: (German—fig)

feijão: (Portuguese—bean)

feijoada: (Portuguese—dish of French beans) Brazilian dish containing beans, meat, and rice in abundance.

fennel: Aromatic herb whose seeds, tasting somewhat like anise, are used to flavor fish, pastries, sweet pickles, etc.

fenugreek: Aromatic herb of the pea family, used in making curries and artificial vanilla.

Fernet-Branca: Brand of Italian bitters used in cocktails.

fersk suppe og kjøtt: (Norwegian—fresh soup and meat) Soup made with beef, carrots, and cabbage.

feta: (Greek—white goat's milk cheese)

fête: (French—festive celebration)

fête champêtre: (French—garden party)

fetticus: Corn salad, an herb.

fettucine: (Italian—egg noodles)

feuilletage: (French—puff paste; pastry)

fève: (French—bean or berry)

fhb: Slang abbreviation for family hold back—wait until guests have been served and offered second helpings.

fiambre: (Spanish—cold meat)

fiasco: (Italian—flask) Round-bottomed straw-covered bottle.

fiber glass: Noninflammable easily washable fabric of which kitchen curtains are often made.

fiddlehead: Edible cinnamon fern so called because the rolled-up tips of its young fronds resemble the scroll at the head of a fiddle; fiddleheads are served as a salad, or steamed and eaten as a hot vegetable.

fideo: (Spanish—thin noodle)

field corn: Fodder corn.

field salad: Corn salad, an herb.

fifth: A unit of measure for liquor equal to ⅕ gallon or ⅘ quart; also a bottle holding this quantity of liquor.

fifty-five: Lunchroom slang for root beer.

fifty-one: Lunchroom or soda fountain slang for one cup of hot chocolate.

fifty-two: two cups of hot chocolate, etc.

fig: Tropical tree whose domesticated species bears edible figs; figs are eaten raw or are preserved in syrup, or used in desserts, cakes, cookies, and crackers.

Figaro sauce: Hollandaise sauce enriched with puréed tomatoes, named after the character Figaro in Rossini's *Barber of Seville*.

fig banana: Small tropical American banana having a figlike flavor.

fig bar: Bar-shaped cooky filled with a kind of fig jam.

Fig Newton: Brand name for a commercial fig bar.

figue: (French—fig)

filbert: Hazelnut.

filbunke: (Swedish—soured milk)

filé: Sassafras-leaf powder used in thickening sauces, soups, and stews; also a seasoner.

filet: (French—fillet)

filet de sole: (French—fillet of sole)

filete: (Spanish—fillet)

filete de ternera: (Spanish—veal fillet)

filet mignon: (French—dainty fillet) Tender steak with the bone removed.

filetto: (Italian—fillet)

filetto di sogliola: (Italian—fillet of sole)

filled cheese: Cheese with butter

fats removed and other fats added; the latter are usually adulterants.

fillet: Piece of lean meat or fish without bones.

fillet of flounder: Boned flounder.

filmjölk: (Swedish—sour milk)

filo: (Greek—paper-thin sheets of pastry dough) Dough used in making many types of pastry such as baklava, honey-and-almond-filled pastry.

filosoof: (Dutch—philosopher) Meat and potato pie.

filter: Porous device for straining particles from liquid.

filter paper: Porous unsized paper for use in a filter apparatus, such as a tea bag, or a funnel; filter papers are specially cut or fluted to fit the strainers of coffee- or teapots.

fine champagne: (French—fine champagne) High grade of brandy distilled from wine produced in the Charente Valley.

fines herbes: (French—delicate herbs) Combination of herbs such as chervil, chives, parsley, tarragon, thyme, chopped fine and used to flavor omelets, salads, soups, and stews.

fingerbowl: Individual basin for rinsing fingers and lips while still at table; fingerbowls are usually served half full of warm water plus a few drops of eau de cologne, florida water, or lemon juice.

finger rolls: Bread baked in long fingerlike rolls.

finnan haddie: Scots term for smoked haddock.

finocchio: (Italian—sweet fennel) Herb often eaten raw by Italians like celery or braised or served *au gratin*.

fired: Oven baked.

firewater: American Indian name for strong liquors, particularly traders' rum.

firkin: Small wooden cask for holding butter or lard, or a unit of capacity equaling about 9 imperial gallons of beer or 56 pounds of butter.

firm-ball stage: Candy-making term meaning when a driblet of cooked syrup forms a firm but not hard ball when it is dropped into cold water; this is possible when the syrup has reached a temperature of between 244 to 250 degrees F.

fish and chips: Boned fried fish and french-fried potatoes.

fishball: Fried cake made of mashed potatoes and shredded fish flakes; usually codfish is used although other fish flakes such as halibut or flounder serve just as well.

fish boiler: Aluminum or stainless-steel utensil for boiling fish atop a rack suspended over water.

fishburger: Hamburger patty made of fish.

fishcake: Somewhat flattened fishball.

fish chowder: Thick fish soup made with onions, potatoes, seasoning, etc.

fish flour: Dried fish meal used as a food.

fish fry: Picnic outing where fish are caught, fried, and eaten.

fish-house cooler: Delaware punch.

fish kettle: Oval-shaped pan for boiling fish whole; sometimes a fish kettle doubles as a clam steamer.

fish knife: Wide-bladed knife.

fishless fish: Engineered food.

fishmonger: Fish dealer.

fish spread: Canapé and tea sandwich spread made of any of various processed fish mixtures such as anchovy and tuna pastes.

fishwich: Slang for fish sandwich.

fishwife: Woman who sells fish.

fisk: (Danish, Norwegian and Swedish—fish)

five B's: Slang for a meal of Boston baked beans and brown bread.

fizz: Any effervescent beverage: soda water and some flavoring; soda water and gin, etc.

flageolet: (French—end-blown flute) Dwarf variety of green bean of Franco-Belgian origin.

flagon: Large bulging vessel of ceramic, glass, or metal provided with a handle, lid, and spout, used for dispensing liquors and wines.

flagroot: Calamus or sweet-flag root sometimes candied and served as a confection.

flake: To separate food into small particles with a fork or other suitable utensil.

flaki: Polish-style tripe.

flamande: (French—Flemish) Served with cabbage, onions, and potatoes.

flambant: (French—aflame)

flambé: (French—flaming) Served flaming; food to be served thus is usually prepared by being coated with some alcoholic beverage such as brandy or rum before being set on fire.

flame tokay: Bright red grape originating in Hungary, now cultivated in America.

flameware: Pyrex or tempered glass designed as cooking ware so it can be exposed to high heats or open flames without breaking.

flaming sword: Menu term for food broiled on a sword-shaped skewer and served flaming.

flan: (French—piecrust with sweet or savory filling; Spanish —custard)

flank: Fleshy part of a side of meat between the hips and the ribs.

flank steak: Steak cut from the interior oblique muscular tissue of beef, calf, lamb, or mutton.

flannelcake: Griddlecake or pancake.

flapjack: Pancake, so called because a skilled cook can turn one in air with a deft twist of a spatula or a toss of the frying pan.

flatfish: Bottom-dwelling fish, such as halibut, flounder, sole, or turbot, which swims on one side of its broad flat body; nearly all flatfish are considered very fine eating.

flatware: Flat silverware such as forks, knives, and spoons.

flaxseed: Mucilaginous seed of the flax plant yielding linseed oil, used in paints, and a coarse meal used as fodder.

flaxseed meal: Nutritive substance containing unsaturated fatty acids; flaxseed meal is normally used for cattle fodder but it can be made palatable for human consumption by being blended with other flours.

Fleisch: (German—meat)

fleishig: (Yiddish—pertaining to the cooking of meat)

flensje: (Dutch—paper-thin pancakes)

flétan: (French—halibut)

flip: Drink concocted of spiced and sweetened ale, beer, cider, or other alcoholic beverage; often an egg is added to the mixture and whipped into an attractive froth.

flipjack: Flapjack.

flitch: Side of bacon.

flitter: Fritter.

floating island: Custard topped with islands of meringue or whipped cream.

fløde: (Danish—cream)

flødeis: (Danish—ice cream)

flødeskum: (Danish—whipped cream)

florence fennel: Sweet fennel.

florentine: (French—Florentine) Served on a bed of spinach, usually said of fish or egg dishes, which then appear on menus as à la florentine.

flounder: Small flatfish celebrated for its fine flavor; some species are called dab or plaice.

flour: Finely ground grain such as barley, corn, rice, rye, oats or wheat.

flourcake: Doughnut.

flower cheese: English rennet whole-milk cheese containing marigold, rose, and violet petals.

fluid ounce: Liquid measure holding two tablespoons.

fluke: Flatfish related to the flounder.

flukie: Scots for flounder.

flummery: Term having several meanings: jellylike food made by the Welsh from soured oatmeal; New England dessert composed of berries, cornstarch, and cream; Maryland custard dessert including grape juice, lemon, sugar, and whipped cream; Scots blancmange of cream, rosewater, and sherry.

flundra: (Swedish—flounder)

flute: To decorate by grooving; pastry dough is often given a fluted edge, vegetables cut into decorative designs; special utensils are available for making fancy-design flutings.

flynder: (Danish—flounder)

flyndre: (Norwegian—flounder)

FNB: Abbreviation for the Food and Nutrition Board of the National Academy of Sciences.

fofo de bacalhau: (Portuguese—codfish puff) Codfish ball.

foie: (French—liver)

foie de veau: (French—calf's liver)

foie gras: (French—rich liver) Goose liver.

fold in: To add ingredients, such as beaten egg whites or whipped cream, by gentle over-and-under movements.

fond: (French—foundation) Stock —liquid in which meat, fish, or vegetables have been cooked.

fondant: (French—melting) Thick creamy sugar paste used as a candy filling and icing.

fond blanc: (French—white foundation) Chicken or veal stock.

fond brun: (French—brown essence) Beef, game, or lamb stock.

fond de cuisine: (French—cooking foundation) Stocks and broths, the basis of all fine sauces, stews, soups, etc.

fondue: Fluffy baked dish containing cheese, eggs, butter, and milk with bread crumbs added for thickening.

fondue fork: Long-handled fork for dipping bread into cheese fondue.

fontina: Soft Italian goat's-milk cream cheese.

food chopper: Food grinder.

food mill: Colander equipped with a pressure plate operated by a rotating handle; food pressed through this mill comes out smooth and lumpless.

food of the loom: Engineered food.

food press: Perforated cone through which food is pressed to make it lump-free and smooth.

foo-foo: African dish made of boiled and mashed plantains, or sometimes of pounded cassava, coco, and yams, or of plain cassava meal.

fool: English dessert made of puréed fruits and whipped cream.

foo yung: Egg foo yung.

Forbidden Fruit: Brand name of an American orange-colored liqueur made of grape brandy flavored with grapefruit juice.

forcemeat: Chopped and ground flesh, usually seasoned and bulked with bread crumbs, oatmeal, and eggs, and used as a filling.

forchetta: (Italian—fork)

forefoot of pork: Meat cut from forequarters of a pig.

Forelle: (German—trout)

forequarters: Neck, shoulders, and breast of a meat animal.

foreshanks: Meat cut from the top part of the front legs of a meat animal.

fork: Tined implement for spearing food and conveying it from the plate to the mouth.

forloren hare: (Norwegian—mock rabbit) Scandinavian hash.

formaggio: (Italian—cheese)

formaggio d'capri: (Italian—goat's-milk cheese)

formosa oolong: Semifermented tea grown on the island of Taiwan (Formosa).

forshmak: (Russian—forcemeat) Mashed potatoes and hashed meat or herrings served as an appetizer.

fortified wine: Wine strengthened by the addition of alcohol.

forum: (Latin—market place)

forum boarium: (Latin—cattle market)

forum olitorium: (Latin—vegetable market)

fourré: (French—covered; furred) Coated with cream and sugar.

fowl: Any edible domesticated bird.

fraise: (French—strawberry)

framboise: (French—raspberry)

frambuesa: (Spanish—raspberry)

frangipane: French-style pastry made with butter, egg yolks, flour, and milk, used with forcemeats and poultry.

frangipane cream: Cream made with eggs, sugar, and macaroons, used in making rich desserts.

frank: Slang for frankfurter.

frankfurter: Beef or beef-and-pork sausage also known as the hot dog.

Frankfurter Wurst: (German—frankfurter sausage)

frappé: (French—whipped) Finely iced drink served in a chilled glass with an iced edging as a frozen milk shake or similar beverage.

freeloader: Slang for a parasitic person who drinks and eats when others pay the bill.

freestone: Fruit whose flesh is almost free of the stony pit.

freezer: Refrigerator compartment for freezing foods, making ice cubes, or storing frozen foods; freezer can also mean a manually or motor operated device for freezing custards, ice creams, and sherbets.

freezing point: Point where water freezes—32 degrees Fahrenheit or 0 degrees Celsius on the centigrade scale.

french bean: String bean or wax bean sliced slantwise.

french bread: Crisp and thick-crusted bread baked in an elongated loaf and made with very little fat or sugar.

french chestnut: Spanish chestnut.

french chop: Trimmed rib chop.

french doughnut: Ring of cream-puff dough fried in deep fat.

french dressing: Salad dressing of olive oil and vinegar flavored with garlic, paprika, sugar, and other seasonings.

french drip: Drip coffee.

french endive: Chicory.

french-fried potato: Potato cut into strips and fried in deep fat.

french-fry cutter: Utensil for reducing a potato to french-fry slivers in one simple operation.

french fryer: Deep pan with wire-basket insert used for deep-fat frying.

french gin: Caramel-colored gin.

french ice cream: Frozen custard made of cream and egg yolks.

french mustard: Mustard sauce plus vinegar and seasoning.

french pancake: Crêpe—thin pancake rolled up and served with jam, jelly, or cinnamon and sugar.

french pastry: Puff pastry filled with custard, preserved fruit, or whipped cream.

french peas: Little peas called *petits pois.*

french roast: Method of roasting coffee beans to yield a very dark brown color but not quite as dark as italian roast.

french roll: French bread baked in a roll-size loaf.

French service: Form of dinner service performed by two waiters: a *chef de rang* (perfect waiter) plus a *commis de rang* who assists him; the *chef de rang* seats the guests and takes their orders, serves drinks, and finishes preparation of foods in front of the guests; the *commis de rang* does the rest of the serving assisted by a captain of waiters and a wine steward.

French service rules: Rules governing the service of food in a fine French restaurant: Serve everything from the guest's right, except bread, butter, and salad plates, which are set at the guest's left.

french toast: White bread soaked in a mixture of egg and milk, fried, and served with syrup, sugar or honey.

french vermouth: Dry vermouth.

french walnut: English walnut.

fresa: (Spanish—strawberry)

fresh butter: Unsalted butter.

fr f: Abbreviation for french-fried potatoes.

fricadelle: (French—small stuffed roll) Roll filled with braised meat.

fricandeau; Larded veal, roasted or braised, and glazed in its own juices.

fricassee: Stew of chicken, turkey, or veal cooked in gravy.

fridge: Slang for refrigerator.

fried bananas: Dessert of sliced bananas sautéed in butter and sprinkled with sugar.

fried cakes: Any sweet bread cooked by frying in deep or shallow fat: crullers, doughnuts, fritters, etc.

fried egg: Whole egg fried in shortening until set.

fried noodles: Noodles cooked in deep fat until crisp and brown.

frigate mackerel: Small marine fish taken on all coasts of the United States, related to the tunny and not a true mackerel.

frijol: (Spanish—bean)

frijoles negros: (Spanish—black beans)

frijoles refritos: (Spanish—refried beans) Dish of beans well cooked, then mashed into a smooth paste.

frikadelle: (Danish—meat ball)

frill: Paper decoration made to hold the bone end of a chop or to embellish the bone ends of a crown roast.

frit: (French—fried)

frito: (Spanish—fried)

frittata: (Italian—omelet)

fritter: Vegetable or fruit fried in egg batter.

fritti di scampi: (Italian—fried prawns)

fritto: (Italian—fried)

fritto misto: (Italian—mixed fry) Assortment of fried foods served as a course.

frizzle: To cook in fat until crisp and curled at the edges.

froid: (French—cold)

desservir: (French—to clear the table)

dessert: Last course of a midday or evening meal, usually some kind of sweet; the name comes from *desservir* (French—to dis-serve) as it was served after the tablecloth had been removed.

dessert fork: Round-tined fork slightly smaller than a dinner fork.

dessert knife: Smallest-size knife used with dessert fork.

dessert plate: Small eating plate about 7 inches in diameter.

dessert spoon: Eating utensil smaller than a tablespoon and larger than a teaspoon.

dessertspoonful: Liquid measure holding about 2 ½ fluid drams, or as much as a dessert spoon will hold.

dessert wine: California term for fortified wine.

detergent: Chemical solvent or similar cleaning agent for emul-sifying fats and greases so they may be washed away easily.

deviled: Highly seasoned.

devil's dozen: Baker's dozen, 13 of anything.

devil's fig candy: Candy made from the prickly pear.

devil's food: Dark rich chocolate cake.

devil's oatmeal: Wild chervil.

devils on horseback: Oysters served under strips of bacon.

devonshire cream: Clotted cream skimmed from scalded milk, an English delicacy usually served with fresh berries or hot scones.

devonshire cream cheese: Cheese made from cow's milk of a type originating in Devonshire, Eng-land.

dewberry: Variety of blackberry.

dewberry flummery: Custardlike dessert made of dewberries, cornstarch, lemon juice, sugar, and water.

diamond flounder: Large food fish caught in California waters.

dice: To cut food into small cubes.

dietary laws: Judaic laws concern-ing the slaughtering of meat animals and the selection, prep-aration, and serving of all foods; dietary laws define both per-mitted (*kosher*) and forbidden (*trefah*) foods.

diet cake: Scots sweet cake sea-soned with cinnamon and lemon.

dill: Aromatic herb of the carrot family, whose leaves and seeds are used in flavoring pickles as well as salads, soups, and stews.

dill pickle: Cucumber pickled in brine flavored with dill seeds.

dill seed: Seed of the dill plant, used for pickling and seasoning many foods.

dilute: To thin by adding liquid.

dimple: New Orleans confection made of blanched almonds, egg whites, and sugar.

dinde: (French—turkey hen)

dindon: (French—turkey cock)

dindonneau: (French—young turkey)

diner: (French—dinner)

dinette: Small-size dining area usually just big enough for the family.

dining car: Railway restaurant car.

dining room: Room where meals are eaten.

dining salon: Room where food is served as aboard a ship.

dinner: Principal meal of the day, served at midday, around sun-down, or in the evening, accord-ing to family custom.

frokost: (Danish—luncheon; Norwegian—breakfast)

fromage: (French—cheese)

fromage à la crème: (French—cream cheese)

fromage bleu: (French—blue cheese)

fromage de chèvre: (French—goat's-milk cheese)

fromage de cochon: (French—hogshead cheese)

fromage de Troyes: (French—cheese made in Troyes)

frosted glass: Glass covered with ice frosting or rimmed with sugar crystal frosting, used in serving hot-weather beverages and many cocktails.

frostfish: Name for three fishes: Tomcod, smelt, and a scabbard fish.

frosting: Sweet covering for cakes and cookies, made either cooked with egg white or uncooked with confectioner's sugar.

frozen custard: Ice milk or similar frozen dessert.

frozen dessert: Ice milk or other frozen custard.

frozen food: Perishables subjected to quick freezing and kept frozen until ready for use.

frozen pudding: Frozen custard filled with candied fruit and nuts and sometimes flavored with rum.

Frucht: (German—fruit)

fructose: Fruit sugar.

frugt: (Danish—fruit)

Frühstück: (German—breakfast)

fruit: (French—fruit; product)

fruitcake: Rich cake containing dried fruit, nuts, and spices and flavored with brandy or rum; fruitcake is a favorite year-end holiday treat.

fruit cocktail: Mixture of diced fruits served in syrup as a first course or as a dessert.

fruit cup: Dessert made of diced assorted fruits, nuts, and ice cream or whipped cream.

fruit de mer: (French—shellfish)

fruit drink: Beverage made of chilled fruit juices, single or blended.

fruiterie: (French—fruit store)

fruit frais: (French—fresh fruit)

fruit juice: Juice extracted from fruit.

fruit knife: Small kitchen knife designed for coring, paring, or slicing fruit, or small dinner-table knives for peeling and cutting fruit.

fruit salad: Salad of assorted fruits, usually arranged to contrast their colors and shapes as attractively as possible.

fruit soup: Summertime soup made of stewed berries and other fruits such as apples, peaches, pears, raisins, etc.

fruit spread: Sandwich spread of mashed avocado, banana and peanut butter, guava jelly, and other similar combinations.

fruit squeezer: Device for expressing fruit juices electrically or manually.

fruit wine: Wine fermented from fruit other than grapes.

fruktvin: (Norwegian—fruit wine)

fruta: (Spanish—fruit)

frutta: (Italian—fruit)

frutta cotta: (Italian—stewed fruit)

frutta di mare: Italian—fruit of the sea) Seafood.

fry: To cook in hot fat or cooking oil, in a pan over a fire.

Frydenlund: Norwegian pilsner beer brewed in Oslo.

fryer chicken: Chicken weighing 2½ to 3½ pounds and tender enough for frying, usually 14 to 20 weeks old.

frying pan: Broad shallow pan with long handle for frying; frying pans are sometimes coated to prevent sticking.

FSEA: Abbreviation for Food Service Executives Association.

fudge: Rich candy made of chocolate or cocoa, sugar, butter, milk, and sometimes added flavoring such as maple sugar, bitter walnut, or vanilla.

fugu: (Japanese—blowfish) The spiny blowfish is made into a stew and served in hundreds of *fugu* restaurants throughout Japan, although the fish contains a deadly poison which must be carefully removed.

fumé: (French—smoked)

fumet: Concentrated essence of fish, flesh, or fowl produced during cooking, used as an additive in making sauces.

funchi: (Papiamento—cornmeal mush) Baked, boiled, or fried cornmeal mush served in Curaçao and other islands of Netherlands Antilles.

funghi ripieni: (Italian—stuffed mushrooms)

fungo: (Italian—mushroom)

funnel: Hollow cone for pouring liquids and powders into narrow-necked containers.

funnel cake: Fried cake made by releasing egg batter from the spout of a funnel; fancy rings can be formed by moving the funnel as the batter is released.

fu yung: Egg foo yung.

fylld blomkal: (Norwegian—stuffed cauliflower)

g: Abbreviation for gram.

g-a-c: Abbreviation for grilled american cheese (sandwich).

gal: Abbreviation for gallon.

galantina: (Italian—galantine)

galantine: Boned fish, flesh, or fowl cooked in broth, pressed in a mold, and served in aspic.

galette: (French—a kind of flaky pastry) Twelfth Night delicacy.

gali: (Malay—galley)

galleta: (Spanish—cracker)

galley: Ship's kitchen, or compact compartment for storing and preparing beverages and foods aboard an airplane.

galley oven: Coal, electric, or oil-fired oven installed in a ship's galley for baking bread, pastry, rolls, etc.

galley range: Coal, electric, or oil stove installed in a ship's galley for cooking food.

gallina: (Spanish—chicken)

gallina en chicha: (Spanish— chicken in chicha) Chicken in red wine sauce, dish of El Salvador.

gallipot: Small earthenware creamer.

gallon: Liquid measure containing 8 pints or 4 quarts or 128 fluid ounces.

Galloway: Hornless beef cattle with curly black coats, first bred in the Galloway district of southwestern Scotland.

galuiha rechiada: (Portuguese— stuffed capon)

galuska: (Hungarian—soft noodles)

gamba: (Spanish—Mediterranean shrimp)

gambrel: Butcher's hook for hanging meat.

game: Wild animals, chiefly mammals and birds, killed for sport and used for food.

game birds: Wildfowl hunted for food: prairie chickens, wild ducks and geese, partridge, pheasant, pigeons, snipe, quail, and woodcock are among those commonly pursued.

gammelost: (Norwegian—old-milk cheese)

gammon: Ham or side of cured bacon.

gans: (Dutch—goose)

Gans: (German—goose)

ganso: (Portuguese and Spanish —goose)

gaper: Large burrowing clam with a shell that gapes at either end; the Pacific Coast bigneck gaper is prized for its tasty qualities.

garavance: Chick pea.

garbage disposal: Electrical device for disposing of food refuse; attached to waste line of kitchen sink, it accepts and disposes by grinding and flushing down the drain with a flow of tap water.

garbanzo: (Spanish—chick pea)

garbure: (French—bacon and cabbage soup) Rich *pot-au-feu* containing bacon, bread, cabbage, smoked sausage, and seasoning.

garçon: (French—boy; waiter)

garden cress: Asiatic herb cultivated for its pungent bottom leaves.

garden egg: Eggplant.

garden mint: Spearmint.

garden pepper grass: Garden cress.

garden sorrel: European herb used as a salad green.

gardevin: (French—wine guard) Large bottle or decanter for holding and serving wine.

garlic: Pungent bulb of the lily family widely used in seasoning; garlic bulbs are composed of smaller bulbs called cloves; the penetrating odor of garlic cannot be mistaken for anything else.

garlic bread: French- or Italian-style bread or rolls spread with garlic butter and heated in an oven.

garlic butter: Butter sauce flavored with crushed garlic cloves.

garlic dill pickles: Cucumbers pickled in brine containing dill and garlic.

garlic mustard: European herb possessing a garliclike smell.

garlic oil: Olive oil or other salad oil infused with garlic.

garlic peppercorn: Garlic-flavored peppercorn used to season corned beef, roasts, stews, etc.

garlic powder: Pure garlic concentrated by dehydrating and grinding.

garlic salt: Salt flavored with powdered garlic.

garlic wine vinegar: Wine vinegar flavored with garlic.

garni: (French—garnished)

garnish: To decorate food, or add a savory touch, as with sprigs of mint or parsley, pitted olives, chopped nuts, marshmallows, etc.

garniture: (French—garnish)

gås: (Danish, Norwegian and Swedish—goose)

gaspergou: Louisiana name for the freshwater drumfish.

gastrology: Humorous term for keeping oneself pleasantly fed.

gastronome: Person learned in matters pertaining to fine beverages and good foods.

gastronomy: Art and science of cooking, dining, and eating.

gâteau: (French—cake)

gâteau chocolat au rhum: (French chocolate cake with rum)

gateaux assortis: (French—assorted cakes)

gaufre: (French—honeycomb; waffle)

gazpacho: (Spanish—salad soup)

Cold vegetable soup composed of salad ingredients such as cucumbers, lettuce, tomatoes, onions, garlic, bread crumbs, and many condiments; *gazpacho* can also mean a watery salad eaten from a bowl with a soup spoon.

gebaken: (German—baked)

gebraten: (German—fried)

gefilte fisch: (Yiddish—stuffed fish) Stewed or baked fish stuffed with a mixture of fish meat, bread crumbs, and eggs.

gefüllt: (German—stuffed)

gefüllte Kalbsbrust: (German—stuffed breast of veal)

gehaktnest: (Dutch—meatloaf nest) Ground beef, pork, or veal stuffed with bread crumbs, eggs, onions, and spices.

gekocht: (German—boiled)

gelatin: Jelly obtained by boiling meat; cattle feet and skins yield much of the commercial gelatin used; dry gelatin is sold in packages, plain or ready colored and flavored, for use in making aspics, desserts, and pie fillings.

gelato: (Italian—frozen; ice cream; sherbet)

gelée: (French—jelly)

gelinotte: (French—hazel grouse)

gemel: Pair of coupled cruets whose pouring spouts and stems diverge but whose bases and sides are fused; one side of a gemel holds oil, the other vinegar.

gemischter Salat: (German—mixed salad)

Gemüse: (German—vegetable)

Gemüsesuppe: (German—vegetable soup)

gemyse: (Danish—vegetables)

genièvre: (French—juniper) Gin.

genipap: Plum-size West Indian fruit with a green skin and purplish juice; the flavor is both tart and sweet, and is captured in many tropical American preserves.

genips: Genipap.

génoise fine: (French) Butter sponge cake.

gentiane: (French—gentian) Liqueur flavored with gentian roots and used as a digestive drink.

Gentsche waterzooi: (Flemish— Ghent-style fish soup) Belgian soup made with small chunks of fish boiled with bay leaves, carrots, cloves, sliced lemons, onions, and seasoning.

geoduck: Large chowder clam taken along the Pacific Coast.

geranium jelly: Jelly made from apple juice and rose-geranium leaves.

german beefsteak: Chopped meat eaten raw with chopped fresh onion and lemon juice or topped with a raw egg, the original hamburg steak.

german duck: Sheep's head boiled with onions.

german-fried potatoes: Parboiled potatoes fried in a skillet.

german mustard: Mustard made with tarragon vinegar or wine and hot spices.

german pancake: Stiff-batter pancakes fried lightly, then baked to a fluffy consistency.

german rum: Highly flavored Jamaica rum prepared for export, particularly to Europe.

german silver: Nickel-silver alloy containing copper, zinc, and silver, used in making shiny flatware and many kitchen utensils.

german toast: French toast.

géromé cheese: Semisoft greenish cheese similar to münster; anise is sometimes added, to flavor this cheese first made in Géromé, a small town in eastern France.

geröstet: (German—broiled)

Gerstensuppe: (German—barley soup)

gervais cheese: Neufchatel type of rennet cheese made with whole milk and cream, originating at the Maison Gervais in Paris.

gevulde kalfsbors: (Dutch— stuffed breast of veal)

gex: Blue-veined French skim-milk cheese.

gezouten haring: (Dutch—salt herring).

gëzuar: (Albanian—happiness to you) A toast.

ghee: Clarified butter used in East Indian dishes.

gherkin: Very small prickly cucumber grown to make pickles; gherkins are used to garnish hot and cold dishes.

ghiaccio: (Italian—ice)

giant bass: Large perchlike food and game fish found in southern California waters, also known as black sea bass.

giant rock: Large chowder and stewing clam of the Pacific Northwest.

giblets: Edible entrails of a fowl such as the heart, stomach, and liver; in French cookery the term includes the head, feet, tail, wattles, and all other discards; hearts and gizzards are used in flavoring gravies, and chicken, duck, and goose livers have long been considered a delicacy in many lands.

gibson: Cocktail made of gin and dry vermouth and served with a cocktail onion.

gigot: (French—leg of mutton)

gigot d'agneau: (French—leg of lamb)

gill: Liquid measure holding a quarter pint.

gilthead: Any of several brilliantly colored marine fish such as the sea bream taken from the Mediterranean or the cunner taken off the coasts of the British Isles.

gimlet: Highball made of carbonated water, lime juice, sugar, and gin or vodka.

gin: Alcohol distilled from grain and flavored, usually with juniper berries but also with anise, fennel, or other additives, including turpentine; hollands (dutch gin) is made by distilling grain mash with a small amount of juniper berries.

gin and It: English for gin and Italian vermouth.

gin and tonic: Drink composed of gin and quinine water served with a lemon or lime peel.

gin buck: Gin-based highball containing ginger ale and lemon or lime juice.

ginebra: (Spanish—gin)

ginep: Genipap.

gingembre: (French—ginger)

ginger: Spicy herb imported from tropical countries in Asia and islands in the South Pacific; a superior grade developed in Jamaica is called Jamaica ginger; ground ginger root is used in flavoring candies, baked goods, and many desserts.

gingerade: Ginger-flavored soft drink.

ginger ale: Carbonated soft drink, sweetened, flavored with ginger, and often spiced with *Capsicum*.

ginger beer: Tart soft drink made of carbonated water, not as sweet and stronger-flavored than ginger ale.

ginger brandy: Ginger-flavored liqueur.

gingerbread: Plain cake flavored with ginger and molasses; gingerbread is often baked in molds.

ginger cake: Gingerbread.

gingernut: Ginger-spiced cookie of Australian origin.

ginger oil: Aromatic essential oil extracted from ginger root, used in flavoring.

ginger pop: Ginger ale.

gingersnap: Thin hard molasses cooky, called a gingersnap because it is ginger flavored and snaps sharply when broken.

ginger wine: Effervescent ginger-flavored beverage.

ginkgo: Nutlike fruit pit of the ginkgo tree, used as a flavoring agent in some Japanese dishes; the ginkgo is of ancient Chinese origin but now widely planted in many other countries including the United States.

gin rickey: Highball composed of gin, soda water, and lime juice.

ginseng: Chinese medicinal herb whose licorice-flavored root is made into soup; ginseng is also the name of a similar plant native to New England whose roots were traded for tea leaves by Yankee skippers of the early 1800's.

girdlecake: Scots for a griddle-cake.

gislev cheese: Danish-type hard rennet cheese made from skimmed cow's milk.

gj: Abbreviation for grapefruit juice.

gjætost: (Norwegian—herdsman's cheese) Sweet-flavored brown cheese.

glacé: (French—frozen; glazed)

glace: (French—ice; ice cream, pastry glaze)

glace à la vanille: (French—vanilla ice cream)

glace de viande: (French—meat glaze) Concentrated meat stock used as an additive in sauce-making and as a glaze.

glass: Transparent or translucent silica-based material made into dinnerware, cooking utensils, and drinking vessels of all kinds.

glassware: Kitchenware and table-ware made of glass.

glaze: Glossy coating; in savory dishes, glaze is usually composed of broth cooked to a gelatinous paste; pastry usually glazed with a topping of syrup made of egg white, sugar, and water.

globe artichoke: Artichoke head.

globe urn: Spherical metallic chafing dish with an alcohol burner used for serving hot beverages.

glögg: Swedish hot drink of spiced red wine served at year-end holidays.

gluten: Protein found in flour after starch is washed away; gluten is also the name of a gummy substance in flour milled from wheat; this substance creates the cohesion required for dough to hold together.

gluten bread: Wheat-flour bread high in gluten and low in starch content.

glutton: Person who habitually overeats; glutton is also a common name for the wolverine.

gnocco: (Italian—dumpling)

gnocchi leggieri: (Italian—light dumplings) Cheese noodles.

goblet: Bowl-shaped stemmed glass holding 6 to 12 ounces of liquid.

Godard: Garnish usually for chicken, containing *quenelles,* sweetbreads, truffles, and cock's combs, named for 19th-century composer Benjamin Godard.

gold apple: Tomato.

gold cake: Cake prepared with egg yolks and not whites.

golden buck: Welsh rarebit topped with a poached egg.

Golden Delicious: Sweet yellow apple produced in the State of Washington.

golden egg roll: Bread roll yellowed with egg yolks, vegetable dye, or saffron.

golden gin: Gin that has been aged in wood, thus picking up a slight coloring.

goldenrod tea: Blue mountain tea.

golden syrup: British term for a blend of sugar, corn syrup, and molasses, used as a table syrup.

gold flakes: Tiny flakes of gold used for garnishing liqueurs and elegant pastries.

Goldwasser: Danziger Goldwasser.

golubtsy: (Russian—cabbage)

gomme: (French—[plant]gum)

goober: Peanut.

goober pea: Peanut.

good beef: Third-best grade of beef as determined by the U.S. Department of Agriculture; *see also* beef.

Good Humor: Trademark name for a confection consisting of cholocate-covered ice cream on a stick.

goose: Waterfowl intermediate in size between ducks and swans; the goose's big eggs are used in baking, and its flesh is usually roasted.

gooseberry: Acid-flavored green, red, and yellow berries used chiefly in pies and preserves; the European varieties may be eaten raw when fully ripe, but American species must be cooked.

gooseberry fool: English dessert made of stewed gooseberries and whipped cream.

gorgonzola: Pungent blue cheese originating in Gorgonzola near Milan in northwestern Italy.

gorgot: (Armenian—wheat kernels)

gouda: Dutch cheese, cannonball-shaped and yellow, first made near the town of Gouda in the Netherlands.

goulash: Hungarian beef stew made with caraway seeds, onions, and paprika.

goumi: Orange-red berry from China and Japan, used in making preserves and sauces.

gourmand: Person who takes excessive pleasure in eating and drinking.

gourmet: Connoisseur of food and drink.

gourmet exotica: Odd and unusual foods, usually canned, pickled, or otherwise preserved: choco-late-covered ants, rattlesnake canapé, tiger meat, bear steaks, crocodile tails, elephant and kangaroo cutlets, etc.

goveda supa: (Yugoslavian—beef soup)

grace cup: Cup used for drinking the final toast at the end of a meal.

graduate: Measuring glass marked to indicate quantities such as cups or ounces.

graham crackers: Crackers made of whole-wheat or graham flour.

graham flour: Whole-wheat flour, as advocated by the 19th-century American food reformer, Sylvester Graham.

grain alcohol: Ethyl alcohol.

gram: Metric unit equal to 0.035 ounce; in India the word means a chick pea.

granada: (Spanish—pomegranate)

grana reggiano: (Italian—Reggian grain) Parmesan-type grating cheese made from whole milk and prized for its pungency; cheese first made in Reggio nell' Emilia in northern Italy.

grande champagne: (French—great champagne) Cognac distilled from wine grown in certain vineyards in the Charente-Maritime department of France.

grande liqueur: Chartreuse type of liqueur.

grand marnier: Orange-flavored golden-brown liqueur.

grand-père: (French—grandfather) Nickname for a French-Canadian dumpling served in maple syrup.

granité: (French—pebbled; granitelike) Light-textured water ice.

Granny Smith's: Canadian green apple.

granoturco: (Italian—Turkish grain; corn)

granulate: To form or crystallize into grains; sugar crystals are granulated by drying and screening.

grapefruit: Largest of the popular varieties of citrus fruits, called grapefruit because it grows in grapelike clusters; some are seedless and some are less pithy and pulpy than others.

grapefruit juice: Juice expressed from the grapefruit, available commercially in sweetened and unsweetened forms.

grapefruit knife: Small kitchen knife with a curved and serrated blade for coring and sectioning grapefruit.

grapefruit spoon: Spoon with a serrated edge for removing sections of citrus fruit without the aid of a knife.

grape juice: Juice expressed from grapes, often sterilized to prevent its fermenting and forming wine or vinegar.

grapevine: Woody vine growing by tendrils and producing clusters of juicy berries called grapes; *see also* grape.

grappa: (Italian—brandy)

grate: To rub food on a grater until it is reduced to small particles.

grater: Utensil with a rough surface, usually formed of perforations, for abrading food into small particles.

Gravenstein: Yellowish or green apple streaked with reddish stripes, characterized by its slightly tart flavor.

graves: Dry red or white table wine, named for this district in France near Bordeaux.

gravlax: (Swedish—marinated or pickled salmon)

gravy: Sauce made from the pan drippings of meat, plus, flour, water, and seasoning.

gravy boat: Boat-shaped receptacle with a pouring lip at one end and a handle at the other, used at table for serving gravy.

grayfish: Dogfish shark or pollock, so called because of its color.

gray goose: Canada goose, or the European graylag.

graylag: European wild goose believed to be the ancestor of domesticated geese.

grayware: Enamelware made with a thin coat of enamel, through which the base material shows in spots.

grease: Rendered animal fat, used in many kinds of cooking.

greasy spoon: Inelegant term for a low-class or low-price lunchroom.

greben: (Yiddish—cracklings rendered from chicken or goose fat)

greek olive: Ripe black olive preserved in brine and olive oil.

greek salad: Salad made of vegetables, feta cheese, anchovies, capers, and other ingredients in an olive-oil-and-vinegar dressing.

green cheese: Name for several kinds of cheese: new cheese with a greenish color; sapsago cheese; skim milk and whey cheese; unripe cheese.

green corn: Tender ears of sweet corn ready for cooking.

green crab: Edible crab found in tidal waters in both Europe and America.

green duck: Young duckling, 9 to 13 weeks old, fattened for market.

greengage: Greenish and greenish-yellow dessert plums named for the 18th-century English botanist Sir William Gage who imported them from Europe.

green goods: Fresh vegetables.

green goose: Gosling 10 to 12 weeks old and fattened for market.

greengrocer: English term for a dealer in fruits and vegetables.

greengroceries: Fresh fruits and vegetables.

green kelsey: One of more than a thousand varieties of plums, relished for its tart flavor.

green laver: Edible seaweed.

greenling: North Pacific food and game fish caught close inshore; the lingcod and the pollack taken from the North Atlantic are also called greenling.

green olive: Unripe olive pickled in brine and vinegar; sometimes pitted and stuffed with almonds or red pimientos.

green onion: Scallion.

green pea: Pea.

green pepper: Immature fruit of the red pepper, used as a garnish in salads, or as a casing for forcemeat.

green tea: Unfermented tea.

grenadin: Small slice of veal, cut into a triangle or rectangle, larded with bacon, and braised.

grenadine: Pomegranate syrup used in making cocktails and in flavoring some baked goods.

greyano vino: Bulgarian spiced hot wine punch.

griblette: (French—broiled forcemeat)

griddle: Flat metal surface on which food is cooked by dry heat.

griddle cake: Pancake.

gridiron: Metal grating on which food is broiled over direct heat.

grill: Gridiron.

grill: To broil over or under an open flame or other direct heat.

grillé: (French—broiled)

grille: (French—grating; gridiron)

grillroom: Restaurant usually specializing in grilled meats and seafoods.

grilse: Young salmon.

Grimes Golden: Sweet eating apple with yellow-orange skin bearing many small dark specks, named for its 18th-century developer Thomas P. Grimes.

grind: To crush food, usually in a chopper or food mill, until it flakes, breaks into small bits, or powders.

grinder: Utensil for grinding foods by manual or motor power; grinders usually have a variety of cutting blades so foods may be ground to varying degrees of coarseness and fineness.

grindstone: Circular stone revolved in a stand and used to sharpen cleavers, knives, and other edged implements.

grits: Coarse part of meal; colloquially, grits usually means hominy grits, served boiled or fried.

groats: Particles larger than grits, usually of hulled grain; in England hominy grits are called groats.

groceries: Produce, green, staples, and food supplies of all kinds.

groentesoep: (Dutch—vegetable soup)

grog: Royal Navy term for a sailor's ration of alcoholic liquor, usually rum, cut with water; grog can also mean a drink made of hot water and rum, or rum flavored with lime juice or lemon juice and sweetened with molasses and brown sugar.

grønnsaker: (Norwegian—vegetables)

grønsager: (Danish—vegetables)

grönsaker: (Swedish—vegetables)

groseille: (French—currant)

grouper: Large relative of the sea bass taken off the Atlantic and Pacific Coasts, a popular food fish.

grovbrød: (Norwegian—coarse bread) Rye or brown bread.

gruau: (French—grit; groat) Oatmeal.

gruel: Thin porridge of hominy or oatmeal boiled with milk, sugar, and water.

grüne Bohne: (German—green bean)

grunt: Any of many tropical food fishes; New England dessert made by dropping biscuit dough on top of boiling berries.

gruyère: Emmenthaler type of cheese made from whole milk, partly skimmed milk, and skimmed milk, originating in this valley in Switzerland; gruyère is often packed in individual metal-foil-covered wedges.

grytstek: (Swedish—pot roast)

guacamole: Salad of mashed avocados, tomatoes, onions, and lime juice, often used as a dip for potato chips or toasted tortillas.

guanabana: Soursop.

guava: Delicious tropical and subtropical fruit made into jams and jellies; fruit grows well in southern California and along the Florida Keys.

guava nectar: Commercial term for canned guava juice.

guayaba: (Spanish—guava)

guéridon: (French—small serving table)

Guernsey: Dairy cattle of a type originally bred on Guernsey in the Channel Islands off the northern coast of France.

Gugelhupf: (Austrian-German—name applied to a type of cake) Yeast cake with raisins and almonds, baked in a fluted form.

guinea fowl: Bird related to the pheasant, native to West Africa but domesticated in many parts of the world; guinea fowl is most commonly served roasted or stewed.

guineo: (Cuban-Spanish—banana)

Guinness stout: Rich dark beer brewed in Dublin, Ireland by the firm of Guinness.

guisado: (Spanish—stew)

guisante: (Spanish—pea)

guiso: (Spanish—dish)

gula batu: (Malay—sugar stone) Kind of candy.

gulf flounder: Flatfish taken from the Gulf of Mexico.

gulyás: (Hungarian—herdsman's stew) Goulash.

GUM: Abbreviation for Gossurdarstvienny Universalny Magasin (Russian—state universal store) Department store and supermarket under Soviet state control.

gum arabic: Acacia gum.

gumbo: Soup thickened with okra pods, a Southern specialty.

gumbo filé: Gumbo thickened with filé powder.

gumdrop: Sugar-coated candy made of cornstarch, corn syrup, gelatin, and gum arabic, plus a variety of colorings and flavorings; gumdrops are usually shaped like rounded cones, and are not to be confused with smooth-coated jelly beans.

gum tragacanth: Exudate of the tragacanth plant grown in the Middle East; the gum is used to make lozenges firm and chewy, also in ice-cream powders and gelatin desserts.

gunpowder tea: Green tea grown in China where each leaf is rolled into a pellet like coarse gunpowder.

Gurke: (German—cucumber)

Gurkensalat: (German—cucumber salad)

gut durchgebraten: (German—thoroughly roasted) Term used of well-done meat.

guten Appetit: (German—good appetite)

gypsy bread: Fruit bread made with black molasses.

gyu: (Japanese—thin-sliced beef) Used in making sukiyaki-type dishes.

haba: Broad bean, specifically lima bean.

habanera: (Spanish—Havana style) Foods prepared with many spices, often listed as *à la Habanera*.

haberdine: Dried and salted codfish.

haché: (French—hashed; minced)

hachis: (French—hash; minced meat)

hackberry: Small sweet berry used for making preserves.

haddie: Scots for haddock.

haddock: Important food fish somewhat smaller than the related cod: lightly smoked, it is called finnan haddie; haddock is served baked, broiled, poached, and in many other ways and is probably the most important food fish taken from the Atlantic Ocean.

hae kün: (Thai—shrimp rolls)

haggis: Scots pudding consisting of chopped heart, liver, and lungs of a calf or sheep seasoned with chopped onions, oatmeal, and suet, and steamed in the stomach of the animal.

hake: Important food fish related to the much larger cod.

half-and-half: In America: half cream, half milk; in Great Britain: half ale, half beer.

half bottle: Liquid measure containing 12 to 15 ounces.

half gallon: Liquid measure containing 2 quarts or 64 ounces.

half liter: Liquid measure containing a little more than 1 pint.

half-moon: Perchlike marine food fish of the Pacific.

half om half: Sweet brownish-red Dutch liqueur.

half pint: Liquid measure containing 1 cup or 8 ounces.

half pound: Dry measure containing 8 ounces.

halibut: Largest of the flatfishes, weighing up to 600 pounds; halibut is taken in both Atlantic and Pacific waters, and because its flesh is tender and tasty, it is often sold as chicken halibut.

Haligonian stew: Seafood specialty of Halifax, Nova Scotia.

hallaca: Venezuelan meat pie boiled in corn husks or banana leaves.

hallaur: Swiss red wine.

halleves: (Hungarian—fish stew) Codfish stew with root vegetables.

Hallgartener: German white wine.

halvah: Flaky Turkish confection made of crushed almonds or crushed sesame seeds mixed with honey or syrup.

halwah: (Turkish—halvah)

ham: Meat from the buttock or thigh of a pig or other animal; salted and smoked hams can be eaten raw or cold after parboiling, but are most often prepared for baking or braising.

ham and: Slang for ham and eggs.

hamantaschen: (Yiddish—Haman's pockets) Three-cornered pastry filled with prunes or poppy seeds, baked for Purim in memory of Haman; the triangular shape of these cookies is supposed to resemble the triangular hat worn by Haman; they are called taschen because they form pastry pockets.

Hamburg: Poultry breed developed around Hamburg, Germany.

hamburg brandy: Beet or potato alcohol flavored with wine to create an ersatz brandy.

hamburger: Meat patty usually made of ground beef, pork, pork and beef combined, or ground vegetables; the patty is fried or broiled and served on a round bun, plain or garnished.

hamburger press: Device for cutting and shaping hamburger patties.

hamburger roll: Soft round white bread bun on which hamburgers are served.

hamburg steak: Hamburger; among many Europeans this means ground beef topped by a raw egg and eaten with a side order of fresh or pickled onion rings.

Hämchen: (German—pig's knuckle)

ham hock: Cut of ham just above the foot and full of tender tissue; ham hocks are usually boiled although they may be sliced and stewed.

Hamm: American beer brewed in St. Paul, Minnesota.

Hammel: (German—mutton)

Hampshire: American breed of white-and-black belted swine and also the name of a large, mutton-producing, hornless sheep originally bred in Hampshire, England.

ham shoulder: Economical cut of pork taken from front leg of the carcass; ham shoulder is the chief ingredient of Spam and other commercial meat preparations.

hamwich: Slang for ham sandwich.

hanche: (French—haunch)

hand cheese: German sour-milk cheese, such as *Alt Kuhkäse, Berliner Kuhkäse, Dresdener Bierkäse*, thuringian caraway cheese, tyrolean sour cheese, etc.

hand of pork: Pork shoulder with blade bone removed.

hang: To age meat by hanging it in a cool but unrefrigerated place until it becomes tender; the more expensive the meat, the long it has probably been hung.

hanpen: (Japanese—fishcake)

Hansa: Norwegian beer brewed in Bergen.

hanya: (Arabic—good health) A toast.

haptule: Ceylon's finest tea.

har chow fun: (Chinese—fried rice with shrimp)

hardbake: English candy made of almonds, molasses, and sugar.

hard-ball stage: Candy-making stage in which the syrup, when dropped into cold water, becomes a hard ball; this occurs between 270 and 290 degrees F.

hard boiled: Cooked until hard, usually said of eggs.

hard candy: Confection of corn syrup and sugar offered in a variety of flavors, shapes, and sizes.

hard cider: Fermented cider, containing less than 10 percent alcohol.

hard clam: Hard-shelled clam or quahog.

hard crab: Hard-shelled crab.

hardekookt eier: (Dutch—hard-boiled egg)

hardkogt æg: (Danish—hard-boiled egg)

hard sauce: Mixture of butter, cream, powdered sugar, and flavoring served on puddings.

hard-shelled clam: Quahog.

hard-shelled crab: Hard-shell phase of the blue crab before it molts.

hardtack: Hard unsalted ship's biscuit or bread made of flour and water; Japanese ship's biscuits are flavored with black sesame seeds.

hardware: Household and kitchen implements such as cutlery, grinding and chopping equipment, and such taken-for-granted items as cabinet catches, knobs, drawer pulls, towel racks, etc.

hare: Large long-eared rabbit often raised for its meat; hare, either wild or domestic, is considered better eating than rabbit, and is served in many of the same ways as chicken.

hareng: (French—herring)

hareng frais: (French—fresh herring)

hareng fumé: (French—smoked herring)

hareng mariné: (French—pickled herring)

hareng saur: (French—kippered herring)

haricot: (French—bean)

haricot de Lima: (French—lima bean)

haricot flageolet: (French—flageolet bean)

haricot rouge: (French—kidney bean)

haricot vert: (French—green bean)

haring: (Dutch—herring)

haringsla: (Dutch—herring salad)

hart: Mature male of the European red deer.

harvard beets: Sweet-and-sour vegetable dish consisting of small whole beets served hot in vinegar-flavored sauce.

harvest fish: Edible fish related to the butterfish and the California pompano, found chiefly in warm Atlantic waters.

Hasenkuchen: (German—hare cake) Pâté of hare.

Hasenpfeffer: (German—peppered hare) Stew made of hare meat soaked for 48 hours in pickling spices and vinegar.

hash: Dish of chopped meat and chopped vegetables, usually potatoes, browned in a frying pan; hash is a popular way of using up leftovers.

hashed-brown potatoes: Parboiled potatoes, chopped and fried brown.

hashed-browns: Hashed-brown potatoes.

hash house: Low-class or low-price lunchroom.

haslets: Edible entrails of the pig.

hasty pudding: English porridge made of boiled flour or oatmeal and water, or a New England dessert made of cornmeal mush and milk and served with molasses or maple syrup.

hatz yev banin: (Armenian— bread and cheese)

Hauptmahl: (German—chief meal; dinner)

haut: (French—high) Term indicating a wine comes from a vineyard farther up the river than others of the same sort.

havercake: Scots oatcake.

haw: Hawthorn berry.

Hawaiian crab: Large edible crab related to the Atlantic blue crab; it is popular in Hawaii and sometimes shipped to markets in California, Oregon, and Washington.

hazelnut: Sweet thick-shelled nut used in flavoring ice cream and garnishing desserts; hazelnuts are European in origin but related to a native American filbert similarly used.

headcheese: Jellied mass made of beef, lamb or pig offal meats: feet, heads, hearts, and tongues; these are seasoned, chopped, and boiled, then pressed into jelly molds.

head lettuce: Variety of lettuce with a compact, well-bunched head.

health foods: Fruits, nuts, and other special vegetable products, sold chiefly in health-food stores and appealing particularly to vegetarians and to persons on restricted diets.

health salad: Salad composed of apples, carrots, and cucumbers cut into thin strips, seasoned with lemon juice and salt, and coated with sour cream.

heart of palm: Edible bud of a palm tree served as a salad; in the U.S. the cabbage palmetto is used; in Brazil, the wax palm; in the West Indies, the cabbage palm.

heather ale: Mild Scots beverage made of heather blossoms, honey, hops, spices, and yeast.

heavy cream: Whipping cream, containing not less than 30 percent butterfat.

Hecht: (German—pike)

hedge garlic: Garlic mustard.

heel: Heel of round cut from the hind shank of a meat animal.

heel pot roast: Inner and upper beef shank cut from between the round and the lower shank.

heifer beef: Meat cut from carcass of a young cow.

heilbot: (Dutch—halibut)

Heilbutt: (German—holy flounder) Halibut — originally so named because it was eaten on holy days.

Heineken: Dutch beer brewed in Rotterdam.

helado: (Spanish—ice cream)

helgeflundra: (Swedish—halibut)

helleflynder: (Danish—halibut)

helleflyndre: (Norwegian—halibut)

helote: (Spanish-American—roasted ear of corn)

helva: (Arabic—halvah)

hen: Female domestic fowl.

hen tureen: Tureen made of glazed pottery in form of a nesting hen atop a basket of eggs.

henware: Honeyware.

herb: Any plant not developing woody tissue such as vines, shrubs, and trees; in cookery the term usually means a plant valued for the aromatic and fla-voring qualities of its seeds, leaves, roots, etc.

herb bouquet: Bunch of three or four herbs tied together and removed after cooking like a *bouquet garni*.

herb of kings: Basil, so called by the ancient Greeks who esteemed its aroma and used it in making perfumes as well as in cooking.

herb shelf: Spice shelf.

herb vinegar: Vinegar made from malt, distilled, or wine vinegar, or a combination of them, and flavored with an assortment of herbs.

herkimer: Cheddar cheese from Herkimer County, New York.

hermits: Cookies made with molasses, brown sugar, and cinnamon.

herring: Probably the most important food fish in the modern world, fished from the colder waters of the North Atlantic; most herrings are salted and smoked, though many Europeans eat it raw; in the U.S., young herrings are canned as sardines.

hete bliksem: (Dutch—heat lightning) Pork chops with apples and potatoes mixed.

hibachi: Portable Japanese brazier for grilling food over a charcoal fire.

hickory cheddar: Hickory-smoked cheddar cheese.

hickory nut: North American relative of the walnut used in cakes, cookies, and many chocolate bar confections; hickory-wood shavings give off a fragrant odor favored in smoking hams, bacon, and cheese.

hielo: (Spanish—ice)

hígado: (Spanish—liver)

highball: Tall drink, usually iced, composed of brandy, gin, rum, vodka, or whiskey plus some mixer such as Coca-Cola, ginger ale, soda water, or plain water.

highball glass: Tumbler containing 8 to 10 ounces of liquid.

high tea: Supper served with tea.

higo: (Spanish—fig)

hind: Mature female of the European red deer.

hindbær med fløde: (Danish—raspberries with cream)

hind foot: Pork cut from the hind foot of a pig.

hindquarter: Hind leg and loin of a side of meat.

hind shank: Rear leg of a meat animal.

hipon: (Filipino—shrimp)

hip steak: Beefsteak cut from the haunches or hips.

Hirn: (German—brains)

hiyar salatasi: (Turkish—cucumber salad)

hochepot: (French—hotchpotch) Stew made of many things such as pig's ears and tails or beef, mutton, and bacon combined with a variety of vegetables.

hock: Hockenheim, a Rhine wine; hock can also mean meat taken from just above the fore or hind foot.

hoe cake: Corn cake, so named because in early days corncake was baked on the heated blade of a hoe.

hog: Domesticated swine; in the pork industry, a hog is a pig exceeding two-hundred pounds and being readied for market.

hog banana: Red-skinned cooking banana, rarely eaten raw.

hog chitterlings: Hog intestines cut up and prepared as food.

hogen-mogen: Strong, said of alcoholic drinks.

hogflesh: Pork.

hog jowls: Pork cut from the lower jaw.

hogmeat: Pork.

hog's grease: Hog fat or pork lard.

hogshead: Cask containing 63 to 140 gallons of liquid; hogshead also refers to a U.S. unit of capacity equaling 63 gallons.

hog trotters: Pig's feet.

holishke: (Russian—stuffed cabbage)

hollandaise: (French—in the Dutch manner) Sauce made of butter, egg yolks, and lemon juice or vinegar.

holland gin: Dutch gin.

Holland Rusk: Popular round-shaped zwieback.

hollands: Dutch gin.

Holstein-Friesian: Black-and-white dairy cattle developed in Friesland, northern Holland, and now found all over the world; Holsteins have the highest milk yield of all dairy breeds, although the milk itself is lowest in butterfat content.

homard: (French—large-clawed lobster)

home-brew: Homemade alcoholic beverage.

home-fried potatoes: Potatoes cooked or uncooked, and fried in a skillet.

home ripener: Utensil for speeding up the ripening of green fruits and vegetables by means of fluorescent light.

hominy: Corn grits.

hominy grits: Uniform-size grains of hominy, boiled and fried in many parts of southern United States, and served at breakfast with bacon and eggs.

homogenized: Blended and made uniform by thorough beating and mixing; homogenized milk is processed so the cream will not separate from it.

høne: (Danish—chicken)

honey: Sweet sticky substance manufactured by bees from the nectar of flowers.

honey bee: Cocktail made of jamaica rum, honey, and lime juice.

honey biscuit: Baking-powder biscuit split, filled with butter-and-honey cream, and reheated.

honeydew: Smooth-skinned muskmelon with sweet greenish flesh.

honeydrop: Honey-flavored candy.

honeyware: Edible seaweed resembling and served like spinach after it is boiled.

hooch: Slang for liquor, usually a poor quality of moonshine.

hood: Metal canopy built above an oven or range to carry off excess heat and the fumes of cooking.

hooker: Big liquid portion, applied especially to alcoholic drinks.

hop: Female flowers of a vine related to hemp, used in brewing beer; young hop shoots are sometimes served in salads or boiled like asparagus.

hopping John: Southern stew of beans or black-eye peas and bacon, seasoned with red peppers.

horchata: Almond-flavored soft drink popular throughout Latin America and Spain.

horehound: Mint-family herb yielding extract for flavoring cakes, cookies, and some stews.

horn chestnut: Water chestnut.

hors d'oeuvre: (French—out of work) Appetizer served during cocktail parties or at the beginning of a meal.

hors d'oeuvre server: Tray with glass, plastic, or pottery sections inserted for serving a variety of appetizers.

horsemeat: Meat cut from the carcass of a horse, in many parts of Europe there are butcher shops that specialize in horsemeat and advertise the fact by displaying a picture of a horse's head over the door of the shop.

horseradish: Herb of the mustard family whose root is ground and made into a fiery relish, served with many meat courses.

horseradish sauce: Finnish sauce of clear meat stock, flour, butter, and vinegar which is poured over grated horseradish and served with meat and boiled potatoes.

horticultural bean: Shell bean whose pods are splashed with red and white, and whose seeds are buff and red.

hot breads: Bread, biscuits, muffins, rolls, etc., served hot.

hot buttered rum: Mixed drink composed of dark rum, hot water, sugar, and cloves, topped with a dab of butter.

hot cake: Pancake.

hotchpotch: Scots mutton broth containing cauliflower, lettuce, peas, and other vegetables.

hotchpotchsoppa: (Swedish—hotchpotch soup) Stew thin enough to be eaten with a spoon.

hot-cross bun: Raisin bun decorated with a cross, usually made of sugar frosting; such buns are featured in bakeries just before and on Good Friday.

hot dog: Slang for a boiled or grilled frankfurter served in a split hot roll and usually seasoned with mustard, sauerkraut, catsup, chopped pickles, or other relishes.

hot-dog stand: Place specializing in serving frankfurters and beverages although other foods may be sold.

hothouse: Grown out of season by special forcing methods; said of such delicacies as berries, grapes, tomatoes, etc.

hothouse lamb: Lamb marketed from January to March as this is out of the normal lambing season.

hot oven: Oven heated from 400 to 450 degrees Fahrenheit.

hot pepper: Any pungent pepper.

hot plate: Portable cooking or warming range; hot plates are usually heated by electricity or gas, although some use solar heat, gasoline under pressure, or solidified alcohol.

hot pot: (Dutch—pork chops and potatoes)

hot toddy: Mixed drink consisting of hot water, whiskey, lemon, cloves, cinnamon, and sugar.

howtowdie: Scots boiled chicken served with poached eggs and spinach.

hr: Abbreviation for hour.

huck: Slang for huckleberry.

huckleberry: Edible black or dark-red berry of a low shrub of the heath family.

huevo: (Spanish—egg)

huevos duros: (Spanish—hard eggs) Hard-boiled eggs.

huevos escalfados: (Spanish—poached eggs)

huevos fritos: (Spanish—fried eggs)

huevos pasados: (Spanish—boiled eggs)

huevos rancheros: (Spanish—ranch-style eggs)

huevos y tocino: (Spanish—bacon and eggs)

Huhn: (German—chicken)

Hühnerbrühe: (German—chicken broth)

huile: (French—oil)

huître: (French—oyster)

huîtres à l'écaille: (French—oysters on the [half] shell)

huîtres marinées: (French—pickled oysters)

hull: To remove the outer covering of a fruit or seed, or to cut off the stem or calyx of strawberries, tomatoes, etc.

hulled millet: Millet.

huller: Metal tweezers for removing berry and other fruit stems.

humble pie: Meat pie made of entrails of a deer or a wild pig.

humita: Hot tamale made of cornmeal and sugar, popular in the port cities of western South America.

hummer: (Danish, Norwegian and Swedish—lobster)

Hummer: (German—lobster)

Hummermayonnaise: (German—lobster with mayonnaise)

hummer salat: (Danish—lobster salad)

humpback salmon: Small pink species of Pacific Coast salmon common in rivers from Alaska to California; in the breeding season, the male develops a large dorsal hump, hence the name.

Hungarian goulash: Goulash.

Hungarian paprika: Red paprika grown in Hungary.

Hungarian pepper: Hungarian paprika.

hush puppy: Cornmeal fritter made of batter containing cornmeal, flour, grated onion, eggs, milk, and baking powder.

hvitkålsoppa: (Swedish—white cabbage soup)

hydrogenated fat: Vegetable oils hardened by exposure to hydrogen in the presence of heat and a catalyst; coconut, corn, cottonseed, peanut, sesame, and soybean oils are all hydrogenated fats.

hydromel: Mixture of honey and water often including herbs and spices; when fermented, hydromel becomes mead.

hyldebærsuppe: (Danish—elderberry soup)

hyson: Variety of Chinese green tea.

hyssop: European mint-family herb whose pungent leaves are used (sparingly) in flavoring liqueurs, soups, and stews; hyssop can also refer to any of several American varieties of wormwood.

i'a ota: (Polynesian—raw fish) Fish marinated in coconut milk and lime juice.

ICA: Abbreviation for International Chefs Association.

ice: Frozen water (melts at 32°F or 0°C), used to chill beverages and many foods, or in making flavored sherbets; in England the term is often synonymous with ice cream or sherbet.

iceberg lettuce: Crisp, firm, and round vegetable with large broad leaves, excellent with cottage cheese, fruit, salads and sandwiches, or served cooked or wilted.

icebox: Insulated refrigerator for keeping beverages and foods cold; many are built with special compartments for holding ice or making ice cubes.

ice bucket: Container for holding ice; usually used to chill a bottle of champagne or other wine.

ice cellar: Underground room where foods and refreshments are kept on ice or near ice.

ice chest: Icebox, ice compartment, or portable icebox.

ice chipper: Ice fork—utensil with a row of short tines for chipping ice off a block.

ice cream: Frozen confection made from a basic mixture of cream, eggs, and sugar, plus flavoring.

ice-cream bonbons: Tiny scoops of ice cream covered with chocolate coating and kept cold until eaten.

ice-cream cone: Crisp conical pastry wafer used for holding ice cream or sherbet.

ice-cream fork: Bowl-shaped short-tined fork used for eating ice cream or sherbet.

ice-cream freezer: Manually or motor operated device for mixing and freezing custards, ice creams, and sherbets.

ice-cream scoop: A device for serving individual portions of ice cream in neat round balls.

ice-cream soda: Mixture of carbonated water, flavoring, ice cream, and syrup, usually sipped with a straw.

ice-cream-soda spoon: Long-handled spoon.

ice crusher: Metallic utensil for crushing chunks or cubes of ice.

ice cube: Small block of ice made in the freezer compartment of a refrigerator or by a commercial device, used principally for chilling drinks.

iced coffee: Coffee served ice cold with cream and sugar, a popular summer beverage.

iced tea: Tea served ice cold, usually with lemon, a favorite summer beverage.

iced-tea spoon: Long-handled spoon.

icefish: Smeltlike fish of China and Japan.

ice fork: Ice chipper.

ice machine: Device for producing ice or ice cubes.

ice milk: Nonfattening skim-milk ice-cream dessert.

ice pick: Taper-pointed steel utensil for chipping ice.

icer decanter: Wine decanter with blow-glass indent for holding ice, so that contents are chilled without being diluted.

ice shaver: Metal-bladed utensil shaped like a wood plane and used for reducing small blocks of ice to compact crystal masses used in sherbets and for frosting beverages.

ice tongs: Hooked tongs for handling large blocks of ice.

ice tray: Shallow tray for forming and storing ice cubes, usually provided with a removable grating.

ice tub: Ice bucket.

ice water: Water chilled with ice.

ichang: Fine-flavored black tea imported from China.

ichiba: (Japanese—market)

icing: Frosting.

icing sugar: Confectioner's sugar.

ic pilav: (Turkish—rice pilaf)

iechyd da: (Welsh—good health) A toast.

IFHE: Abbreviation for International Federation of Home Economics, worldwide organization founded in 1908.

iguana: Tropical American lizards, whose tail meat often substitutes for chicken in many Latin American lands, where their eggs are also eaten fried, dried, or pickled.

ihlefeld: Hand cheese.

IIA: Abbreviation for International Institute of Agriculture, founded in Rome in 1905 to protect farmers against sudden drops in the produce market.

ikang: (Malay—fish)

il conto, per piacere: (Italian—the bill, please)

Imbiss: (German—snack)

Imbiss-stube: (German—snackbar)

immersion heater: Electrical device whose heating element is designed to be immersed in the water it is to boil; immersion heaters are used mainly to heat small amounts of water quickly.

Imo: Imitation sour cream made with carrageen, gelatin, lactic acid culture, and vegetable oil; Imo does not contain milk fat, is used like dairy sour cream, and is especially good for restricted diets.

imperial club: Canadian cheddar cheese.

imperial gallon: Five-quart liquid measure used in Canada and throughout the British Commonwealth, containing 277¼ cubic inches, which makes it one fifth larger than the four-quart, the American gallon (231 cubic inches).

imperial tea: Green tea of China made from older tea leaves.

imrek helva: (Armenian—farina dessert) Dish made with farina, milk, and sugar.

in.: Abbreviation for inch.

incinerator: Device for reducing trash to ash by burning it in an air-vented destructor chamber; incinerators are no longer allowed in many communities where air pollution is a problem.

indian arrowroot: Starch extracted from the roots of a tropical herb.

indian bread: Cornbread.

indian corn: Corn or maize.

indian fig: Cactus fruit.

indian gram: Chick pea.

indian kale: Taro.

indian maize: Indian corn.

indian meal: Cornmeal.

indian mustard: Asiatic cabbage-like plant whose pods are used as a potherb.

indian nut: Betel nut of the East Indies; pine nut of the American Southwest.

indian pear: Shadbush berry.

indian pudding: Baked pudding of milk, molasses, cornmeal, sugar, spices, butter, and eggs, served with vanilla ice cream or whipped cream.

indian rice: Wild rice.

indian shuck bread: Cornmeal batter wrapped in corn husks and boiled, a favorite dish of many Oklahomans.

indian tea: Tea substitute brewed from dried leaves of the yaupon tree, a holly of the southern U.S.; indian tea is also another name for labrador tea and for new jersey tea.

Indische kruiderij: (Dutch—Indonesian spice)

indonesian isinglass: Agar.

infrared cooker: Propane-fired cooker for use in house trailers, campers, and tents, which cooks without flame.

inkfish: Cuttlefish or squid.

insalata: (Italian—salad)

insalata di lattuga: (Italian—lettuce salad)

insalata di legumi: (Italian—vegetable salad)

insalata mista: (Italian—mixed salad)

insalata verde: (Italian—green salad)

instant food: Commercial products prepared by dehydration or by fine grinding and pulverization; cocoa, coffee, cream, garlic, onion, potatoes, cake, and pie, and many other foods come in instant form.

intercostata di manzo: (Italian— rib steak of beef)

intingolo: (Italian—gravy; stew)

invert sugar: Small-crystal sugar, created during the process of making candies and jellies; invert sugar is a mixture of glucose and fructose.

in vino veritas: (Latin—in wine there is truth) Truth uttered under alcoholic stimulus.

involtini: (Italian—rolled)

irish coffee: Hot coffee and Irish whiskey topped with whipped cream.

irish mist: Irish honey-and-whiskey liqueur.

irish moss: Carrageen.

irish potato: Large white potato, cultivated in many parts of the world but a dietary staple among the Irish poor.

irish soda bread: Round loaves of leavened white bread flavored with caraway seeds and raisins.

irish stew: Stewed boneless lamb and potatoes flavored with onions, salt, and pepper.

irish turkey: Slang for corned beef and cabbage.

irish whiskey: Barley-malt-and-grain whiskey distilled in Ireland.

irish wine: Nickname for Irish whiskey.

ironware: Cooking utensils made of iron: dutch ovens, iron pans, pots, and skillets; muffin pans, etc.

ise-ebi tempura: (Japanese—deep-fried lobster)

isvand: (Danish—ice water)

isvann: (Norwegian—ice water)

isvatten: (Swedish—ice water)

italian chestnut: Spanish chestnut.

italian dressing: Salad dressing made of olive oil and wine vinegar plus pepper, salt, and other seasoning.

italian paste: Alimentary paste or *pasta,* chief ingredient of macaroni and spaghetti.

italian roast: Method of roasting coffee beans to yield a brownish black color, darker than a french roast.

italian turnip: Broccoli rab.

italian vermouth: Sweet vermouth.

italian walnut: English walnut.

jabalí: (Spanish—wild boar)

jackfish: Pike or pickerel.

jackfruit: Edible tropical fruit related to the breadfruit; the seeds are eaten roasted.

jack plum: Java plum.

jack salmon: Wall-eyed perch.

Jacks' cheese: Jacks' Monterey.

Jacks' Monterey: Soft cow's-milk cheese first produced by a Scots immigrant named Jacks who settled in Monterey, California, where much of this cheese is still produced.

jaggery: East Indian term for the crude brown sugar used in many tropical countries.

jagging iron: Metallic or plastic wheel with a zigzag or fluted edge, attached to a short handle; jagging irons are used for edging or cutting dough into fancy shapes.

jaiba: (Cuban-Spanish—crab)

jak: Jackfruit.

jalapeño: Hot green and yellow Mexican capsicum pepper.

jalea de guayaba: (Spanish—guava jelly)

jam: Sweet preparation made by boiling berries or fruits with sugar until they attain a thick consistency.

jamaica apple: Cherimoya.

jamaica banana: Large yellow commercial banana of Central America and the West Indies.

jamaica cucumber: Gherkin.

jamaica ginger: Superior grade of ginger, originally developed on the island of Jamaica.

jamaica pepper: Allspice.

Jamaica rum: Heavy-bodied dark rum produced on the island of Jamaica; its flavor is valued in baking and candy making.

Jamaica tangelo: Ugli.

jam-and-butter dish: Divided dish for serving jam and butter or jelly on one side and cream cheese on the other.

jambalaya: Spicy creole dish of rice and vegetables cooked with meat, usually ham.

jam biscuit: Baking-powder biscuit dough filled with jam and rolled up before baking.

jambon: (French—ham)

jambonneau: (French—foreleg of ham)

jamoke: java + mocha—strong black coffee.

jamón: (Spanish—ham)
jamón gallego: (Spanish—
Galician-style ham) Thin-sliced
smoked ham.
jantar: (Portuguese—dinner)
japanese date plum: Japanese persimmon.
japanese gelatin: Agar.
japanese ginger: Export grade of
ginger sold in crystallized sugar
coating or in oriental preserves.
japanese horseradish: Wasabi.
japanese isinglass: Agar.
japanese medlar: Loquat.
japanese oyster: Large oriental
oyster transplanted from the
Orient to the Pacific Coast of
North America.
japanese persimmon: Large luscious persimmon once native to
Japan although now grown in
Hawaii and elsewhere.
japanese radish: Daikon.
Japan tea: Light unfermented tea
characteristic of Japan.
japanware: Lacquer-coated boxes,
canisters, trays, lazy susans,
bowls, plates, cups, and saucers,
etc.
jar: Wide-mouthed neckless container usually provided with a
lid or top.
jarabe: (Spanish—syrup)
jardinière: (French—gardener's
wife) Vegetables served in a
savory sauce or soup, usually
labeled *à la jardiniere.*
jar opener: Utensil consisting of
opposing grips for grasping
and turning hard-to-open screw
caps.
jasmine tea: Tea whose leaves are
mixed and fired with jasmine
petals, imported from oriental
countries.

Jause: (German—light meal) Aus-
trian-style four o'clock tea consisting of coffee with whipped
cream, pastries, sandwiches, and
tea.
java: Slang for coffee, so called because much was cultivated and
shipped from the island of Java.
Java plum: Large East Indian tree
of the myrtle family yielding a
plumlike fruit.
Java tea: East Indian plant of the
mint family whose dried leaves
were made into a medicinal
drink.
javelina: North American peccary
hunted and eaten in many parts
of the Southwest; the hams of
this native member of the swine
family are tough and not at all
like those of domestic pigs.
Jax: American beer brewed in
Jacksonville, Florida.
jellied: Congealed, gelatinous.
jellied bouillon: Clear soup jellied
with gelatin and served cold.
jellied consommé: Clear broth jellied with gelatin and chilled until firm.
jellied soup: Gelatinized broth,
consommé, puree, or soup
served cold.
Jell-O: Brand name for a fruit-flavored gelatin dessert.
jelly: Semitransparent preparation
of fruit juice and pectin boiled
with sugar to produce a gelatinous spread; the term jelly is
also used to describe gelatinous
dishes such as aspics, jellied
consommé, jellied ham, etc.
jelly beans: Small oval candies of
a jellylike consistency covered
with a harder glazed coating;
jelly beans are multiflavored
and varicolored.

jelly doughnut: Jelly-filled doughnut.
jelly glasses: Medium-size tum-
blers for holding homemade
jelly; the top is usually sealed
with a coating of paraffin wax.
jelly powder: Powdered gelatin.
jelly roll: Thin layer of sponge
cake spread with jelly or jam
and rolled up while warm;
sometimes the roll is topped
with powdered sugar, whipped
cream, or frosting.
jelly roll pan: Shallow rectangular
pan for baking jelly roll cake,
usually less than ¾-inch high.
jerez: (Spanish—sherry wine)
jerky: Beef jerky.
jeroboam: Wine bottle containing
four fifths of a gallon.
Jersey: Tan-and-gray milk cattle
of a type bred on Jersey in
Channel Islands off the northern
coast of France.
Jersey lightning: Slang for applejack.
Jersey tea: Wintergreen.
jerusalem artichoke: Edible tuber
related to the American sunflower; the jerusalem artichoke,
an artichoke in name only, is not
from Jerusalem either, but is
now cultivated in Israel because
of its food value.
jerusalem cucumber: Gherkin.
jerusalem pickle: Pickled gherkin.
jerusalem potato: Jerusalem artichoke.
jicama: Mexican turnip plant of
the morning-glory family, having a sweet water-chestnut flavor; it is used sliced in salads or
served boiled with melted butter sauce.
jigger: Liquid measure containing
1½ ounces.

Johannisbeersosse: (German—
red-currant sauce)
John Barleycorn: Nickname for
intoxicants.
john collins: Tom collins made
with Dutch gin.
johnnycake: American-style country bread made of cornmeal,
eggs, milk, and some leavening
agent; in Australia johnnycake
means a country bread made of
baked or fried wheat meal.
Jonathan: Bright-red late-autumn
apple sold for eating and for
baking in pies.
jonnycake: Johnnycake.
jordan almond: Candy-covered almond ranging from snow white
through popular pastel tones to
deep violet.
jordbær: (Norwegian—strawberry)
jueye: (Puerto Rican-Spanish—
land crab)
jug: Large vessel of earthenware
or glass with a handle and a narrow lip for pouring.
jugged: Cooked in an earthenware
or stone vessel, usually said of
hare.
jug-jug: Barbados-style aspic of
chopped ham or salt beef with
green peas.
jugo: (Spanish—juice)
jugo de naranja: (Spanish—
orange juice)
jugo de piña: (Spanish—pineapple juice)
jugo de tomate: (Spanish—tomato
juice)
juice: Natural fluid expressed from
foods such as fruits, meats, vegetables, etc.
juicer: Utensil for expressing juices
from fruits and vegetables.
juicy: Juice filled.

jujube: Chewy and somewhat gummy candy, offered in various colors, sizes, and shapes.

julekake: (Norwegian—yule cake)

julep: Mixed drink of bourbon, sugar, and fresh mint served in a frosted glass.

Jules Verne: Garnish made of chopped mushrooms, potatoes, and turnips, named after the 19th-century French science-fiction writer.

julienne: Matchlike strips of vegetables, or a clear soup or consommé containing julienned carrots, onions, and potatoes.

jumble: Sugar cooky filled with jam or mincemeat.

jumbo peanuts: Large-size peanuts.

jumbo size: Biggest size offered, often described as the big economy size.

jump seat: Collapsing, folding, or portable seat; a folding jump seat is sometimes hinged to the leg of a kitchen table or to the side of a working counter.

juniper: An evergreen with aromatic berries that are used in flavoring gin; juniper-berry juice is also used in flavoring sauces and stuffings.

juniper juice: Slang for gin.

junket: Term for several different milk dishes: flavored milk set with rennet and served cold when jellylike; cream cheese packed in a wicker basket; dish of curds and whey.

junket tablet: Rennet tablet for curdling milk when making junkets or puddings.

jus: (French—gravy; juice)
jus de fruit: (French—fruit juice)
jus de tomates: (French—tomato juice)
jus d'orange: (French—orange juice)

k: Abbreviation for kilo or kilogram.

kaas: (Dutch—cheese)
kaastruffel: (Dutch—cheese truffle)

kabâb: (Persian—roast; roast meat)
Kabeljausteak: (German—codfish steak)
kabiljo: (Swedish—codfish)

Kabinett Wein: (German—cabinet wine)

kabob: Chunks of meat marinated and roasted on a skewer over an open fire.

kabuni: (Albanian—raisin and rice dessert)

kadayif: Middle Eastern shredded-wheat dessert.

kadota: (California dottatos) Yellow fig developed by the University of California from dottato Italian figs.

kærnemælk: (Danish—buttermilk)

kærnemælkskoldskal: (Danish—buttermilk cold bowl) Cold buttermilk soup.

kaffe: (Danish, Norwegian and Swedish—coffee)

Kaffee: (German—coffee)

Kaffeeklatsch: (German—coffee gossip) Gossipy gathering where coffee is served.

Kaffeekuchen: (German—coffeecake)

Kaffee mit Milch: (German—coffee with milk)

Kaffee mit Schlagobers: (Austrian-German—coffee with whipped cream) Viennese-style coffee.

kage: (Danish—cake)

kahlúa: Coffee-flavored liqueur.

kahvi: (Finnish—coffee)

kail: Scots for kale.

kail brose: Scots broth made of kale, oatmeal, vegetables, and meat such as an ox head or a cow heel.

kail gully: Large Scots knife for cutting kale.

kailyard: Scots for kitchen garden.

Kaiserfleisch: (Austrian-German—meat for the emperor) A Viennese dish of smoked pork, which may be eaten raw or cooked.

kaiser roll: Raised round roll with top folds or creases appearing like the iron cross bestowed upon German warriors in Imperial times.

Kaiserschmarrn: (Austrian-German—the emperor's omelet) A Viennese-style omelet which is gently pulled apart and sprinkled with sugar and raisins.

kajmar: Serbian cream cheese popular in Yugoslavia.

Kakao: (German—cocoa)

kakku: (Finnish—cake)

kakoretsi: (Greek—sausage roasted on a spit)

kalakukko: (Finnish—baked fish) Whole fish baked slowly so its bones become soft enough to eat.

Kalb: (German—calf)

kalbasá saséski: (Russian—salami sausage)

Kalbfleisch: (German—calf meat; veal)

Kalbsbraten: (German—roast veal)

Kalbsfrikassee: (German—veal fricassee)

Kalbsgulasch: (German—veal goulash)

Kalbskotelett: (German—veal chop)

kaldomar: (Swedish—stuffed cabbage rolls)

kale: Curly-leafed, loose-headed cabbage often served in broths and soups.

kalfkott: (Swedish—veal)

kalops: (Swedish—collops)

kal rulader: (Norwegian—stuffed cabbage) Ground meat rolled in cabbage leaves and served with cucumbers and dill.

kålsoppa: (Swedish—cabbage soup)

kaltes Geflügel: (German—cold poultry)

kalvehjerte: (Danish—veal heart)

kalvekjøtt: (Norwegian—veal)

kalvkød: (Danish—veal)

kamano lomi: (Hawaiian— mashed salmon) Salted salmon mashed with tomatoes, onions, and a little water.

kamar makan: (Malay—dining room)

kan bei: (Chinese—a toast)

kanpai: (Japanese—a toast)

kanten: Agar.

kapuśniak: (Polish—cabbage soup)

karab: *Eriwani*.

karidopita: (Greek—nut cake)

karnemelk: (Dutch—buttermilk)

Karotte: (German—carrot)

karp: (Swedish—carp)

Karpfen: (German—carp)

kartoffel: (Danish—potato)

Kartoffel: (German—potato)

Kartoffelbrei: (German—mashed potatoes)

Kartoffelpuffer: (German—potato pancakes)

Kartoffelpüree: (German— mashed potatoes)

Kartoffelsalat: (German—potato salad)

Kartoffelsuppe: (German—potato soup)

Käse: (German—cheese)

Käsebrot: (German—cheese bread)

Käseplatte: (German—cheese plate) Assorted cheese.

kasha: (Russian—buckwheat groats) Mush made from barley and buckwheat mixture or from buckwheat alone.

kasha varnishkas: (Yiddish— buckwheat groats mixed with noodles)

kashkaval: Balkan corruption of *caciocavallo*—loaf-shaped rennet cheese made from sheep's milk or goat's milk and similar to the original Italian cheese.

Kasseler Rippchen: (German— smoked pork chops)

kasza: (Polish—buckwheat groats)

Katahdin: Cobblestone-shaped white potato originally cultivated around Mount Katahdin in Maine.

katjang: (Malay—peanuts)

Katzenjammer: (German—cat's whining; misery) Hangover.

kaukauna: American gouda-type processed cheese made in Wisconsin, filled with caraway seeds and flavored with hickory smoke.

kava: Polynesian intoxicant made by fermenting the root juices of a true pepper plant.

KC steak: Slang for a steak in Kansas City style.

kebab: (Turkish—roast meat) Usually a chunk of skewered lamb.

kechap: (Malay—catsup) Spicy sauce served with fish and seafood dinners.

kedgeree: Rice boiled with butter, curry powder, eggs, fish, and peas; a favorite in India.

kedju: (Malay—cheese)

Kellner: (German—waiter)

kelner: (Dutch—waiter)

kelp: Large brown seaweed sometimes used in oriental soups.

Kelsey plum: Large reddish-purple Japanese species perfected by 19th-century California botanist John Kelsey.

Kennebec: Smooth-skinned large white potato of a type raised along the Kennebec River in Maine.

Kentucky bass: Black bass.

Kentucky ham: Ham salted and hung in a smokehouse for several days, where a smudge fire of corn cobs, hickory bark, or sassafras wood is kept burning.

kereta makan: (Malay—dining car)

kernmilk: Scots for buttermilk.

kerosine: Petrochemical product burned in oil stoves and lamps.

kerosine stove: Kitchen stove with heat provided by burning kerosine.

kerrie kool sla: (Dutch—curried coleslaw)

kerupuk: (Malay—jumbo-size fried shrimp) Shrimp fried in peanut oil and expanded to about twice their normal size.

kesäkeitto: (Finnish—vegetable soup) Summer soup made from fresh vegetables.

ketchup: Catsup.

kettle: Agateware or metallic caldron or pot for boiling liquids.

Key-lime pie: Lime pie made with the small limes found in the mangrove thickets of the Florida Keys.

kg: Abbreviation for kilo or kilogram.

khana: (Hindi—dinner; food)

khleb: (Russian—bread)

kichel: (Yiddish—cookie)

kickshaw: Fancy food, delicacy.

kid: Young goat.

kid-glove orange: Mandarin orange or any of its varieties such as the tangerine.

kidney: Offal meat from a meat animal; the least alkaline and pungent come from small animals such as calves, heifers, and lambs; beef kidneys can be made palatable by parboiling in salt water; kidneys are braised, sautéed, or stewed.

kidney bean: Dark-red kidney-shaped shell bean served in salads, soups, and succotash.

kidney chop: Loin chop containing part or all of the kidney; kidney chops are usually cut from lamb or veal.

kielbasa: Red-cased Polish sausage, similar to knockwurst, often served with sauerkraut and diced green peppers.

kiliç baligi sisde: (Turkish—swordfish on a spit)

kill-devil: Slang for primitive West Indian rum.

kilo: Kilogram, a unit of metric measure equaling 2.21 pounds (about 2¼ pounds).

kingfish: Name applied to several types of excellent-flavored fishes such as the whiting found along the Atlantic coast of North America, and a small, silvery California fish which is also called chenfish.

king salmon: Chinook or quinnat salmon, one of the most important food fishes of the North Pacific, taken from Alaska to Monterey Bay.

kip: (Dutch—chicken)

Kipferl: (Austrian-German—crescent roll)

kipper: Split dried herring salted and smoked.

kippis: (Finnish—cheers) A toast.

Kirin: Japanese rice beer brewed in Tokyo.

Kirsch: (German—cherry) Usually means cherry brandy.

Kirschwasser: (German—cherry water) White cherry brandy.

kishka: (Yiddish—sausage) Beef intestines stuffed with various savory fillings and roasted.

Kitchen Bouquet: Brand name for a commercial product used to color and flavor gravy.

kiss: Bite-size piece of candy or pastry, usually wrapped individually; coconut-filled meringue shells are also called kisses, especially if the shells are small.

kitchen brush: Bristled implement for cleaning dishes, glasses, and sinks; nylon brushes are best for dishware and glassware; wire brushes for scouring pans, pots, and metalware; natural-fiber brushes for scrubbing vegetables and many fruits.

kitchen car: Railway kitchen car usually coupled to the dining car of a railroad train.

kitchen shears: Heavy-duty shears with serrated edges for poultry-bone shearing, meat trimming, and vegetable cutting; some models can also be used for removing screw tops.

kitchen tool set: Rack holding cooking implements — usually long-handled fork, spoon, spatula, slotted spoon, ladle, rotary beater, etc.

kitchen utensil: Household device or implement used in food preparation.

kitchenware: Essential utensils and hardware used in the kitchen when preparing food.

kizel: (Russian—soft jelly) Fruit purée thickened with cornstarch.

kjøttpudding: (Norwegian—meat pudding) Hash made of ground meat.

Klim: Milk spelled backward, the brand name of a dried milk.

Kloss: (German—dumpling)

Klosterkäse: (German—cloister cheese) Small pungent cheese.

knäckebröd: (Swedish—rusk)

knaidel: (Yiddish—dumpling; matzo ball)

knead: To work dough with the hands, folding and pressing until the required consistency is attained.

knekkebrød: (Norwegian—clop bread) Thick rye cracker.

knife: Cutting instrument with a blade and a handle; kitchen cutlery includes special knives for cutting bread or cake, carving meat, chopping and dicing all kinds of food, coring and sectioning fruit, opening oysters, paring, etc.

knifeboard: Board for cleaning and scouring knives; the term also means a rack for holding kitchen knives.

knife box: Compartmented open-top box or drawer divider for holding knives, forks, and spoons.

knife case: Decorative box container for displaying and storing a carving set.

knife grinder: Emerystone or paired steel wheels used for sharpening knives.

knish: (Yiddish—baked, boiled, or fried dumpling) Dough filled with cheese, kasha, or seasoned chopped meat, and potatoes.

Knoblauch: (German—garlic)

Knödel: (German—dumpling)

knuckle: Ankle joint of a meat animal, usually pork or veal knuckles which are boiled and eaten with mashed potatoes and sauerkraut.

kobu: Large Japanese seaweed popular is soups and stews.

kød: (Danish—meat)

koekje: (Dutch—sweet biscuit; cooky)

koffie: (Dutch—coffee)

koffietafel: (Dutch—lunch)

kogt oksebryst: (Danish—boiled brisket of beef)

Kohl: (German—cabbage)

kohlrabi: Variety of cabbage with a turnip-shaped stem; kohlrabi stem is eaten raw in salads or boiled and served with a sauce.

Kohlsprossen: (German—brussels sprouts)

kokanee: Land-locked sockeye salmon of British Columbia.

koláčeki: (Czechoslovakian—little cakes) Buns filled with a cooked mixture of apples, apricots, and prunes, dates and nuts, poppyseeds, or prunes and cinnamon.

koldt bord: (Danish—cold table) Cold collation consisting of a variety of dishes from smoked fish to meats, salads, and many cheeses.

kombu: (Japanese—variety of kelp)

komijnekaas: (Dutch—cumin cheese) Spicy cheese flavored with cumin.

Kompott: (German—compote) Stewed fruit.

kona coffee mousse: Hawaiian dessert containing unsweetened chocolate, coffee extract, crème de cacao, sour cream, gelatin, chopped macadamia nuts, and sugar.

kona crab: Polynesian shellfish featured in many Hawaiian, Guamanian, and Samoan recipes.

Konditorei: (German—pastry shop)

Königinsuppe: (German—queen soup) Cream of chicken soup.

Königsberger Klops: (German—meatball) Spiced sweet-and-sour meatball stewed in caper sauce.

konjak: (Swedish—brandy; cognac)

kool: (Dutch—cabbage)

Kopfsalat: (German—head salad) Boston lettuce.

koppen: Bohemian or Silesian goat's-milk cheese made in cup-like shapes.

Koppen: (German dialect—cup)

korf: (Swedish—sausage)

Korkbrand: (German—branded cork) Cork bearing a marking denoting a particular vineyard.

koromiko flan: New Zealand apricot and almond dessert named for a local species of the herb veronica.

kosher: (Yiddish—permitted; proper) Prepared according to Judaic dietary laws, as first determined in Biblical times, said of many foods.

kosher pickle: Fresh cucumber cured in brine-filled wooden kegs containing garlic, spices, and vinegar.

Kotelett: (German-chop)

köttbullar: (Swedish—meatballs)

kouglof: (French—a kind of Alsatian raised-dough pastry) Sponge cake laced with toasted almonds and seedless raisins; *kouglof* is also called *kugelhupf*.

koulibiak: (Russian—pastry loaf stuffed with fish or meat)

koulitch: Russian-style currant bread traditionally baked just before the Russian Easter.

k-p duty: Military slang abbreviation for kitchen-police duty—doing such kitchen chores as peeling potatoes, scrubbing floors, washing dishes, cleaning up, etc.

Kraftbrühe: (German—strong broth) Consommé.

Kraut: (German—plant; vegetable, specifically the cabbage)

Krebs: (German—crayfish)

kreeft: (Dutch—crayfish)

kreplach: (Yiddish—small noodle-dough dumplings) Triangular dumplings filled with cheese, chicken, liver, or chopped meat and served in soup.

kringle: (Norwegian—ring-twisted cake)

Krokette: (German—croquette)

kromeski: Bacon-wrapped croquette.

krupnik: (Polish—hot mead) Holiday drink made of honey and hot vodka flavored with cinnamon, citrus rind, cloves, and vanilla.

Kuchen: (German—cake; coffee cake; tart)

kuchen dough: Dough prepared with a rich topping of jam, nuts, and a traditional streusel.

kufta: (Egyptian—meat croquettes)

kugel: (Yiddish—little ball) Pudding made of bread, noodles, or potatoes.

kumle: (Norwegian—raw potato dumpling)

Kümmel: (German—caraway) Liqueur flavored with caraway and anise.

kumminost: (Swedish—cumin cheese)

kumiss: Fermented milk often served in carbonated water, originally made by the Tartars who used camel's milk or mare's milk.

kumquat: Plum-size citrus fruit used chiefly in marmalades, pickles, and preserves, and sometimes candied.

kurini: Eriwani.

kurkkukeitto: (Finnish—cucumber soup)

kvass: Thin Russian beer, brewed by fermenting bits of rye bread in a mixture of sugar and water, or by adding yeast to a cooked mixture of rye flour and barley sprouts.

kyckling: (Swedish—chicken)

kylling: (Danish and Norwegian—chicken)

kypare: (Swedish—waiter)

l: Abbreviation for liter.

labrador herring: Common herring of the North Atlantic.

labrador tea: An evergreen of eastern North America, the leaves of which are used for making tea.

la carte: (French—the menu)

Lachs: (German—salmon)

lacquerware: Japanned ware.

lacrima christi: (Latin—tear of Christ) Sweet dessert wine grown from grapes raised on the slopes of Mount Vesuvius, sometimes offered in a sparkling variety.

lactose: Milk sugar.

la cuenta, por favor: (Spanish—the bill, please)

l'addition, s'il vous plait: (French —the bill, please)

ladle: Deep-bowled dispensing spoon made of ceramic, glass, or metal, used for ladling out liquid or semiliquid food.

Lady Baltimore cake: White layer cake frosted and filled with chopped figs, nuts, and raisins.

lady finger: Small finger-shaped sponge cake; lady fingers are eaten with ice cream or used as a foundation for custards and fancy puddings.

lafite-rothschild: Claret of the Médoc region near Bordeaux in southwestern France.

lager: Light-bodied light-colored beer of low alcoholic content; brewed by slow bottom-fermentation method, and stored, or lagered, for some months before clarification.

lait: (French—milk)

laitue: (French—lettuce)

laitue printanière: (French— spring lettuce)

lake chub: Lake herring or cisco.

lake herring: Cisco.

lake perch: Common yellow perch.

lake salmon: Large trout found in many Canadian and Alaskan lakes.

lake whitefish: Whitefish.

laks: (Danish and Norwegian— salmon)

lamb: Sheep less than a year old; when the animal is older than one year, its meat is called mutton; spring lamb is the meat of a very young lamb slaughtered shortly after its birth in the spring of the year.

lamb-and-kidney-pie: Pastry containing lamb shank or shoulder meat and kidneys.

lamb chop: Chop cut from various parts of a lamb carcass: leg, loin, rack, or shoulder.

lamb fries: Lamb testicles.

lamb kidney: Kidney sliced and seasoned with spices.

lamb loaf: Meat loaf made of ground lamb seasoned and baked.

lamb mint: Peppermint or spearmint.

lamb pie: Stewed lamb and vegetables baked in a pastry shell.

lamb shoulder: Meat cut from the upper foreleg of a lamb, economical compared to leg of lamb.

lamb's wool: Mixed drink of mulled ale, mashed apples, spices, and sugar heated and served in a copper vessel.

Lamm: (German—lamb)

lammestek: (Norwegian—roast lamb)

Lammkeule: (German—leg of lamb)

Lammkotelett: (German—lamb chop)

lampone: (Italian—raspberry)

lamponi con crema: (Italian— raspberries with cream)

lamproie: (French—lamprey)

lancashire: Hard rennet-type cheese made in high and round loaves, originally made in Lancashire, England. When fresh, lancashire is easy to spread.

langosta: (Spanish—rock lobster; spiny lobster)

langostino: (Spanish—baby crayfish)

langouste: (French—rock lobster; spiny lobster)

langoustine: (French—baby crayfish)

langres: Soft square rennet cheese famed for its full flavor and pungency, originating in Langres, France.

lapereau: (French—wild rabbit less than four months old)

lapereau rôti: (French—roast baby rabbit)

lapin: (French—rabbit)

lapin de garenne: (French—wild rabbit)

lapje: (Dutch—steak)

lapland: Reindeer-milk cheese shaped like a dumbbell, made in Lapland.

lapskaus: (Norwegian—hash)

lap tray: Rattan, plastic, or wooden tray fitted with short folding feet used to serve people in bed.

lard: Soft white animal shortening rendered from hog fat.

lard: To insert strips of fat into meat before it is cooked, or to cover it with strips of bacon or fat to help keep it moist while cooking.

larder: Kitchen cabinet, pantry or storeroom where food is kept; *see also* pantry.

larding needle: Large needle with hollow-tube tip for larding meat.

lardon: (French—lardoon) Fat strip used for larding.

lardoon: Larding strip of fat.

large jigger: Liquid measure containing 2 ounces.

lasagna: (Italian—noodle)

lasagne: (Italian—noodles) Wide ribbonlike *pasta* usually prepared with tomato-and-meat sauce plus mozzarella cheese.

lasagne fresche: (Italian—fresh lasagne)

lasagne verdi: (Italian—green lasagne) Noodles dyed green with spinach water.

latke: (Yiddish—pancake) Griddle cakes of grated potatoes, buckwheat flour, matzo meal, etc.

latte: (Italian—milk)

lattuga: (Italian—lettuce)

lattuga all'aceto: (Italian—lettuce with vinegar)

lau lau: (Hawaiian—dish combining meat and fish) Combination of meat and fish wrapped in banana leaves, then roasted and steamed in a bed of coconut charcoal.

lax: (Swedish—salmon)

layer cake: Cake baked in shallow pans and stacked in two or three layers separated by filling or frosting.

layer-cake pan: Shallow round pan made in various diameters.

lazy susan: Revolving service tray; some have compartments for various items: cheeses, condiments, jellies, nuts, spices, etc.

lb: Abbreviation for pound; the abbreviation is derived from *libra* (Latin—pound)

leaf lettuce: Variety of lettuce characterized by a loose head and incised, crisp, and curly leaf margins.

lean: Fat free or having little fat.

leather cheese: German round cheese made from skimmed cow's milk and containing many small openings or eyes.

leaven: Fermentation agent such as baking powder, sourdough starter, or yeast; leaven makes a gas causing the batter or dough to rise.

lebanon: Spiced red sausage originally made by Pennsylvania Germans around Lebanon, Pennsylvania.

lebban: Arab beverage of coagulated sour milk.

Leber: (German—liver)

Leberknödel: (German—liver dumpling)

Leberwurst: (German—liver sausage)

Lebkuchen: (German—spice cake) Traditional Christmas cookie containing citron, honey, nuts, and spices.

leche: (Spanish—milk)

leche asada: (Spanish—roast milk) Peruvian custard made with cognac, eggs, and milk.

lechón: (Spanish—suckling pig)

lechuga: (Spanish—lettuce)

leckach: (Yiddish—honey cake)

lecythos: Narrow-necked Greek vase for holding oil; its classic shape is sometimes reproduced in ornamental kitchenware.

leechee: Litchi nut.

leek: Garden herb of the lily family, less pungent than its cousins, the garlic and the onion; leeks are used in salads, sauces, soups, and stews.

lees: Wine dregs.

Leghorn: Domestic poultry of a type originating near Leghorn (Livorno) on the northwest coast of Italy; the fowls are usually white feathered with yellow legs and are good egg producers.

leg of lamb: Cut of meat from the hind leg of a lamb, usually roasted.

legumbre: (Spanish—vegetable)

legumbres frescas: (Spanish—fresh vegetables)

légume: (French—vegetable)

legume: (Italian—vegetable)

legume: Plant group comprising the various beans and peas, as well as such animal-fodder foods as alfalfa.

legumi all'aceto: (Italian—vegetables with vinegar) Antipasto of vegetables with oil and vinegar.

leipa: (Finnish—bread)

leitão assado: (Portuguese—roast suckling pig)

leite: (Portuguese—milk)

leite creme con farófias: (Portuguese—custard with meringue)

lemon: Light-yellow acid citrus fruit whose tart juice and grated rind are popular flavoring agents; some lemons are smaller than a golf ball while a few are as large as grapefruit.

lemonade: Iced summer beverage composed of lemon juice, sugar, and water.

lemon balm: Ancient perennial herb of the mint family; used for flavoring beverages, salads, and sauces, as well as after-dinner liqueurs.

lemon curd: Tart filling or cookie spread made of butter, eggs, lemon juice, lemon rind, and sugar.

lemon gin: Gin flavored with lemon instead of juniper berries.

lemon phosphate: Soda water flavored with lemon syrup.

lemon pickle: Condiment used with fish, fowl, and other meats.

lemon twist: Thin slice of lemon slit so it can be twisted over the edge of a cocktail glass as a garnish.

lemon verbena: Small South American shrub whose leaves are used to flavor cold drinks; lemon verbena grows wild along the

Pacific Coast from California to Chile.

lengua: (Spanish—tongue)

lenguado: (Spanish—sole; flounder)

lenoxware: Fine translucent china produced in the U.S. by Walter Scott Lenox in the early 1900's.

lenteja: (Spanish—lentil)

lentil: Herb of the pea family whose tiny seeds are used in salads, soups, and stews.

lentille: (French—lentil)

lepre: (Italian—hare)

lesso: (Italian—boiled)

lettuce: Any of several plants with succulent leaves which are used raw in salads. Some varieties of lettuce are also cooked.

leverpostei: (Norwegian—liver pie)

leverpostej: (Danish—liver paste) Pâté made of cooked and seasoned liver meat.

liaison: (French—junction) Sauce thickener such as agar, arrowroot, cornstarch, or flour.

lichee nut: Litchi.

licor: (Spanish—liquid; liquor)

licorice: A perennial herb of the Mediterranean region, the dried roots of which are used in preparing licorice extracts and powders for flavoring candies and beverages.

liebre: (Spanish—hare)

liederkranz: German-American cheese somewhat like limburger in consistency, flavor, and pungency, accidentally created by a New York delicatessen owner who was trying to imitate Schlosskäse; he named his product in honor of a German-American singing society, Liederkranz (song wreath).

lièvre: (French—hare)

lièvre en civet: (French—jugged hare)

light bread: Southern and Midwestern term for ordinary white bread.

lights: Animal lungs, often served in soups and stews.

lima: (Spanish—lime)

lima bean: American shell bean found in green pods, widely cultivated in many parts of the Americas.

Limabohne: (German—lima bean)

limande: (French—lemon sole or sand dab)

limburg: Creamy white Belgian cheese first made near Limburg and long famous for its pungent aroma.

lime: Greenish-yellow citrus fruit sometimes as small as a playing marble and sometimes as large as an orange, depending on the species; the juice is widely used as a flavoring agent.

limeade: Iced summer beverage composed of lime juice, sugar, and water; often made with brown sugar sweetening and carbonated water.

Limejuicer: Nickname for a British ship or seaman, as lime juice was formerly served aboard British ships to prevent scurvy.

lime juicer: Utensil for expressing juice from limes.

lime phosphate: Soda water flavored with lime syrup.

lime pickle: Pickled lime condiment flavored with cloves and served with soups, meats, and various cheese dishes.

limequat: Lime + kumquat—Citrus hybrid.

limewater: Calcium carbonate solution used in making tortillas, or a mixture of lime juice and water used in beverages.

limo: Slang for lemonade.

limogesware: Fine porcelain of a type produced in Limoges, France.

limon: Lime + lemon—hybrid citrus fruit.

limón: (Spanish—lemon)

limonata: (Italian—lemonade)

limone: (Italian—lemon)

lincoln: Soft cream cheese originally produced in Lincolnshire, England.

ling: Name applied to numerous unrelated species of fish such as a slender codlike food fish of northern Europe and Greenland, or any of several American hakes.

lingonberry: Scandinavian evergreen yielding a dark-red berry widely used in cooking and dessert making.

lingua: (Italian—tongue)

linguine: (Italian—tonguelets) Narrow macaroni ribbons.

Linse: (German—lentil)

Linsensuppe: (German—lentil soup)

Linzertorte: (German—Linz-style cake) Austrian cake first made in Linz, baked with almonds, apricots, and ground hazelnuts or walnuts.

liptauer: Hungarian sharp cheese made of goat's milk and heavily flavored with condiments such as paprika, capers, and peppers.

lipto: (Hungarian—sheep's milk cheese)

liq: Abbreviation for liquid.

liqueur: Heavy-bodied alcoholic beverage flavored with herbs or spices; cordials are also heavy bodied but are fruit flavored.

liqueur d'or: (French—gold cordial) Colorless French liqueur containing little flecks of gold leaf.

liqueur glass: Small tumbler containing ¾ to 2 ounces of liquid.

liqueur jaune: (French—yellow liqueur) French liqueur made in imitation of yellow chartreuse.

liqueur verte: (French—green liqueur) French liqueur made in imitation of green chartreuse.

liquid pepper seasoning: Tabasco sauce.

liquor: Distilled beverage of high alcoholic content such as gin, rum, vodka, or whiskey; the term also denotes a broth or gravy.

liquorist: Maker of liqueurs.

lista delle vivande: (Italian—list of food; menu)

lista de platos: (Spanish—list of dishes; menu)

lista de pratos: (Portuguese—list of dishes; menu)

litchi: Asiatic soapberry tree yielding an edible fruit whose flesh when dried is sweet and black.

liter: Liquid measure containing about 1 quart 2 ounces.

littleneck: Smallest-size hardshell clam; usually served on the half shell.

liver: Reddish-brown abdominal gland used as food; beef liver is less choice than calf, chicken, or lamb liver, but costs less; can be prepared in many ways.

liver pudding: Liver sausage.

liverwurst: Liver sausage.

l'khíam: (Hebrew—to life) A toast or salute.

llapingacho: Ecuadorean cheese and potato patty.

loaf: Molded or shaped mass of bread or other doughlike mixture.

loaf cake: Cake baked in a rectangular loaf pan, rather than in a circular one.

loaf cheese: Loaf-shaped process cheese.

loaf sugar: Sugar molded in cubes or loaves.

lobscouse: Hash or stew made of hardtack, meat, and vegetables, often served aboard ships.

lobster: Edible marine crustacean whose tail meat is considered a delicacy in most parts of the world; rock or spiny lobsters are found in many oceans and seas; large lobsters with great pincer fore claws are taken from the cold waters off the coasts of Maine and Norway.

lobster biscuits: Baking-powder dough rolled out, filled with chopped and seasoned lobster meat, rolled up, and baked.

lobster newburg: American dish of lobster meat cooked with cream, egg yolk, and sherry, and labeled a la Newburg.

lobster thermidor: Creamed lobster baked in its shell, a dish named for the eleventh month of the French revolutionary calendar: July 19 to August 17.

lobster tureen: White earthenware tureen topped by a ceramic cover made in the shape and color of a lobster.

locksoy: Type of macaroni made with rice flour and flavored with soy sauce, originally imported from China.

locro: Argentinian stew.

Lodi: Green-skinned variety of cooking apple grown in Pacific

Northwest orchards, or a grape grown in central California.

lofschotel: (Dutch—praise dish) Baked endive.

loganberry: Natural hybrid of the dewberry and the red raspberry named for Judge J. H. Logan who discovered it in 1881; loganberries are used in flavoring ice creams and puddings, and in making wine.

loin: Lower back meat.

loin chop: Chop cut from the lower back or loin.

loksh: (Yiddish—noodle)

lollipop: Hard candy on a stick.

lolly: British word for candy.

lombata di vitello: (Italian—loin of veal)

lombo di bue: (Italian—fillet of beef)

lo mein: (Cantonese Chinese— soft noodles)

lomo de cerdo: (Spanish—fillet of pork)

lonche: (Mexican-Spanish— lunch) Word borrowed from English, originally along Mexico's border with the United States but now used in many parts of Latin America.

loncheria: (Spanish-American— lunchroom)

london broil: Large flank steak broiled, then cut in thin slices diagonally across the grain for serving.

Lone Star: American beer brewed in San Antonio, Texas.

long bean: Kidney bean.

long clam: Soft clam.

long drink: Drink served in a tall glass, usually a highball.

longe: (French—loin)

longe de veau: (French—veal loin)

longlick: Slang for molasses.

loquat: Tart fruit of the Japanese medlar tree used in preserves, now common in many parts of the American Southwest.

lotvarik: (Pennsylvania-German— lot of work) Apple butter, so named because its preparation was a lot of work.

louie dressing: Dressing of vegetable oil, tomatoes, vinegar, sugar, onions, lemon juice, garlic and other spices; louie dressing can also mean a seafood sauce, and crab louie, a popular dish along the West Coast.

Louisiana cala: Cala.

Louisiana coffee: Blend of ground coffee beans and roasted chicory.

loukoumades: (Greek—sweet fritters)

loukoumi: (Greek—confection) Oriental delight made of chopped almonds and corn syrup.

lovage: Herb with a celery flavor used in preparing meats and stews.

love apple: Old name for tomato.

low-calorie food: Foods low in fats and starches, such as many dietetic foods sold in markets and health-food stores.

low carbo: Slang for low in carbohydrates or starches.

Löwenbräu: German beer brewed in Munich.

lox: (Yiddish—salmon) Kosher-style smoked red salmon, usually served with bagels and cream cheese.

lozenge: Hard candy or cough drop usually sharply flavored.

ls and d: Abbreviation for liquor store and delicatessen.

luau: Hawaiian or other Polynesian picnic where guests sit on the ground as they drink and eat to the accompaniment of dancing and music making.

Lucky: Lager beer brewed in San Francisco, California.

luganiga: (Italian—spiced pork sausage)

lumacha: (Italian—snail)

lunchbox: Metal or plastic container for carrying lunch to school or work.

luncheon: Light noonday meal.

luncheonette: Place where snacks are served together with standard beverages such as coffee, milk, tea, and soft drinks.

lunchmobile: Mobile lunch wagon designed for serving people at small plants.

lunchroom: (Dutch—tea room) Place where tea and cakes, ice cream and ices, sandwiches and soft drinks are served.

lunchroom: Place where quick-to-prepare and ready-to-serve food is offered—not as small as a luncheonette and not as big as a restaurant.

lunch wagon: Diner or restaurant styled to look like a mobile kitchen and lunchroom.

lunel: French dessert wine made in the Lunel district in the south of France.

lusterware: Highly glazed earthenware with an iridescent sheen.

lutfisk: (Swedish—lye fish) Codfish prepared by soaking in mild solution of lye until the bones become so softened they are part of the flesh.

lye hominy: Grits hulled by soaking in lye solution; the hominy is thoroughly washed and dried before it is packaged for home use.

lyonnaise: (French—Lyons style) Sautéed with sliced onions, said usually of sliced cooked potatoes.

m: Abbreviation for *mit* (German—with) and *med* (Norwegian—with).

maatjes haring: (Dutch—mate herring) White herring pickled in spices, sugar, and vinegar.

macadamia: Australian evergreen yielding an edible nut named for Scotch chemist John Macadam who initiated their cultivation in the Hawaiian Islands; macadamia nuts taste somewhat like the sweet almond and are used in candies or eaten roasted and salted.

macaron: (French—macaroon)

macaroni: Semolina pasta made in a variety of shapes: alphabets, bow ties, elbows, sea shells, etc.; the most common shape is the short elbow-shaped tube, served hot with cheese and cold in salads.

macaroni salad: Cooked and cooled macaroni combined with salad dressing, salad herbs, and various spices.

macaroni vongole: Macaroni, spaghetti, or other pasta served with a clam sauce.

macaroni wheat: Durum, whose purified middlings, called semolina, are used to make macaroni, spaghetti, and other pastas.

macaroon: Cake or cookie made with almond paste, egg white, flour, and sugar.

macassar mace: Mace produced from the macassar nutmeg and used as a spice.

macassar nutmeg: East Indian tree related to the true nutmeg, whose fruit seed is sometimes used as a substitute.

maccherone: (Italian—macaroni)

maccherone alla chitarra: (Italian—macaroni in guitar style) Macaroni cut on coiled steel wires to give the look of guitar strings.

maccherone alla marinara: (Italian—sailor-style macaroni) Mac-

aroni cooked with garlic and olive oil.

macchli: (Hindi—fish)

mace: Aromatic spice derived from the dried external covering of the nutmeg.

mace butter: Nutmeg butter.

macédoine: (French—medley) Mixture of fruits or vegetables in a cocktail, dessert, garnish, sauce, or salad.

macédoine de fruits: (French—fruit salad)

macedonia di frutta: (Italian—fruit salad)

macerate: To separate or soften food by steeping in liquid.

mácére: (French—macerated) Pickled or steeped in wine.

mâche: (French—corn salad [the herb])

machinetta: Neapolitan drip coffee maker made in three snug-fitting parts; a bottom with a long spout; a middle part where fine-ground or pulverized coffee is placed in a perforated metal basket, and the top into which boiling water is poured.

MacIntosh: Sweet bright red apple grown chiefly in Canada and northern U.S., used for cooking and eating.

mackerel: Important food fish of the North Atlantic; these medium-size and nearly scaleless fish are eaten fresh, salted, or smoked, and are prepared in many ways.

madagascar bean: Hyacinth bean.

mad apple: Old name for the eggplant.

madeira: Sweet dark fortified wine of a type originating on the Portuguese island of Madeira off the West African coast.

madeira nut: English walnut.

madeleine: Small French cooky baked in an oval mold and exhibiting a crisp brown glazed surface, named in honor of 19th-century French pastry cook—Madeleine Paulmier; madeleines contain butter, eggs, flour, sugar, and almond or vanilla flavoring.

madras tea: Black tea of type originally raised in Madras province of southern India.

madrilène: (French—Madrid style) Flavored and colored with tomato juice, said of consommé, served hot, cold, or jellied.

mælk: (Danish—milk)

maggiordomo: (Italian—majordomo; butler, chief steward)

magnum: Wine bottle containing about two fifths of a gallon.

magnum platters: Large wooden serving platters designed for extra heavy duty so they can also be used as carving boards.

maguey: Mexican cactus cooked as a vegetable or fermented to make tequila.

Mahlzeit: (German—mealtime)

Maine lobster: Large-clawed cold-water species of lobster found from Labrador to Cape Cod but chiefly off the coast of Maine, also called American lobster.

maïs: (French—maize; Indian corn)

maito: (Finnish—milk)

maitre d': Slang for *maitre d'hotel* (French—master of the house; butler; headwaiter).

maitre d'hotel butter: Sauce made of melted butter, lemon juice, chopped parsley, and seasonings.

maíz: (Spanish—corn)

maize: Corn, Indian corn.

maize oil: Corn oil.

majarete: Puerto Rican dessert made from milk, rice flour, and sugar.

majolica: Richly ornamented Majorcan pottery used to decorate festive banquet tables.

majordomo: Butler or head steward.

makan malam: (Malay—supper)
makan pagi: (Malay—breakfast)
makan siang: (Malay—luncheon)
Makrele: (German—mackerel)

malabar almond: Edible East Indian almond first found on the Malabar coast of southwestern India.

málaga: Sweet red or white dessert wine of a type produced in the Spanish province of Málaga in southern Spain.

malaxe: Mixture of brandy, butter and cheese popular in Normandy.

mallard: Common wild duck of Europe and North America, ancestor of most domestic breeds.

malmsey: Sweet Madeira wine produced from the malvasia grape.

malpeque: Oyster found in the waters around Prince Edward Island.

malt: Grain, usually barley, softened in water, allowed to germinate, then kiln dried; germination produces an enzyme useful in brewing and distilling, high in carbohydrates and protein; malt is also used in malted milk powder and many ice-cream desserts.

malted milk: Milk drink containing malt powder and flavoring, often with ice cream added and blended in.

maltese orange: Blood orange.
maltose: Malt sugar.
malt vinegar: Vinegar made from fermented barley malt, used in preparing seafood dishes, fish and meat sauces, and salad dressings.
malt whisky: Whiskey made from malted barley in a pot still, one of the sources from which Scotch and Irish whiskies are blended.
mamaliga: (Roumanian—cornmeal)
mämmi: (Finnish—pudding) Traditional Easter dish of rye malt and rye meal which is boiled, seasoned, and baked; mämmi is served cold with cream and sugar.
mandarijntje: (Dutch—tangerine)
mandarin: Mandarin orange.
mandarine: (French—tangerine)
mandarin oil: Flavor extracted from mandarin oranges.
mandarin orange: Chinese citrus tree yielding small dark-orange fruit with a loose skin; the tangerine is a cultivated variety of the mandarin orange.
Mandel: (German—almond)
Mandelbrot: (German—almond bread) Almond-flavored pastry roll baked, cut in slices, and browned.
mandelbund: (Norwegian—almond cake)
Mandeltorte: (German—almond pastry)
mandioc: Manioc, cassava.
mandlen: (Yiddish—almonds) Marble-size rounds of dough baked and eaten with soup.
mandorla: (Italian—almond)
mango: Tropical Asiatic tree of the cashew family, yielding a sweet yellow fruit; mangoes are

eaten raw, prepared as chutney, or canned in their own syrup; many are now cultivated in Florida and Hawaii.
mangue: (French—mango)
manhattan: Cocktail made of sweet vermouth, rye whiskey, and a dash of angostura bitters.
Manhattan-style clam chowder: Chowder made with tomatoes instead of with cream or milk.
manicotto: (Italian—muff) Spinach-flavored tube-shaped pasta filled with beef, chicken, or cheese, and served with various sauces.
man-made meat: Engineered foods.
manos de ternera: (Spanish—calf's hands) Calf's feet.
mansikkatorttu: (Finnish—strawberry tart)
manteca: (Spanish—fat, lard)
mantelikokkare: (Finnish—almond custard) Dessert served with fruit sauce.
mantequilla: (Spanish—butter)
manzana: (Spanish—apple)
manzanilla: Pale Spanish sherry.
manzo: (Italian—beef)
manzo arrosto: (Italian—roast beef)
manzo bollito: (Italian—boiled beef)
maple cream: Candy made by boiling maple syrup and cream.
maple honey: Light-colored maple syrup condensed to the thickness of honey.
maple sugar: Sugar obtained by boiling down maple syrup; cooking the sap is called sugaring off.
maple syrup: Maple sap boiled down to syrupy consistency, popular on pancakes and as a flavoring for baked goods, ice creams, and many confections.

maquereau: (French—mackerel)
marasca: Dalmation cherry
liqueur; marasca cherries are
used in making maraschino.
maraschino: (Italian—cherry
brandy)
maraschino cherry: Cherry pitted
and preserved in maraschino liqueur, used in garnishing baked
goods, ice cream desserts, cup
custards, etc.
marble cake: Cake made with
dark and light batters semi-
blended so as to appear marble-
ized.
marché: (French—market)
margarine: Vegetable-oil butter
substitute.
margarita: Cocktail concocted of
tequila, lime juice, and sugar;
served with a wedge of lime and
a small mound of salt.
marguerite: Small cupcake made
with pecans and brown sugar or
molasses.
marinade: Liquid blend of herbs
and vinegar or wine in which
meat is marinated to be flavored
and tenderized.
marinara: (Italian—sailor style)
Served with garlic and tomato
sauce, usually labeled *alla marinara.*
marinara sauce: Sauce made with
olive oil, onions, parsley, plum
tomatoes, salt, and other seasoning.
marinate: To soak in a brine or
seasoning marinade.
mariné: (French—marinated)
marisco: (Spanish—shellfish)
marjoram: Herb of the mint family
widely used in seasoning salads,
soups, and many other dishes.
marknad: (Swedish—market)
markt: (Dutch—market)

Markt: (German—market)
marmalade: Jelly containing fruit
or fruit rind; oranges are the
most common of marmaladed
fruits although grapefruit, mangoes, papayas, pineapples, and
other fruits are also used.
marmellata: (Italian—jam)
marmite: Earthenware or metal
soup kettle; small or petite mar-
mites are often used for serving
soups and stews.
marron: (French—chestnut)
marron glacé: (French—iced
chestnut) Glazed chestnut confection.
marrow: Delicate tissue extracted
from the hollow bones of animals, excellent jellied, and in
sauces, soups, and stews; in
England marrow is also the
name for a summer squash.
marrow scoop: Long thin spoon
used for extracting marrow from
bones.
marsala: Wine fortified with
brandy and grape juice, produced near the Sicilian town of
Marsala.
Marsh: Pale-yellow medium-size
seedless grapefruit characterized
by their tart flavor.
marsh hare: Small hare found
along the southeastern American coast; marsh hare is also the
market name for muskrat sold
as game flesh.
marshmallow: Confection made
with albumen, corn syrup, gelatin, and sugar, beaten to a
spongy consistency and coated
with powdered sugar.
martini: Cocktail made of gin and
vermouth and served with a
lemon twist or a small green
olive.

marzipan: Confection of ancient origin, made from almond paste or crushed almonds, egg whites, and sugar, usually colored and shaped to resemble small fruits.

mashburn: Mixture of ground barley, bran, and oats.

mashelson: Rye and wheat mixture.

masher: Utensil, usually flat-bottomed for mashing potatoes and other foods; mashers are made of plastic, wood, stainless steel, or chrome-plated wire.

maslin: Bread made with mixed flours such as rye and wheat.

mason jar: Wide-mouth glass jar used for home canning and named for its inventor, John L. Mason; mason jars are made of tempered glass to withstand boiling and sterilizing, and are provided with rubber-gasketed screw tops or glass lids held in place by a spring.

masquer: (French—to mask) To cover food with mayonnaise or some other thick sauce.

masséna: Garnish made with artichoke hearts and *sauce béarnaise,* served with *tournedos* and eggs and named for André Masséna, one of Napoleon's marshals; it usually appears on menus as *à la Masséna.*

massenet: Garnish made of artichoke bottoms filled with beef marrow, string beans, and potatoes, named in honor of 19th-century French composer Jules Massenet.

mast: (Persian—yogurt)

maté: Beverage tea made from the dried leaves of the Paraguay tea tree native to Misiones Province, Argentina, and to southern Brazil, Paraguay, and Uruguay; maté is brewed in a gourdlike container and sipped through a metal tube with a fine strainer at its tip, the *bombilla.*

matelote: (French—sailor's wife) Fish stew prepared in wine.

matsal: (Swedish—dining room)

matzo: Unleavened crackerlike bread traditionally eaten during Passover by the Jews, in remembrance of the fact that the Jews did not have time to let their bread rise before the exodus from Egypt; matzos are now consumed by many other people who eat them plain, flavored with cheese, eggs, onions, and even with chocolate.

matzoon: (Armenian—fermented milk)

mayo: Slang for mayonnaise.

mayola: Slang for mayonnaise.

mayonnaise: Sauce made from egg yolks and olive oil or of raw eggs, vegetable oil, and vinegar; widely used for dressing salads and seafoods; the name is derived from the Minorcan seaport town of Port Mahon where mayonnaise originated.

May wine: German punch consisting of champagne, claret, and Rhine or Moselle wine flavored with the herb woodruff; slices of apple, orange, or pineapple are sometimes added as a garnish.

mazapán: (Spanish—marzipan)

mazarin: Benedictine-type liqueur; a cake filled with candied fruit and glazed with kirsch-flavored apricot coating; and a deep serving dish, usually pierced and used as a liner for a larger dish.

mead: Ancient beverage made of fermented honey and water; sometimes beer, cider, or malt is added.

mealie: South-African for an ear of corn or a cornmeal cake.

mealie-mealie: South-African staple consisting of coarse-ground cornmeal, often used in making mealies.

measuring cup: Glass or metal graduate marked to indicate common cooking measurements: ⅛ cup, ¼ cup, ½ cup, full cup, 2 cups or pint, 3 cups, 4 cups or quart, etc.

measuring pitcher: Glass or enamel-coated graduate marked to show cup and pint divisions and provided with a pouring lip.

measuring spoons: Nest of spoons made in graduated sizes to measure ¼ teaspoon, ½ teaspoon, full teaspoon, full tablespoon.

meatball: Ground meat compressed into a ball; meatballs are broiled, fried, steamed, and stewed, and served alone or in combination with noodles, spaghetti, and many other dishes.

meat chopper: Grinder.

meat grinder: Utensil or attachment for grinding meat, usually provided with a variety of cutting blades for different grinds.

meatless meat: Engineered foods.

meat loaf: Ground meat, bread crumbs, and other ingredients shaped into a loaf and baked.

meat spread: Canapé and sandwich spread such as chicken liver, chicken salad, deviled ham, ham-cheese, liverwurst, pâté de fois gras, etc.

médaillon: (French—medallion) Small round slice of meat: *tour-*

nedo of beef; scallop of mutton, beef, or poultry.

medlar: Eurasian tree of the apple family, yielding small, crabapplelike fruit; medlars are often served with ice cream in Scandinavian homes and restaurants.

Meerrettig: (German—see radish; horseradish)

mejillón: (Spanish—sea mussel)

mekong: Siamese rice whiskey.

mela: (Italian—apple)

mélange: Cream-and-coffee mixture served in a tall glass, lined and topped with whipped cream.

melanzana: (Italian—eggplant)

melanzana alla parmigiana: (Italian—Parmesan eggplant) Eggplant baked with cheese and tomatoes.

melba: Peach melba or melba toast.

melba sauce: Raspberry sauce as served with peach melba.

melba toast: Very thin slice of toast.

melk: (Dutch and Norwegian—milk)

melocotón: (Spanish—peach)

meloen: (Dutch—melon)

melon: Large succulent fruit of various plants of the cucumber family, such as muskmelon or watermelon.

melón: (Spanish—melon)

melon baller: Utensil with a small very round bowl for scooping out balls of melon flesh for compotes and salads.

melon d'eau: (French—watermelon)

melone: (Italian—melon)

melon fruit: Papaya.

melongène: (French—eggplant)

melon musqué: (French—muskmelon)

melt: To heat a solidified substance until it becomes liquid.

melting point: Temperature at which something melts; ice turns to water at 32 degrees Fahrenheit (zero degrees Celsius on the centigrade scale).

melts: Edible spleen glands of a meat animal.

membrillo: (Spanish—quince)

menta: (Portuguese, Spanish, and Italian—mint)

Mentha: Genus of the mint family comprising the true mints: peppermint, spearmint, applemint, etc.

menthe: (French—mint)

menu: Bill of fare.

menudo: (Spanish—small; minute) Mexican-style stewed tripe.

mercado: (Portuguese and Spanish—market)

mercato: (Italian—market)

mercatus: (Latin—market)

merenda: (Italian—snack)

merendero: (Spanish—lunchroom)

merienda: (Spanish—afternoon snack)

meringa: (Italian—meringue)

meringue: Egg-white and sugar mixture used to top cream pies, or baked to form a delicate white shell.

merlan: (French—whiting) Saltwater food fish.

merluche: (French—hake; stockfish, dried cod)

merluza: (Spanish—cod; hake)

merluzzo: (Italian—hake; codfish)

mermelada: (Spanish—marmalade)

merrythought: Wishbone.

merry widow: Cocktail made of dry vermouth, Dubonnet, and lemon twist.

mescal: Mexican alcoholic beverage distilled from the fermented sap of an agave plant; *see also* tequila.

mesero: (Spanish—waiter)

metal waiter: Serving salver or tray used for bringing breakfast to the bedside or tea to the tea table.

metaxas: Sweet Greek brandy liqueur.

metélt: (Hungarian—dry noodles)

methuselah: Wine bottle containing 6½ quarts.

Mettwurst: German—bologna)

Mexicali: Mexican beer brewed in Mexicali, Baja California Norte.

mexicanburger: Hamburger containing chili.

mexican rabbit: Baked dish of cheese, eggs, green peppers, and tomatoes.

Mexican skipjack: Frigate mackerel.

Mexican snapper: Red snapper.

mezcal: (Spanish—mescal.

meze: (Greek—appetizers)

mezzo fiasco: (Italian—half flask) Round-bottomed straw-covered wine bottle, containing one liter.

mickey finn: Slang for liquor containing a drastic purgative or a stupefying drug, usually knockout drops (chloral hydrate).

middagmåltid: (Danish—midday meal)

middagsmål: (Swedish—midday meal)

midia dolma: Armenian-style mussels, stuffed with seasoned rice and cooked with olive oil.

miel: (French and Spanish—honey)

mignardise: (French—delicacy) Decorative pastry puff.

mignon: (French—delicate; dainty)

mijoté: (French—slowly simmered)

Milanese: (Italian—Milan style) Breaded and fried with parmesan cheese.

Milch: (German—milk)

milch cow: Dairy cow.

milchik: (Yiddish—dairy dishes)

Milchkaffee: (German—coffee with milk)

mild-and-bitter: English beverage consisting of a mixture of mild and bitter ales or beers.

milk: Mammary fluid of female mammals; animals domesticated as milk producers include the cow, goat, sheep, water buffalo, reindeer, yak, and others.

milk bar: Snack bar specializing in milk drinks.

milk chocolate: Confection made from chocolate liquor, milk, and sugar; sometimes nuts or dried breakfast cereals are added.

milk fat: Butterfat.

milkfish: Popular food fish of the Pacific, allied to the herring; the Philippine species is often smoked and canned for export to the United States.

milkglass: Opaque or translucent glassware having a milk-white appearance.

milk powder: Dried milk.

milk punch: Mixture of milk and rum or whiskey with sugar and nutmeg.

milk shake: Milk beverage made of ice cream and some flavoring syrup such as chocolate or vanilla, well blended.

milk toast: Hot buttered squares of toast served in warm milk and seasoned or sweetened.

mille-feuille: (French—thousand-leaf) Thin pastry leaves made of puff paste and filled with whipped cream or other filling as in a napoleon.

millefoglie: (Italian—thousand leaves) *Mille-feuille.*

Miller High Life: American beer brewed in Milwaukee.

millet: Small-seeded cereal grain grown in Europe and Asia; hulled millet is used in cereals, casserole dishes, puddings, etc., and is valued for its high protein content.

millet meal: Meal ground from hulled millet.

min: Abbreviation for minute.

mince: To chop as fine as skill and utensils permit.

mincemeat: Cooked meat chopped fine and mixed with fruits, nuts, spices, and sugar, and sometimes flavored with brandy or rum; mincemeat is most commonly used in pies.

mince pie: Pie filled with mincemeat.

mincer: Hand-mill grinder for mincing parsley, hard-boiled eggs, cheese, citrus peel, vegetables, etc.

mineral water: Any water containing minerals believed to be of medicinal value.

minestra: (Italian—soup)

minestrone: (Italian—thick soup) Vegetable soup containing beans, chick peas, macaroni, vermicelli, and Parmesan cheese.

minestrone fiorentino: (Italian—Florentine minestrone) *Minestrone* garnished with tomato and onion sauce.

minestrone genovese: (Italian—Genoan minestrone) *Minestrone* with macaroni.

minguiche: Mexican soup containing cheese, sour cream, onions, green peppers.

Minorca: Domestic fowl of a type somewhat larger than Leghorns, and originating on the island of Minorca.

mint: Aromatic herb such as peppermint or spearmint, popular flavoring agents in many candies, liqueurs, and preserves; mint sprigs make an attractive garnish for cocktails and highballs.

mint julep: Mixed drink made of bourbon whiskey, sugar, sprigs of fresh mint, enough water to dissolve the sugar, and ice.

minuta: (Italian—bill of fare)

minute steak: Boned steak about a quarter-inch thick, which can be cooked in a minute or two.

mirabelle: (French—a small yellow variety of plum) Liqueur made from mirabelle plums and noted for its fine flavor.

mirepoix: Vegetable mixture made by cooking diced carrots, celery, leeks, onions, etc., in butter; mirepoix is added to braising liquid to enhance the flavor of meat.

mirin: Japanese rice wine resembling sherry.

mirliton: (French—cream roll) Pastry tartlet filled with an egg-and-sugar mixture flavored with orange-blossom water.

miroton: (French—stew made from previously cooked meats)

mise en place: (French—putting things in place) Preparing the kitchen for cooking a meal.

mission olive: California olive used for oil and for pickling.

misticanza: (Italian—mixed salad)

misto: (Italian—mixed)

mistra: Anise-flavored Italian liqueur.

Mittagessen: (German—lunch)

mix: Commercial term for anhydrated foods.

mix: To stir until ingredients are well blended.

mixed grill: One-dish meal of assorted fish and meats, grilled.

mixed-herb vinegar: Vinegar flavored with a combination of herbs such as basil, bay leaf, rosemary, tarragon and thyme; mixed-herb vinegars are used in sauces and salad dressings, on cooked greens, or in coleslaw.

mixed whole spices: Blend of unground spices used for pickling and preserving meats, vegetables, relishes, etc.

mixing bowl: Plain round kitchen bowl for preparing foods, usually one of a graduated and nested set.

mixing glass: Heavy-walled glass for mixing drinks, often graduated.

mixto: (Spanish—mixed)

mizú: (Japanese—water)

mjölk: (Swedish—milk)

moa: (Polynesian—fowl)

moa niu: (Polynesian—coconut chicken) Fried chicken served with coconut-milk, chopped macadamia nuts, and greens.

mocha: Blend of chocolate and coffee flavors.

mocha whip: Whipped dessert mixture made from powdered chocolate, instant coffee, and heavy cream; mocha whip is used for fillings and toppings or eaten by itself.

mochi: (Japanese—rice cake)

mock chicken: Iguana, tuna, veal, or other meat prepared so it will taste like chicken.

mock duck: Meat, such as pork chops, shoulder of lamb, carved to resemble a duck.

mock meats: Engineered foods.

mock turtle soup: Soup made of calf's head or veal and seasoned to simulate green-turtle soup.

Moelle de boeuf: (French—beef marrow)

Mohn: (German—poppyseed)

Möhre: (German—carrot)

mojarra: Ball-like food fish of the Caribbean.

moka: (French—a special coffee grown near Mocha in Yemen)

molasses: Dark viscous by-product of sugar refining; New Orleans molasses is lighter, sweeter, and less rumlike in flavor than Puerto Rican molasses; molasses is used as a flavoring agent and sweetener in baking, candy making, and cooking.

molé: (Spanish—mass; bulk) Mexican sauce containing chili and bitter chocolate.

molé de guajalote: (Mexican-Spanish — turkey with mole sauce)

mongole: (French—Mongolian) Cream of tomatoes and peas.

monosodium glutamate: Crystalline salt used for accenting the flavor of food.

monteith: Punchbowl of the 18th century, designed with a scalloped edge and usually made of silver.

Monterey Jacks: Jacks' Monterrey.

montilla: Dry bitter sherry produced near Córdoba in southern Spain.

montone: (Italian—mutton)

moonshine: Illegally distilled liquor often made by the light of the moon.

morango: (Portuguese—strawberry)

morcón: (Filipino—mixed meat roll) Ham and sausage meat rolled up in steak and braised with vegetables and seasoning.

morgenmad: (Danish—breakfast)

morg polo: (Persian—chicken with rice) Chicken cooked with apricots, raisins, and rice.

mortadella: (Italian—myrtle) Sausage made of finely chopped beef and pork meat, seasoned with pepper and garlic; name is derived from an ancient Roman sausage flavored with myrtle berries.

mortar and pestle: Paired utensils of ancient origin used for crushing solid substances to powder; the mortar is the bowl and the pestle is the club-shaped grinder.

morue: (French—codfish)

moscovite: (French—Moscow style)

moscow mule: Mixed drink of ginger beer, lime juice, and vodka.

moselle: German wine somewhat like Rhine wine but grown in the valley of the Moselle River.

mossberry: European cranberry.

Most: (German—cider; new wine)

mostarda: (Italian and Portuguese —mustard)

mostaza: (Spanish—mustard)

mou: (French—soft; slack) Farm cheese.

mouflon: Mountain sheep.

mou goo gai peen: (Cantonese Chinese—chicken with mushrooms) Sautéed chicken with water chestnuts, mushrooms, cabbage, snow peas, and other ingredients.

moule: (French—mussel)

mountain cranberry: Lingonberry.

mountain herring: Whitefish.

mountain mint: Aromatic herb of the mint family native to America; also called basil mint.

mountain oysters: Edible testicles.

moussaka: (Greek—name for an eggplant dish) Dish made of alternate layers of eggplant, ground meat, and white sauce.

mousse: (French—moss; foam) Molded dish, either savory or sweet, stiffened with whipped cream, gelatin, or white of egg; a molded dish containing ice cream is called a *bombe*.

mousse au chocolat: (French—mousse with chocolate) Chocolate mousse containing coffee, sweet chocolate, egg, sugar, and heavy cream.

moussec: English sparkling wine made from French grape juice.

moutarde: (French—mustard)

mouton: (French—sheep; mutton)

mozo: (Spanish—waiter)

mozzarèlla: (Italian—small wheel) Rubbery white unsalted cheese used in making pizza.

mozzarèlla in carrozza: (Italian—small wheel in carriage) Mozzarella cheese sandwich dipped in egg batter and fried.

msg: Abbreviation for monosodium glutamate.

muddler: Utensil for mixing drinks, particularly alcoholic.

muffin: Quick bread baked from egg batter in a muffin tin.

muffin pan: Baking pan containing extruded cavities for holding cupcake or muffin batter.

mufle de boeuf: (French—ox cheek)

mulberry: Tart and somewhat acid berry sometimes eaten raw but usually preserved or fermented to make wine.

mull: To heat, usually cider or wine, with spices or sugar.

mullet: Shallow-water fish of the Atlantic and Pacific oceans valued as food fish; some species of mullet are found in freshwater streams.

mulligans Hobo stew, made of whatever is available and edible.

mulligatawny: Highly seasoned curry soup of East Indian origin.

mum: Strong ale brewed from malted wheat, cereals such as oatmeal, or ground beans.

mung bean: Bushy Asiatic legume, grown for food and forage.

münster: Whole-milk cheese flavored with anise and caraway seed, often molded in a red-wax-covered cylinder and originally made around Münster in Germany.

mûr: (French—ripe)

mûre: (French—mulberry)

muscade: (French—nutmeg)

muscadet: Light white wine.

muscadine: Native American grape found from Virginia to Florida and other parts of the South; cultivated muscadine grapes are used in making scuppernong wine; the term is also applied to muscatel wine.

muscatel: Dessert wine made from muscat grapes.

muscolo: (Italian—mussel)

muscovado: Unrefined raw sugar.

mush: Boiled cornmeal seasoned with salt.

mushimono: (Japanese—steamed food)

mushroom: Edible fungi, prepared in many ways and served in many dishes.

mushroomburger: Vegetarian hamburger made of ground and seasoned mushrooms.

muskellunge: Large North American freshwater pike—sometimes seven feet long—prized as a game fish.

muskmelon: Broad term for several varieties of round, sweet-fleshed melons, including cantaloupe and winter melon.

mussel: Bivalve mollusk found in American streams and rivers and along seacoasts of America and Europe; mussels are usually prepared by boiling in olive oil, wine, or wine vinegar, and sometimes the saltwater species are eaten on the half shell—very popular in many Middle Eastern dishes.

mussel brose: Scots dish consisting of mussels cooked with milk, oatmeal, and water.

must: Unfermented grape juice; sterilized must is imported into England from France, and is treated with yeast and turned into wine.

mustard: Plant of the cabbage family widely cultivated for use as a condiment or as a flavoring agent.

mustard greens: Large pungent green leaves of various mustard plants, used in salad making.

mustard pot: Small jar of ceramic, glass, plastic, or pottery, for storing and serving mustard sauce; mustard pots are often provided with matching spatulas or serving spoons.

mustard sauce: Pungent yellowish condiment made of ground mustard seeds, salt, spices, and vinegar (french mustard) or with spices, and tarragon vinegar, or Rhine wine (german mustard).

mustard seed: Mustard seed ground into powder for use in gravies, on meats, in pickling, and in making sauces.

mustard spinach: Indian mustard.

mutton: Meat of a sheep more than one year old.

muttonburger: Hamburger made of mutton.

mutton chop: Chop cut from various rib portions of mutton.

myrtille: (French—bilberry)

mysost: (Norwegian—whey cheese) Scandinavian cheese made from whey; this light-brown cheese is regarded as the national cheese of Norway.

Nabisco: Trade name for the National Biscuit Company.
nabo: (Spanish—turnip)
nach amerikanischer Art: (German—American style)
nach berliner Art: (German—Berlin style)
nach französischer Art: (German—French-style cooking)
nach hamburger Art: (German—Hamburg style)
nach italienischer Art: (German—Italian style)
nach jäger Art: (German—hunter style) Sautéed with onions.
nach kölnischer Art: (German—Cologne style)
nach limburger Art: (German—Limburg style)
nach munchiner Art: (German—Munich style)
nach russischer Art: (German—Russian style)
Nachtmahl: (German—night meal; supper)
nach ungarischer Art: (German—Hungarian-style)
nagelkaas: (Dutch—nail cheese) Cheese made with skimmed milk and flavored with cloves and cumin seeds.
nagerecht: (Dutch—dessert)
nahit: (Yiddish—chick peas)

naleśnik: (Polish—pancake) Rolled pancake similar to a *crêpe suzette*.
namaycush: Lake salmon.
Nantaise: (French—in the manner of Nantes)
napery: Table linen—napkins and tablecloths.
napkin: Fabric or paper square for wiping the hands and lips during and after eating.
napkin holder: Metal or plastic device for holding a supply of paper napkins.
napkin ring: Cylindrical ring for holding an individual cloth napkin.
naples biscuit: Ladyfinger.
napoleon: *Mille-feuille* filled with custard or whipped cream.
Napoleon brandy: Liqueur casked during the era of Napoleon I, and over a hundred years old, applied to any very old brandy.
napolitain: (French—Neapolitan)
nappé: (French—napkined) Lightly coated with jelly, icing, or sauce.
nappe: (French—tablecloth)
nappy: Shallow serving dish sometimes provided with a single handle and sometimes handleless.

naranja: (Spanish—orange)
naranjada: (Spanish—orangeade)
naranjillada: (Ecuadorean-Spanish—orange-juice drink)
naseberry: Sapodilla.
nasello: (Italian—whiting)
nasi: (Malay—boiled rice)
nasi goreng: Spicy Indonesian dish consisting of fried rice enriched with bits of chicken, fish, or seafood.
nasturtium: Fragrant herb whose seed is sometimes used in pickling.
natillas: (Spanish—custard)
native: English term for an oyster taken from the old oyster beds off the coast of Essex and Kent.
natural brown rice: Rice hulled by a special process, preserving the germ at the tip of the kernel to retain its high-protein content.
Naturschnitz: (German—natural chop) Veal cutlet fried.
navarin aux pommes: (French—mutton stew with potatoes)
navel orange: Seedless orange with a navel-like pit on the exterior.
navet: (French—turnip)
navy beans: White kidney bean.
navy-bean soup: Thick vegetable soup made of navy beans, carrots, celery, milk, onions, parsley, tomatoes, and seasoning.
nazdar: (Czechoslovakian—good luck) A toast.
na zdorovie: (Russian—to your health) A toast.
ndizi na nyama: (Swahili—banana with meat)
neapolitan ice cream: Ice-cream brick containing several flavors arranged in contrasting color layers, usually chocolate, vanilla, and strawberry.

nebuchadnezzar: Wine bottle containing sixteen quarts.
nectar: Mythical beverage imbibed by the Greek gods whose name has been given to the sweet liquid of flowers, used by bees in making honey; nectar is also applied to various commercial fruit juices.
nectarine: Small smooth-skinned variety of peach.
negus: Hot-water beverage containing claret, lime juice, port wine, or other wine plus brown sugar; negus is named for Colonel Francis Negus, a British colonial, who concocted this drink in the early 1700's.
Nessel cheese: English, thin, round, soft rennet cheese made from whole milk of cows.
nesselrode: ice cream, pie, or pudding of creamy custard rum-laced filling containing candied fruits, named in honor of Count Karl Nesselrode, Russian diplomat at Congress of Vienna (1814-1815).
nests: Sets of kitchen bowls, casseroles, or measuring spoons in graduated sizes, fitting one into another.
neufchâtel cheese: Soft rennet cheese made from whole milk, originating in this town in France; Neufchâtel resembles the popular white cream cheese.
neutral brandy: Liquor of high proof—170 to 190—used in fortifying other brandies or wines.
neutral foods: Fats and sugars, which are generally devoid of minerals having either an acid or an alkaline makeup.
neutral spirits: Ethyl alcohol of 190 proof or more used in blending liquors.

newburg sauce: Brandy, butter, cream, egg yolk, and wine sauce; see also a la Newburg.

New England clam chowder: Chowder made with milk rather than tomatoes.

New England codfish cakes: Fish flakes combined with mashed potatoes, shaped into patties, and fried or sautéed.

New England dinner: Corn beef boiled with vegetables.

New Hampshire Red: Fast-maturing breed of domestic poultry developed from Rhode Island Red chickens, valued for heavy winter egg production.

new jersey tea: Deciduous shrub of the eastern U.S., formerly used as a tea substitute.

New Orleans molasses: Light-colored, sugary grade of molasses.

Newtown Pippin: Albemarle apple.

New York cut: Cut of beef including the hipbone.

New York dressed: Prepared for market with feet, head, and viscera included, said of poultry.

New York sour: Variety of whiskey sour.

New York State wine: Wine produced in New York State, often from native American varieties of grapes.

nice cuppa: English slang for a nice cup of tea.

nicht durchgebraten: (German— rare)

Nieheimer Hopfenkäse: (German —Nieheim hop cheese) Slightly tart cheese made with sour milk and originating in the north German town of Nieheim.

Niederungskäse: (German—a rennet-type cheese)

Niere: (German—kidney)

niersoep: (Dutch—kidney soup)

nightcap: Drink, usually alcoholic, taken before going to bed.

nimono: (Japanese—boiled food)

nip: Sip or small serving of some drink.

niu: (Polynesian—coconut)

njure: (Swedish—kidney)

noce: (Italian—walnut)

noce de cocco: (Italian—coconut)

Nockerln: (German—little dumplings)

noggin: Small cup or mug, or a liquid measure equal to a quarter pint.

noisette: (French—hazelnut) Round individual cut of lamb taken from the rib or loin.

noix: (French—nut)

noix de Brésil: (French—Brazil nut)

noix de coco: (French—coconut)

noix de veau: (French—veal knuckle; veal loin)

nokedli: (Hungarian—dumplings)

nøkkelost: (Norwegian—key cheese) Dark-colored cheese made of goat's milk and flavored with caraway.

nopal: (Spanish—edible prickly-pear cactus)

nopalitos: Mexican dish made of prickly-pear cactus leaves.

nonpareil: Chocolate droplet coated with white sugar and wrapped in foil; nonpareil is also the name for multicolored decorative pellets used in decorating cake icings.

noodles: Alimentary paste made with eggs, rolled flat, cut into ribbons, and dried; commercial noodles are made from semolina flour (purified durum middlings), and must contain at least 5.5 percent egg solids to be called egg noodles—otherwise they are water noodles; noodles are used to fortify soups and as a base for ragouts and other stews.

nordost: (Swedish—northeast or north cheese) Whole-milk cheese of tangy and mellow flavor.

Norgold Russet: Large oblong-shaped white baking potato.

normande: (French—Norman) Term applied to a number of different dishes, prepared in various ways, particularly fish or shellfish, appearing on menus as *à la Normande*.

Northern Spy: Bright-red striped winter apple prized for cooking and eating because of its juiciness.

norvégienne: (French—Norwegian) Term for a hot surprise pudding or for a method of serving cold seafood, appearing on menus as *à la norvégienne*.

Norwegian lobster: Big-clawed lobster similar to the American variety but smaller and slenderer.

nougat: Candy made of nuts and sugar or honey.

nougatine: Chocolate-covered nougat.

nouilles: (French—noodles)

noyau: Brandy flavored with fruit-pit kernels imparting an almond-like taste.

NRA: Abbreviation for the National Restaurant Association.

nubbin: Imperfect or small ear of corn.

nubian: Dark-purple plum.

Nudeln: (German—noodles)

Nudelsuppe: (German—noodle soup)

nuez: (Spanish—nut)

nun's toast: Fried bread.

Nuss: (German—nut)

Nussbügel: (German—nut crescent) Nut-filled pastry with almond, hazelnut, or walnut flavor.

Nusskipfer: (German—nut crescents) Nut cooky.

Nusskuchen: (German—nutcakes)

Nusstorte: (German—nut cake)

nut: Hard-shelled dry fruit or fruit seed.

nut butter: Paste made from crushed nuts.

nut chopper: Glass jar with a wooden bottom insert and a set of chopping blades operated by rotating the lid handle.

nutcracker: Jawed device for cracking nuts.

nutcracker bowl: Deep wooden bowl fitted with a nutcracker center, for serving unshelled nuts.

nutcracker set: Set of implements consisting of a nutcracker and three nutpicks.

nutlet: Small nut or object similar to a nut in appearance.

nut margarine: Margarine made from coconut and peanut oils.

nutmeat: Kernel of a nut.

nutmeg: Tropical tree of the myrtle family native to the Moluccas or Spice Islands of Indonesia; the aromatic fruit pit of this tree is the nutmeg and its coating is mace; both mace and nutmeg are used for flavoring baked goods, custards, drinks, puddings, and sauces.

nutmeg grater: Tinware utensil for grating whole nutmegs; some are made to hold nutmegs in the top part of the grater.

nut oil: Oil expressed from nuts: coconut oil, peanut oil, walnut oil, etc.

nutpick: Sharp-pointed implement for picking nut meats from their shells.

nut pine: Piñon seed or other edible seed from pines.

nutritionist: Specialist in the science of nutrition.

NY steak: Short form for a New York cut.

oatcake: Oatmeal pancake baked on a griddle.

oat groats: Hulled oats used for cereal.

oatmeal: Ground or rolled oats, widely used in baking breads, cakes, and cookies, and in making breakfast porridge.

oatmeal cake: Any of a wide variety of Scots breads, cakes and buns.

oatmeal porridge: Oatmeal breakfast cereal.

OB: Abbreviation for *Oranjeboom* (Dutch — orange tree), beer brewed in Rotterdam.

obed: (Russian—dinner)

Oberkellner: (German—head waiter)

obiad: (Polish—dinner)

oblong roaster: Roasting pan of oblong shape.

o'brien potatoes: French-fried potatoes cooked with chopped onions, peppers, and pimientos.

Obst: (German—fruit)

Obstkuchen: (German—fruit tart)

Obstsalat: (German—fruit salad)

ocean perch: Rosefish.

Ochsenschwanz: (German—oxtail)

Ochsenschwanzsuppe: (German—oxtail soup)

Ochsenzunge: (German—ox tongue)

oeuf: (French—egg)

oeufs à la coque: (French—eggs in shell) Boiled eggs.

oeufs brouillés: (French—scrambled eggs)

oeufs durs: (French—hard eggs) Hard-boiled eggs.

oeufs farcis: (French—stuffed eggs) Deviled eggs.

oeufs frits: (French—fried eggs)

oeufs mollets: (French—tender eggs) Soft-boiled eggs.

oeufs pochés: (French—poached eggs)

oeufs sur le plat: (French—eggs on the plate) Fried eggs.

offal: Edible discards and entrails of meat animals: feet, heads, hearts, intestines, kidneys, livers, lungs, tails, etc.

Ohio wine: Wine produced in Ohio, often from native American varieties of grapes; some of the finest are grown on islands in Lake Erie.

oie: (French—goose)

oignon: (French—onion)

oilstone: Whetstone kept moist with oil, for sharpening cutlery.

oiseau: (French—bird)

oison: (French—gosling)

oj: Abbreviation for orange juice.

Oka cheese: Trappist cheese made by monks at Oka, Quebec, Canada.

okole maluna: (Hawaiian—bottoms up) A toast.

okra: Mallow whose seed pods are used extensively in the United States and the West Indies as vegetables and the basis of many gumbos and stews; okra is a favorite vegetable in much creole cooking.

oksesteg: (Danish—roast beef)

øl: (Danish and Norwegian—beer)

Öl: (German—oil)

öl: (Swedish—beer)

old fashioned: Cocktail made of whiskey and soda plus bitters, sugar, lemon peel, and some fresh fruit.

old-fashioned glass: Squat tumbler for serving old-fashioned cocktails.

old hare: Deceptive term for rabbit meat.

old tom gin: Gin sweetened with sugar syrup:

oleomargarine: Margarine.

olio: (Italian—oil)

oliva: (Italian, Portuguese, and Spanish—olive)

olive: Semitropical tree yielding a valuable fruit; olives are used for their oil, eaten green or ripe, and canned in many forms.

olive cream cheese: Soft cream cheese filled with bits of green olive.

olive oil: Oil expressed from olive pulp for use in cooking and in dressing salads; pure olive oil is expensive, and consequently many so-called olive oils are a mixture of olive and other vegetable oils such as corn oil and peanut oil.

olla: (Spanish—jar) Earthenware jug or stewpot with wide mouth and looped handles.

olla podrida: (Spanish—rotten pot) Highly seasoned Spanish stew cooked in an *olla* and containing ingredients such as chick peas; fish, chicken or other meat; chopped vegetables, etc.

oloroso: (Spanish—fragrant) Full-bodied, golden, sweet sherry, famous for its bouquet and flavor.

Olympia: American beer brewed in Olympia, Washington.

omelet: Egg dish made by beating well-seasoned eggs and frying them, then folding the omelet in half before serving; sometimes a filling is added before the egg mixture is folded.

omelet pan: Half-round hinged pan for making omelets; the omelet mixture is poured into the bottom half and covered by the top half, which helps to retain heat and shape the omelet.

omelette: (French—omelet)

omelette alla parmigiana: (Italian—omelet in Parmesan style) Cheese omelet.

omelette au fromage: (French—cheese omelet)

omelette au lard: (French—omelet with bacon)

omelette aux champignons: (French—omelet with mushrooms)

omelette aux confitures: (French —omelet with jam)

omelette aux fines herbes: (French —omelet with herbs)

omelette aux pointes d'asperges: (French—omelet with asparagus tips)

omelette di funghi: (Italian— mushroom omelet)

omelette Norvégienne: (French — Norwegian omelet) Baked Alaska.

onion: Edible bulb of the lily family famed for its flavor and its pungent aroma; onions are used in many ways and in nearly every kind of dish.

onion chopper: Nut chopper, particularly useful when preparing onions because its closed top shuts off pungent odors.

onion powder: Concentrate derived from fresh onions by dehydration.

onion tureen: Pottery tureen fashioned like a huge onion and used for serving sauces and soups.

ontbijt: (Dutch—breakfast)

on the rocks: Served with ice cubes but without water or soda, said usually of alcoholic drinks.

oolong: A tea which is partially fermented before it is dried and which combines the characteristics of green and black teas.

oporto: (Spanish—port wine)

oppenheimer: One of several varieties of white table wine, originating near the town of Oppenheim in the Rhineland, Germany.

oppvarter: (Norwegian—waiter)

orange: Sweet round citrus fruit from several varieties of trees growing in the subtropics and especially cultivated in southern California, Florida, and Texas; oranges are eaten raw, used for juice or flavoring agent and in marmalades.

orangeade: Iced summer beverage composed of orange juice and water.

orangeado: Candied orange peel.

orange ambrosia: Sliced oranges dotted with flaked coconut and sprinkled with rum.

orangeat: (French—candied orange peel)

orange biscuit: Biscuit dough flavored with orange juice and orange peel; sometimes cut-out biscuits are spread with orange marmalade before baking.

orange bitters: Extract of bitter-orange.

orange blossom: Cocktail containing gin, orange juice, and honey or sugar plus ice.

orange blossom water: Essence distilled from bitter-orange flowers and used in baking as an aromatic flavoring agent.

orange drink: Beverage artificially colored and flavored to simulate orange juice, usually made of citric acid, orange oil, sweetener, and water.

orange gin: Orange-flavored gin.

orange juice: Juice expressed from an orange, the essential staple of many breakfasts, cocktails, highballs, and soft drinks; orange juice is probably the most popular of all fruit juices.

orangelo: Orange + pomelo—hybrid citrus fruit.

orange mint: Bergamot mint.

orange oil: Flavoring extract derived from the peel of both bitter and sweet oranges.

orange pekoe: Orange-colored small-leaved black tea from Ceylon and India as well as tea-growing districts of East Africa.

orange phosphate: Carbonated water artificially flavored with orange.

orange spoon: Spoon whose bowl has a serrated edge for removing sections from halved oranges.

orange whiskey: Orange-flavored liqueur made with a whiskey base.

orange wine: Wine made by fermenting orange juice or orange peels.

orangine: French orange pastry.

orasky: Orange-flavored whiskey cordial.

orata bollita: (Italian—boiled gilthead)

oregano: Bushy herb of the mint family, native to the subtropical Americas; oregano is widely used in Italian sauces as well as in such Spanish-American dishes as *chili con carne*.

orge: (French—barley)

orgeat: (French—barley beverage) Drink made originally of barley water, now from an emulsion of almonds.

Originalabfüllung: (German—wine bottled where the grapes were grown)

orohova potica: (Yugoslavian—raisin-and-nut pie)

Orpington: Domestic poultry of a large, deep-breasted type developed around Orpington in Kent, England.

ørred: (Danish—trout)

ørret: (Norwegian—trout)

ortaggio: (Italian—vegetable)

os à moelle: (French—marrow bone)

Oscar of the Waldorf: Oscar Tschirky, general manager of the fine restaurants in the old Waldorf-Astoria: Palm Garden, Peacock Alley, Rose Room, etc.

oseille: (French—sorrel)

osmazone: Liquid extract of meat or meat essence.

ossobuco: (Italian—marrow bone)

ost: (Danish, Norwegian and Swedish—cheese)

ostión: (Spanish—large oyster)

ostra: (Spanish—oyster)

ostrica: (Italian—oyster)

oswego cheddar: Cheddar cheese made in western New York State.

oswego tea: Native American member of the mint family, the leaves of which were brewed into a medicinal tea by the Oswego Indians.

ounce: Unit of measurement equal to 1/16th pound or 28 grams.

ouzo: Anise-flavored Greek brandy.

oval waiter: Serving tray of ceramic or metal for holding a coffee or tea set.

ovár: Reddish-yellow Hungarian cow's-milk cheese, middling hard.

oven: Heavily insulated chamber for baking, usually a part of the kitchen stove.

oven dressed: Poultry prepared for market and ready for baking, boiling, broiling, or roasting as all bleeding, cleaning and removal of inedible offal is accomplished.

ovenware: Tempered glass and

pottery cooking utensils made to withstand oven heat.

ovo: (Portuguese—egg)

ox: Adult male bovine castrated so it can be yoked and used as a draft animal or for food; a young ox is called a steer.

ox cheeks: Fleshy sides of ox heads.

oxe: (Swedish—beef)

oxheart: Term for certain varieties of cherries and for a kind of cabbage with a large oval head.

ox liver: Beef liver similar to calves' liver but not so delicate.

oxtail: Skinned tail meat used for soups and stews.

oxtunga: (Swedish—ox tongue)

oyster: Marine bivalve mollusk prized for its flavor; oysters are eaten raw, baked in their shells, fried, stewed, or served in chowders, stews, soups, and seafood cocktails.

oyster bar: Restaurant specializing in serving oysters.

oyster bay: Special counter in a restaurant, where oysters and other seafoods are prepared and served.

oyster cracker: Small round cracker served with chowders and seafood cocktails.

oysterette: Small flaky cracker served with seafoods, soups, stews, etc.

oyster fork: Small three-tined fork for eating seafoods.

oyster knife: Heavy-bladed short and narrow knife set in a thick wooden handle, heavy enough to provide leverage in opening clams, oysters, and other bivalves.

oyster plant: Salsify.

oysters rockefeller: Oysters baked or broiled in the New Orleans manner on a bed of rock salt and spread with a highly seasoned sauce made in any one of many ways.

oz: Abbreviation for ounce.

Pablum: Brand name of an infant cereal mix.

Pabst: American beer brewed in Milwaukee, Wisconsin.

pabulum: (Latin—food) Nourishment; physical or intellectual.

Pacific halibut: Halibut occupying a range north of the California halibut.

Pacific herring: Herring species found in the North Pacific, differing only slightly from its Atlantic cousin.

Pacific mackerel: Popular food fish found along the entire Pacific Coast.

Pacific sardine: California sardine.

paella: (Spanish—small pan or pot) Classic Spanish dish of rice with meat, poultry, seafood, saffron, and other seasonings, usually prepared one˘ day and served the next.

paella a la valenciana: (Spanish—Valencian paella) Clams, chicken, meat, mussels, peppers, shrimp, and tomatoes on a bed of saffron-colored and saffron-flavored rice.

pago: Rennet cheese made from sheep's milk, originating on the island of Pago off the coast of Yugoslavia.

pah jook: (Korean—rice and beans)

pain: (French—bread)

pain bis: (French—brown bread)

pain d'épice: (French—spice bread) Gingerbread.

pain de seigle: (French—rye bread)

pain doré: (French—golden bread) French toast.

pain grillé: (French—toast)

pain rôti: (French—roast bread) Toast.

palacsinta: (Hungarian—pancake)

palais de boeuf: (French—ox palate)

Palatschinken: (Austrian-German—pancakes) served with fruit, jam, jelly, marmalade, cottage cheese, or nuts and chocolate.

palestinian citrus: Citron.

palm butter: Palm oil.

palm sugar: Sugar made from the sap of certain species of palm trees.

palm wine: Beverage made of fermented palm sap, popular in many tropical countries.

paloma: (Spanish—pigeon)

palpuszta: Highly aromatic Hungarian soft cheese.

pámpano: (Spanish—pompano)

Pampelmuse: (German—grapefruit)

pamplemousse: (French—grapefruit)

pan: Baking or cooking utensil made of metal or heat-resistant glass.

pan: (Japanese and Spanish—bread)

panaché: (French—variegated) Two or more kinds mixed together, said of fruits, meats, vegetables, or ice creams.

panade: (French—something made with bread) Soup or stew of bread and stock, or boiled bread used as a binding for forcemeat.

panais: (French—parsnip)

Panama chicken: Slang for iguana meat.

panbroil: To broil under an open flame with the food in a pan to catch the juices.

pancake: Thick or thin batter made of eggs, milk, flour, with or without leavening, and baked on a griddle; in America pancakes are usually served hot with butter and syrup; in Scotland they are served cold; on the continent they are usually thin, filled, and rolled.

pancake skillet: Griddle for frying pancakes and other foods.

pancit guisado: Filipino meat and seafood dish served with noodles.

pancit molo: Filipino triangular turnover stuffed with spiced pork and shrimp.

pan de centeno: (Spanish—rye bread)

pandekage: (Danish—pancake)
pan de maíz: (Spanish—cornbread)
pane: (Italian—bread)
pané: (French—breaded)
panecillo: (Spanish—roll)
panela: Low-grade brown sugar
of a type produced in many
Latin American countries—an
inferior muscovado but never-
theless tasty in baked goods,
confections, and many soft
drinks.
paner: (French—to cover with
bread crumbs)
panettone: (Italian—a kind of
cake bread) Often orange flavored and raisin filled.
pan-fired tea: Green tea grown
chiefly in Japan; the name refers to the method of preparing
the leaves for market.
panfish: Any fish suitable for frying, usually hand-caught fish
like sunfish or catfish.
panfry: To fry in a pan with very
little fat.
paniert: (German—breaded)
panino: (Italian—roll)
panna: (Italian—cream)
panna montata: (Italian—
whipped cream)
pannekake: (Norwegian—
pancake)
pannekoek: (Dutch—pancake)
pannhaas: (Pennsylvania-German
—scrapple)
pannkaka: (Swedish—pancake)
Pancake baked in an oven
rather than on a griddle; *see
also plättar.*
panocha: (Mexican-Spanish—raw
sugar) Penuche.
panthay khowse: (Burmese—
chicken and noodles)

pantry: Small storage room adjacent to the dining room and
connecting it to the kitchen,
used for storing chinaware, silver, glassware, etc.; a kitchen
pantry is usually a larder where
food supplies are stored.
pão: (Portuguese—bread)
pap: Soft pulpy food such as
bread soaked in milk.
papa: (Spanish American
potato) Latin American slang
for *patata* (potato).
papas rellenas: (Spanish—stuffed
potatoes)
papaw: Any of numerous American shrubs with a large yellowish sweet fruit; it is sometimes
called pawpaw, although the
early English explorers used
this word for the papaya.
papaya: Tropical American shrub
or small tree producing large
yellow fruit with a sweet pulpy
flesh, which is eaten raw, boiled
as a vegetable, preserved, or
pickled.
papboat: Boat-shaped dish for
holding pap fed to infants and
invalids.
papershell: Soft-shell pecan.
paper towel: Rolled absorbent
paper, perforated in sections for
kitchen use: drying hands,
cleaning up messes, draining
greasy foods, etc.
paper-towel holder: Plastic or
metal device for dispensing
paper towels.
pappilan hätävara: (Finnish—
parson's emergency dessert)
Triflelike dessert of berries,
crumbs, and whipped cream.
paprika: Mildly pungent capsicum
pepper made from bonnet pepper; Hungarian paprika is usu-

ally made from the flesh of the pepper after all the seeds and stalks are removed; king's paprika is ground with seeds and stalks and therefore is sharper in flavor; paprika peppers are also called pimientos.

paprika butter: Butter sauce colored and flavored with paprika.

Paprika Hühner: (Austrian-German—chicken paprika)

paprikás: (Hungarian—made with paprika) Containing paprika and sour cream, said of any dish.

Paradiessosse: (German—paradise sauce) Tomato sauce.

Paradiessuppe: (German—paradise soup) Tomato soup.

paraffin: Translucent wax obtained from petroleum and used for sealing homemade preserves.

Paraguay tea: Tree of the holly family whose leaves are made into maté.

parboil: To boil partially as a preparation for baking, roasting, or other manner of cooking.

parched: Sun dried or subjected to dry heat.

parched corn: Roasted or dried ears of corn.

pare: To remove the outer skin of fruits and vegetables.

parer: Implement for paring fruits and vegetables, usually consisting of a sharp blade within a semirotatable shaft.

pareve: Jewish term indicating a food, such as eggs, fruit, matzos, and vegetables which is neither a dairy nor a meat product, and hence may be eaten with either type of meal without breaking any dietary law.

parfait: Dessert made of alternate layers of ice cream, fruit, syrup, and whipped cream; parfait is also the name of a frozen custard rippled with syrup and whipped cream.

parfait-amour: (French—perfect love) Violet-colored liqueur flavored with citron, coriander, and cinnamon.

parfait glass: Tall narrow glass used for serving parfaits.

pargo: (Spanish—porgie)

paring knife: Small-bladed knife used for paring fruits and vegetables.

parkerhouse roll: Rolled yeast dough cut two inches in diameter and folded off center, named for the Boston hotel where these rolls were first served, the Parker House.

parkin: Oatmeal gingercake.

parliament cake: Thin ginger cookie.

parmesan: Italian cheese originating in Parma in northern Italy, excellent as a grating cheese for garnishing pasta dishes, soups, and salads.

parmesan: (French—Parmesan) Served with grated parmesan cheese.

parmigiano: (Italian—Parmesan) Served or seasoned with parmesan cheese.

parsley: Aromatic herb of the carrot family used as a garnish and flavoring agent.

parsley flakes: Dehydrated parsley leaves used as seasoning in cooked dishes.

parsley jelly: Parsley and sugar mixture boiled until it jells.

parsley sauce: Combination of butter, flour, lemon juice, nut-

meg, chopped parsley, seasoning, and hot water, used with
poultry, fish, and meat courses.
parsnip: Herb of the carrot family whose turnip-like root is
commonly boiled with butter
or used as a soup vegetable.
parsnip chips: Parsnip prepared
and fried somewhat like potato
chips.
parsnip wine: Wine made by fermenting very small parsnip
pieces in a mixture of brown
sugar and yeast.
parson's nose: Slang for poultry
rump.
pasa: (Spanish—raisin)
pascal: Green-stalk celery of a
type developed in Utah.
pashka: (Russian—Easter sweetmeat) Cottage cheese, honey,
and ground nuts packed in
cone-shaped molds.
passata: (Italian—mash; purée)
passata di mele: (Italian—applesauce)
passata di patate: (Italian—
mashed potatoes)
Passover bread: Matzo.
Passover wine: Traditional sweet
red wine specially prepared for
Jewish Passover holidays.
pasta: (Italian—paste) Alimentary paste, including such foods
as macaroni, spaghetti, vermicelli, etc.
pasta alimentaria: (Italian—alimentary paste)
pasta asciutta: (Italian—dry
dough)
pasta in brodo: (Italian—spaghetti in broth)
pasta italiana: (Spanish—Italian
paste) Macaroni, spaghetti, etc.
pastel: (Spanish—pastry; pie;
tart)

pastel de carne: (Spanish—meat
pie)
pastel de choclo: (Spanish—corn
pie) Chilean corn and meat pie.
pastel de pescado: (Spanish—fish
pie)
pastelería: (Spanish—pastry)
pastelillo: (Spanish—small
pastry)
pastelito: (Spanish—small
pastry)
pastelito de coco: (Spanish—coconut tart)
pastèque: (French—watermelon)
Pastete: (German—patty; pie;
tart)
pasteurization: Process of sterilizing by raising and lowering the
temperature to prevent fermentation and growth of harmful
bacteria without altering the
substance being pasteurized, a
method developed by the 19th-
century French chemist Louis
Pasteur.
pasteurized milk: Milk sterilized
by heating to 145 degrees Fahrenheit (63 degrees Celsius—
centigrade scale), and rapidly
cooling to below 50 degrees F,
(46 degrees C).
pastille: Medicated lozenge or a
candylike cough drop containing aromatics, gums, and sugars.
pastina: (Italian—tiny pasta
shape) Used in soups.
pastrami: Peppered smoked beef.
pastry: Sweet unleavened dough,
usually rolled thin and used as
a case for a sweet or savory filling; by extension, pastry has
come to mean any type of sweet
baked goods.
pastry bag: Funnel-shaped bag for
expressing pastry dough or
sugar icings in a variety of fancy
forms.

pastry blender: Yoke-handled implement with series of wire blades for blending shortening into flour.

pastry brush: Long soft-bristle brush for applying beaten eggs, melted shortening, or other glazes to the top of bread dough or pastry just before baking.

pastry flour: Flour made from finely milled wheat low in gluten.

pastry fork: Four-tined fork, one tine sharp-edged for cutting.

pastry gun: Trigger-activated mechanism for expressing pastry dough or frosting through a shaped nozzle producing ornamental designs.

pastry jagger: Device for trimming piecrust.

pastry mix: Piecrust mix.

pastry syringe: Device similar to a pastry bag or gun but operated with a plunger; various nozzles permit pastry doughs and icings to be expressed in different designs.

pastry tube: Nozzle of pastry bag, syringe, or gun.

pastry wheel: Pastry jagger.

pasty: English term for a small meat pie or savory turnover.

patata: (Italian and Spanish—potato)

patata bollita: (Italian—boiled potato)

patata dolce: (Italian—sweet potato)

patata foglia: (Italian—potato leaf) Potato chip.

patata passata: (Italian—mashed potato)

patate: (French—sweet potato)

pâté: (French—paste) Liver paste, meat paste, etc.

pâte: (French—pastry) Term applied to most rich or fancy French baked goods, and to paste or dough.

pâte à chou: (French—pastry in cabbage style) Puff paste baked in round shapes; the *chou* is usually filled with *crème* mixture.

pâté à la flamande: (French—Flemish-style) Liver paste.

pâté d'amandes: (French—almond paste)

pâté d'anchois: (French—anchovy paste)

pâte de bifteck: (French—beefsteak pie)

pâté de foie gras: (French—fat liver paste) Goose liver paste.

pâte de guimauve: (French—marshmallow pastry)

patent peeler: Parer.

pâtisserie: (French—pastry; pastry shop)

patna rice: Ganges Valley variety of rice whose firm kernel holds its shape when boiled and therefore is widely used in canned soups and stews.

pato: (Portuguese and Spanish—duck)

patty: Small flat piece of food: small pie, hamburger patty, candy patty, fish-cake patty, potato-cake patty, etc.

patty pan: Muffin pan or pan for baking patty pies.

patty shell: Circular shell of puff pastry baked to hold a creamed savory filling.

paua: New Zealand abalone.

paupiette: (French—thin slice of meat stuffed with forcemeat and rolled)

pavé: (French—paving stone) Savory mixture set in a square mold and coated with jelly.

pavo: (Spanish—turkey)

pawpaw: English term for the papaya.

paysanne: (French—peasant style) Braised and garnished with bacon and buttered vegetables, said of meat or poultry; such dishes appear on menus as *á la paysanne*.

pazar: (Turkish—market)

pazuly leves: Hungarian-style bean soup.

pea: Nutritious seed of a leguminous plant, grown in pods, considered one of the most popular vegetables; peas come in many varieties: garden peas, black-eyed peas, chick peas, etc.

pea bean: Small white variety of shell bean.

peach: Fruit of a tree of the almond family, served raw, preserved, stewed, or dried, or in pies, jams, ice creams, and many other dessert dishes.

peach leather: Confection made of dried and sugared peach pulp; a favorite dish in Georgia where peaches are an important crop.

peach melba: Half a peach topped with vanilla ice cream and melba sauce, named for Australian soprano Dame Nellie Melba.

peanut: Tropical herb of the pea family, native to Brazil and cultivated in most subtropical and tropical countries; peanuts are eaten like nuts, made into peanut butter, and used in baked goods and candy.

peanut brittle: Crunchy confection made by stirring peanuts into a hot syrup or molasses mixture and cooling until hardened.

peanut butter: Rich spread made of ground peanuts, salt, vegetable oil, and dextrose, sold commercially in smooth or chunky styles.

peanut flour: Flour made from relatively oil-free ground peanuts, sold largely in health-food stores.

peanut oil: Oil extracted by pressing peanuts and used as an olive-oil substitute in canning and cooking.

pear: Small tree of the apple family yielding a pear-shaped fruit; pears are eaten raw or preserved in syrup, pickled, made into salads, or fermented into perry (pear cider).

pearl barley: Round pellets of ground barley; used chiefly in soups.

pearl hominy: Medium-size pellets of hominy.

pearl onion: Tiny white onion usually pickled and served in cocktails or used to garnish salads and stews.

pearl tapioca: Round fine-ground pellets of tapioca.

pearlware: Pearly white china.

pease porridge: Pea soup.

pease pudding: *Timbale* consisting of eggs, butter, and puréed peas, baked in a mold.

pea soup: Thick soup of dried split green peas soaked and cooked with a hambone or turkey carcass.

pebbleware: Pebble-patterned wedgwood china.

pecan: Tree of the walnut family, first cousin to the hickory, yielding a rich-flavored nut; pecans are eaten by themselves or used in many different confections.

pecan pie: Open-faced pie filled with rich mixture of pecans, butter, corn syrup, eggs, and sugar.

peccary: Native American piglike mammal; the North American species—the collared peccary, also called the javelina—still inhabits many parts of the American Southwest, where it is hunted and eaten.

pêche: (French—peach)

pêche melba: (French—peach melba)

peck: Dry measure containing 8 solid quarts.

pecorino: Italian sheep's-milk cheese.

pectin: Jelly-forming substance extracted from plant tissue: commercial pectin is derived from apples, citrus fruits, and sugar beets, and is used in making jelly.

peensoep: (Dutch—carrot soup)

peixe: (Portuguese—fish)

Pekin: Large white duck of a type originally imported from Peking, China.

pekoe: Originally black tea made from the first three leaves of the plant's spray, today black tea of the same size obtained by firing and screening; pekoe and orange pekoe teas are grown chiefly in Ceylon and India.

pemmican: American Indian food concentrate made of dried buffalo or deer meat mixed with melted fat; pemmican is also the name of a modern emergency ration of dried beef, flour, molasses, and suet.

pennyroyal: European mint somewhat less aromatic than peppermint or spearmint.

penuche: Brown-sugar candy.

pepato: (Italian—peppery) Grating cheese of Sicilian origin, made from mixture of cow's and goat's milk; pepato is characterized by its spicy peppercorn flavor.

pepe: (Italian—pepper)

peperone: (Italian—capsicum; chili)

peperoni: Highly seasoned Italian sausage.

pepino: (Spanish—cucumber)

pepita: (Spanish—pip; seed) Roasted and salted pumpkin seed.

pepper: Tropical climbing shrub whose seed-filled berries are important flavoring agents in cooking and food preserving; whole ground seeds become ground black pepper; decoated ground seeds become white pepper; unground seeds are used in pickling; powdered pepper—black or white—is used in nearly every kind of dish except desserts.

pepperbox: Pepper shaker.

peppercorn: Dried black-pepper berry used for flavoring and pickling; whole peppercorns are sometimes ground over salads from a peppermill.

peppergrass: Spring herb of the cabbage group similar to watercress and also used for garnishing salads.

peppermill: Hand mill for grinding whole peppercorns, often part of a set with a matching salt shaker.

peppermint: Dark-green aromatic true mint; fresh or dried peppermint leaves are used in sauces, beverages, and vinegar.

peppermint glacial: After-dinner cordial made of wine alcohol flavored with mint essence.

peppermint oil: Flavoring extract derived from peppermint.

peppernut: Christmas confection made of highly spiced and sugared dough.

pepper pot: Highly spiced West Indian stew of fish or meat and vegetables such as okra and white yams.

pepper sauce: Sauce made by immersing hot peppers in vinegar and replacing the vinegar as it is used.

pepper shaker: Container with a perforated top for sprinkling pepper.

peppersteak: Beefsteak baked in pepper sauce.

pepsin: Digestive enzyme obtained from the mucous lining of cattle stomachs, often used as a digestive aid and sometimes substituted for rennet in cheese making.

pequeno almoço: (Portuguese—little lunch) Breakfast.

pera: (Italian, Portuguese, and Spanish—pear)

perch: Freshwater food and game fish.

perche: (French—perch)

percolate: To filter liquid through a permeable substance to extract its essence.

percolator: Two-level coffeepot in which boiling water in the lower pot ascends and percolates over the coffee grounds contained in a perforated metal basket on the upper level until the brew is strong enough to suit.

perdrix: (French—partridge)

Perrier: French mineral water.

perry: Pear cider, a fermented beverage.

persian melon: Muskmelon having a netted but unribbed rind; some of the finest are raised in the American Southwest.

persian walnut: English walnut.

persil: (French—parsley)

persillade: (French—garnish of chopped parsley)

persimmon: Fruit of a tree of the ebony family which has two varieties: the native American species is very astringent when green but palatable when it ripens to a golden yellow, whereas the Japanese variety is sweet and without astringency.

pesca: (Italian—peach)

pesca alla Melba: (Italian—peach Melba)

pescado: (Spanish—caught fish) Fish no longer alive, a *pez pasado*—a past or dead fish; in Spanish a live fish is a *pez*.

pescado frito: (Spanish—fried fish)

pesce: (Italian—fish)

petite beurre: (French—little butter) Sweet butter biscuit.

petite gruyère: (French—little gruyère) Tinfoil-wrapped process cheese.

petite marmite: (French—little porridge pot) Meal-in-one soup containing beef broth, pieces of lean beef, marrow bones, vegetables, and cabbage balls, served in a small pottery casserole.

petit four: (French—small oven) Small cake frosted and decorated.

petit pain: (French—little bread) Roll.

petit poussin: (French—baby chick)

petits pois: (French—little peas) Small green peas.

pewterware: Serving utensils made of pewter: sugar-and-cream sets, serving platters and trays, mugs and tankards, display ware.

pez: (Spanish—live fish)

Pfannkuchen: (German—pancake; doughnut; fritter)

Pfeffer: (German—pepper)

Pfeffernuss: (German—pepper nut) Traditional spicy, ball-shaped Christmas cookie, frosted in various colors; the name is derived from black pepper included in the batter along with other spices.

Pfirsich: (German—peach)

pg: Slang abbreviation for pure gin.

Philadelphia pepper pot: Highly seasoned stew of tripe, meat, and dumplings.

phosphate: Carbonated water flavored with cherry, lemon, lime, orange, or some other flavored syrup.

p'house steak: Contraction for porterhouse steak.

picadillo: (Spanish—meat and vegetable hash)

piccalilli: Pickle relish often made with cabbage, chopped green and red peppers, green tomatoes, onions, vinegar, pickling spices, and brown sugar plus seasonings.

pichola: Arizona-style stew of fresh pork, sliced onions, tomatoes, chilis, and hominy.

pickerel: Freshwater fish of the pike family.

pickle: Brine or vinegar solution for preserving foods such as cucumbers, peaches, tomatoes, watermelon rind, etc.

pickle fork: Flared-tine fork for spearing pickles in jars or serving bowls.

pickling cabbage: Cabbage of a type suitable for pickling, such as red-leaf cabbage.

pickling cucumber: Cucumbers suitable for pickling; pickle cucumbers are usually small, spine free, and of fairly uniform shape and size.

pickling spices: Premixed blend of whole spices suitable for pickling: allspice, bay leaf, cardamom seed, celery salt, chili, cinnamon stick, clove, coriander, dill, mace, mustard, black pepper, fenugreek, ginger root, etc.

picnic: Outing where guests eat in the open air and each provides some of the food or refreshments.

picnic ham: Ham cut from pickled pork shoulder and trimmed into a ham shape; sometimes called a cala.

picnic hamper: Basket for holding picnic supplies: beverages, bread, cold cuts, cutlery, dishes, glasses, napkins, etc.

picnic-size can: Commercial can containing 10 ounces or 1¼ cups.

pie: Food baked in open or closed layers of pastry; meat pie (American style) usually has only a top crust, cream pie only a bottom, fruit pie both top and bottom.

pièce de résistance: (French—piece of resistance; solid portion) Main course or principal dish of a meal.

pie crust: Pastry dough—basic mixture of flour, shortening, and water, rolled to fit a pie pan.

pie-crust mix: Commercial preparation of flour, salt, and shortening, to which water is added to form pastry dough.

pieds de porc: (French—pig's feet)

pie pan: Shallow utensil for baking a pie.

pie plate: Pie pan.

pie prick: Utensil for pricking unbaked pie shells to keep them from shrinking during baking; a sharp-tined fork is often used.

pierna de cabrito asado: (Spanish —roast kid leg)

pierna de cordero asado: (Spanish —roast leg of lamb)

pie shell: Baked pie crust ready to be filled with any prepared filling or with creamed mixtures.

pig: Immature swine.

pigeon blood: Chinese-restaurant slang for soybean sauce.

pig fries: Pig entrails or testicles.

piggvar: (Swedish turbot)

pig in a blanket: One food wrapped up and cooked in another: oysters or cube steak in bacon; pork sausage in biscuit dough; frankfurter encased in a batter, etc.

pignola: Pine nut.

pig's feet: Feet of a pork carcass, usually boiled or pickled, and served with potatoes and sauerkraut.

piirakka: (Finnish—rice pastry) Rye crust filled with a rice cream.

pike: Large long-nosed freshwater food and game fish found in lakes and streams throughout the Northern Hemisphere and also called northern pike; pike is also the name of numerous other fishes unrelated to the northern pike.

pikelet: Crumpet.

pilaf: Dish originally from the Middle East, consisting of cooked rice with meat and prepared in various ways in different countries.

pilau: (French—pilaf)

pilchard: Soft-finned fish of the herring family whose young are called sardines.

pilé s kesteni: (Bulgarian— chicken with chestnuts)

pilot biscuit: Hardtack.

pilot bread: Hardtack.

pilot burner: Small flame kept burning continuously in gas appliances, where it is used to light larger burners.

pilot cracker: Hardtack.

Pilz: (German—mushroom)

piment: (French—green or red pepper)

pimienta: (Spanish—black pepper)

pimiento: (Spanish—green or red pepper)

pimento cheese: Cheese of any kind, usually process, flavored with pimiento.

piña: (Spanish—pineapple)

piña colada: (Spanish—chilled pineapple) Cuban pineapple drink.

pinbone steak: Steak cut from between the beef short loin and the sirloin.

pinch: Amount of seasoning that can be held between the forefinger and thumb.

pineapple: Large bromeliad fruit valued for its sweet flesh and its juice; the pineapple is cultivated in Florida, Hawaii, Puerto Rico, and many other subtropical places, and is eaten raw or canned.

pineapple cheese: Native American cheese molded and colored like a pineapple, or a cream cheese flavored with pineapple.

pineapple stick: Pineapple flesh cut into a stick shape for use in cocktails, long drinks, or salads.

pine nut: Edible seed of various nut pines or piñons, low-growing pine trees of western North America.

pink lady: Cocktail made of apple brandy, gin, grenadine syrup, lemon juice, and egg white.

piñon nut: Pine nut.

pint: Liquid measure containing 2 cups or 16 ounces.

pinto bean: Dotted pink shell beans grown in western United States as a vegetable and to feed livestock.

pinwheel: Cookie or canapé filled, rolled up like a jelly roll, and cut into slices.

pipe: Wine cask of varying capacity, sometimes regarded as equivalent to two hogsheads (about 126 gallons).

piperade: (French—decoy) Basque omelet made of onions, sweet peppers, and tomatoes with eggs added to make a light puree.

pippin: Dessert apple with greenish yellow skin tinged with red.

piqué: (French—pricked) Term applied to larded meat.

pirok: Alaskan-style salmon pie made with grated cheddar cheese, hard-boiled egg, sliced onions, steamed rice, and cream sauce.

piroshki: (Russian—small meat pasties)

Pischinger Torte: (Austrian-German—Pischinger cake) Viennese chocolate wafer named after its inventor.

pisco: Chilean or Peruvian grape brandy of high alcoholic content.

pisco sour: Mixed drink of pisco and lime juice.

pisello: (Italian—pea)

pismo: Hard-shell clam found along the coast of central and southern California, first discovered at Pismo Beach, California.

pissaladière: (French—a kind of savory tart) Pizza-like dish filled with anchovies, onions and black olives, a specialty of Nice.

pistache: (French—pistachio)

pistachio: Small tree of the sumac family native to southern Europe and Asia Minor, the fruit of which yields a green almond-like kernel eaten or used as a coloring and flavoring agent in many confections, desserts, ice cream dishes, etc.

pivni polevka: (Czechoslovakian—beer soup)

pizza: Italian-style open-faced pie filled with spiced tomato sauce, cheese, and some olive oil, and garnished with anchovies, sliced sausage, mushrooms, olives, or any of many other combinations.

pj: Slang abbreviation for prune juice.

pk: Abbreviation for peck.

place mat: Oblong mat of cotton, woven grass, linen, plastic, or straw placed at each diner's place in lieu of a tablecloth; a place mat is usually large enough to hold the main plate, flatware, and a tumbler or teacup.

plaice: Name applied to two varieties of flatfish: the summer flounder in America and in Europe a large flounder.

plaki: Greek dish of codfish baked in oil with garlic and raisins or currants.

planked steak: Restaurant term for a steak broiled and served on a well-seasoned plank and garnished with a border of mashed potatoes, mushroom caps, tomato slices, and sometimes julienned carrots.

plantain: First cousin of the banana but not as sweet; plantains served boiled, baked, or fried as a vegetable, are raised in many parts of the tropical world, as well as in south Florida, Hawaii, and Puerto Rico.

planter's punch: Mixed drink of dark rum, grenadine, curaçao, pineapple sticks, maraschino cherries, and carbonated water.

plastic mesh sponge: Scouring pad made of plastic findings for cleaning sticky pans, pots, and other cooking utensils.

plat: (French—dish)

plat de jour: (French—dish of the day) Ready-to-serve specialty.

plátano: (Spanish—banana or plantain)

plate of beef: Forequarters of beef.

plato: (Spanish—plate; serving)

Platte: (German—plate)

plätter: (Swedish—flats) Pancakes made on a griddle rather than in an oven; see also pannkaka.

platter: Large flat plate for serving main course.

plombière: (French—plumber's wife) Rich ice cream made with almonds, eggs and whipped cream, also called glace plombière (French—ice plumber's wife).

pluck: To remove the feathers from a fowl.

plucks: Entrails plucked from an animal or bird: heart, liver, lungs, etc.

plum: Any of several species of trees of the almond family yielding plums, damsons, green gages, prune plums, etc.; plums are eaten raw, dried as prunes, preserved in jam or syrup, and used in cakes and cookies.

plum brandy: Distillate of plum wine, called slivovitz in Slavic countries.

plumcot: Plum + apricot—hybrid fruit.

plum duff: Plain flour pudding containing currants or raisins but no plums.

plum pudding: Holiday pudding containing many ingredients but no plums; recipes usually include currants, figs, seeded raisins, citron, eggs, suet, bread crumbs, spices, and some brandy or wine.

plum tomato: Small oval cherry tomato, popular in salads.

pluto water: Purgative.

Plymouth Rock: Poultry of a type developed for eggs and meat, named for the rock where the Pilgrims landed; Plymouth Rocks are barred, buff, or white feathered.

poach: To cook in liquid kept simmering just below the boiling point.

poached eggs: Eggs broken and cooked in gently boiling water until the outsides are firm.

poacher: Shallow two-level pan: the lower level is used for boiling water; the upper level is a tray or trays for holding the eggs.

po'-boy sandwich: Poor-boy sandwich made with half a loaf of french bread cut horizontally and filled with lettuce, cheese, ham, relish, etc.; said to have originated in New Orleans.

poché: (French—poached)

podvarku: (Yugoslav—baked sauerkraut)

poffertje: (Dutch—fritter)

poi: Polynesian taro-root paste popular in many South Sea dishes, including those served in the Hawaiian Islands, Guam, and Samoa.

pointes d'asperges: (French—asparagus tips)

poire: (French—pear)

poireau: (French—leek)

pois: (French—pea or peas)

pois cassés: (French—split peas)

pois chiche: (French—chick pea)

pois et riz: (French—peas and rice) Favorite dish in Haiti.

poisson: (French—fish)

poisson d'eau douce: (French—freshwater fish)

poisson de mer: (French—marine fish; saltwater fish)

poitin: (Irish—potlet) Poteen—illicit whiskey distilled from barley, potatoes, or molasses.

poitrine: (French—breast)

poivrade: (French—peppery sauce)

poivre: (French—pepper)

poivré: (French—peppered)

Poland China: Black pigs with white markings, an American breed of swine representing a cross of Polish and Chinese types.

polar cattle: Muskoxen, native ungulates of the Far North.

polenta: (Italian—cornmeal pudding) Mush made so thick that a spoon will stand upright in it.

polenta dulce: (Spanish—sweet *polenta*) Paraguayan cornmeal cream flavored with anise, cinnamon, and vanilla.

polished rice: White rice parboiled to retain its nutritive qualities, then machine-hulled and polished.

polish ham: Ham of a type imported from Poland, usually strong flavored and thoroughly smoked and aged.

polish pickles: Cucumbers pickled in alum, garlic, onions, vinegar, and such spices as tumeric.

polish sausage: Polish ground beef and pork sausage flavored with garlic.

pollack: Green food fish of the cod family, eaten fresh or salted.

pollo: (Italian and Spanish—chicken)

pollo alla cacciatore: (Italian—chicken in hunter style) Stewed chicken.

pollo al vino blanco: (Italian—chicken in white-wine style)

pollo arrosto: (Italian—roast chicken)

pollo asado: (Spanish—roast chicken)

polpetta: (Italian—croquette)

polpettone saporito: (Italian—tasty hash)

pølse: (Norwegian—sausage)

polynee: Swiss tart filled with almond-flavored meringue.

polyunsaturate: Fat, oil, or shortening containing many insoluble fat globules; the use of poly-unsaturates reduces the tendency of fats to remain in the system.

pomace: Mashed fruit pulp or residue such as the seeds, skins, and stems of apples, left over from cider making.

pomato: Potato + tomato; *see also* potomato.

pome: Pulpy fruit of the apple family, such as apple, haw, pear, and quinces, whose seeds are contained in a central core.

pomegranate: Tropical tree of the myrtle family, whose fruit is eaten raw or drunk as juice; an ancient fruit, the pomegranate is found in many parts of the world, including the American Southwest and the Mediterranean area.

pomelo: Name for either of two citrus fruits: the shaddock or the grapefruit.

pomme: (French—apple)

pomme au four: (French—apple in the oven) Baked apple. Also colloquially: baked potato.

pomme de terre: (French—apple of the earth) Potato.

pomme de terre en robe de chambre: (French—potato in its dressing gown) Potato in its skin.

pommes allumettes: (French—matchstick potatoes)

pomme sauvage: (French—wild apple; crab apple)

pommes chips: (French—potato chips)

pommes de terre duchesse: (French—duchess potatoes)

pommes frites: (French fried potatoes)

pommes purée: (French—mashed potatoes)

pommes sautées: (French—sautéed potatoes)

pomodoro: (Italian—tomato)

pompano: Name applied to several species of tropical marine food fishes taken from the Atlantic and the Caribbean; pompano is also a small bluish or greenish fish found along the Pacific coast; the various species called pompano are considered excellent food fishes.

pompano en papillote: (French—pompano in curl paper) Pompano cooked in metal foil or special paper.

pompelmo: (Italian—grapefruit)

ponche: (Spanish—punch)

ponche de piña: (Spanish—pineapple punch)

pone: Cornmeal bread or cake, hand-shaped into an oval and cooked.

pontet-canet: Fine-quality dry red wine produced near Bordeaux in southwestern France, a claret long favored by English and American experts.

pont-l'évêque: Fermented cheese usually packed for export in flat wood-chip boxes, originally produced in a town of the same name in northern France.

pony: Small liqueur or whiskey glass, holding an ounce of liquid.

poor boy: Po'-boy sandwich.

poor knights of windsor: Fried slices of bread spread with jam, or wine-flavored slices of french toast.

pop: Soft drink of any flavor charged with carbonated water.

popcorn: Variety of corn whose kernels pop open when heated, extruding a white puffy mass; popcorn is usually served with melted butter and salt or coated with a carmelized sugar.

popcorn popper: Hinge-lid wire basket with a long handle for popping corn over an open flame.

pope's nose: Slang for poultry rump.

popover: Quick-bread puff made of egg batter and baked in muffin tins at high heat, so that expanding steam will blow them up to balloonlike hollows.

popper: Popcorn popper.

poppyseed: Seed of the opium poppy used in flavoring and in decorating breads, rolls, and pastries.

poppyseed oil: Oil extracted from poppy seeds for use in cooking and salad dressings.

porc: (French—pork)

porcelain: Delicate and beautiful grade of translucent ceramic used in making ornamental dishware and decorative pottery.

porgy: Marine food fish of the sea-bream family, found along the Atlantic and Mediterranean coasts; porgy is also the name of many other fishes related (pinfish and scups) and unrelated (margate, spadefish, surf fish, menhaden).

pork: Swine meat classified in three grades: butcher, bacon, and packer; butcher—highest grade—is used for choicest cuts; bacon—medium grade—for bacon and wiltshire sides; packer —lowest grade—for low-priced pork products.

porkburger: Pork patty fried and eaten like a hamburger.

pork loin: Side cuts of pork.

pork side: Pork loin.

porridge: Oatmeal or other boiled cereal.

porringer: Bowl for eating porridge.

port: Fortified Portuguese wine originally shipped to England from Oporto, and made from grapes grown in the Douro valley.

port du salut: Rennet cow's-milk cheese of a type made at the Port du Salut abbey in northeastern France, tasting somewhat like swiss cheese.

porter: Weak and somewhat sweetish stout.

porterhouse: T-bone steak cut from the center of the beef loin; the name is derived from a New York tavern where porter was served on tap; the French call this steak a *chateaubriand.*

porto: (Portuguese—port) Port wine.

posset: Spiced milk curdled with ale, molasses, sherry, or other wine, and served as a beverage.

possum fruit: Persimmon, from its being a favorite of the opossum.

postre: (Spanish—dessert)

pot: Ceramic, enamelware, or metal cooking vessel; pots are usually deep welled and provided with handles.

potac: (French-Canadian— potato)

potage: (French—thick soup)

potage au vermicelle: (French— noodle soup)

potage bavarois: (French—Bavarian soup) Sliced sausage in lentil soup.

potage crème d'orge: (French— cream of barley soup)

potage danois: (French—Danish soup) Cucumber soup.

potage de volaille: (French—chicken soup)

potage mongol: (French—Mongolian soup) Creamed pea and tomato soup)

potage Parmentier: (French—Parmentier soup) Potato soup, named for the man who popularized the potato among the French people.

potage portugais: (French—Portuguese soup) Tomato soup.

potage purée à la reine: (French —queen-style purée soup) Cream of chicken soup.

potage purée de lentilles: (French —lentil soup)

potage purée de marrons: (French —chestnut soup) Chestnuts cooked with chicken consommé, celery, and spices.

potage purée de pois frais dite Saint Germain: (French—fresh pea purée soup called Saint Germain)

potage Rossini: (French—Rossini soup) Onion cream soup with grated cheese, named for the Italian composer who spent many years in Paris.

potage velours: (French—velvet soup) Smooth carrot and tapioca soup.

potaje: (Spanish—thick soup)

potaje de garbanzos: (Spanish—chicken-pea soup)

potato: Root vegetable of the nightshade family, native to the highlands of Central America and Mexico but now known throughout the world; potatoes are prepared and served in countless ways.

potato alcohol: Distillate of fermented potato mash.

potato apple: Seed ball of the potato.

potato ball: Small potato croquettes.

potato bean: Yam bean.

potato cake: Mashed potatoes, eggs, and flour fried like a patty.

potato cheese: Thuringian sour-milk cheese made with boiled grated potato mash and flavored with caraway seed; sometimes beer is used to cover the ripening curd of this cheese.

potato chips: Sliced white potatoes crisped in deep fat and dried; many commercial varieties feature special flavors such as cheese, hot sauce, bacon, and so forth.

potato flakes: Anhydrated potatoes finely flaked.

potato flour: Flour prepared from potatoes by cooking, drying, and grinding; potato flour is considered very nutritious and is sometimes used in place of wheat flour.

potato masher: Masher.

potato pancake: Pancake made from batter containing grated raw potato.

potato salad: Salad mixture made of cubed boiled potatoes garnished with salad dressing, chopped celery, onions, and seasoning.

potato whiskey: Potato alcohol.

pot-au-feu: (French—pot on fire) Meat and vegetable soup.

pot ball: Dumpling.

pot barley: Hulled barley.

pot cheese: Dry cottage cheese.

pot de crème: (French—pot of cream) Vanilla- or chocolate-flavored custard topped with whipped cream.

potet: (Norwegian—potato)

pot herb: Any herb eaten as a vegetable or used as seasoning.

pot liquor: Southern term for broth made by boiling meat or vegetables; in the South it is often served with vegetable greens.

potomato: Potato + tomato—hybrid made by grafting a tomato on a potato plant.

pot pie: Chicken or meat, potatoes, and other vegetables, covered with a pie crust, and baked in a casserole or dutch oven.

potpourri: (French—rotten pot; hodgepodge) Many foods cooked together.

pot roast: Braised meat, usually beef; pot roasts are served with thick gravy, celery, and cranberries; cider is sometimes added for flavor.

pottage: Thick soup or meat and vegetable stew.

potted: Ground into a fine paste, seasoned, and canned, said of fish or meat.

potted cheese: Cheese made from ripened cheddar, butter, condiments, wine, or other spirits.

pottery: Coarse type of ceramic ware used in making kitchen utensils such as cooky jars, casseroles, and bean pots.

pottle: Old dry or liquid measure equal to a half gallon or a drinking cup containing a half gallon.

potware: Crockery.

pouchong tea: Oolong tea scented with gardenia, jasmine, or magnolia.

pouchouse: Bouillabaisse made of freshwater fish.

pouding: (French—pudding)

pouding au pain: (French—bread pudding)

pouding de Noël: (French—Christmas pudding) Plum pudding.

poularde: (French—fattened pullet)

poule: (French—hen)

poule au pot: (French—chicken in the pot) Boiled chicken.

poule au riz: (French—chicken with rice)

poulet: (French—chicken; pullet)

poulet de grain: (French—corn-fed chicken)

poulet froid: (French—cold chicken)

poulet rôti: (French—roast chicken)

poulette: (French—young hen)

poultry: Domesticated species of birds raised for their eggs or their meat.

poultry needle: Long heavy needle for sewing up fish, meats, and poultry that have been stuffed.

poultry seasoning: Commercially packaged blend of marjoram, sage, savory, and thyme used in seasoning many dishes but particularly chicken and turkey stuffing.

poultry shears: Heavy-duty scissors for cutting up a poultry carcass.

pound: Unit of mass equaling 16 ounces.

pound cake: Sweet, fine-grained buttery cake, so called because the chief ingredients were originally measured in equal quantities of one pound.

pour batter: Batter thin enough to be poured.

pousse-café: (French—push coffee) Mixed drink made in layers of various liqueurs and spirits in contrasting colors; the layers do not blend because the ingredient liqueurs have different specific gravities.

poussin: (French—chick; very young chicken)

powdered coffee: Instant coffee.

powdered milk: Dehydrated milk, skimmed or whole.

powdered sugar: Confectioner's sugar.

powdered tea: Instant tea.

prairie oyster: Hangover remedy consisting of a whole raw egg, one-half teaspoon of vinegar, pepper, and salt, to be swallowed in one gulp.

praline: (French—burnt almond) French confection made of almond kernels roasted in boiling sugar; in New Orleans this candy is made in the shape of a water-tumbler coaster, and studded with pecan halves.

pranzo: (Italian—meal)

pranzo di legumi: (Italian—vegetable platter)

pranzo di manzo: (Italian—beef dinner) Pot roast with Italian sauce.

prawn: Large marine crustacean resembling a big shrimp.

prefab meat: Engineered food.

preheat: To turn on an oven before it is actually used so it will have the correct temperature when the food is ready to be put in.

Preisselbeere: (German—cranberry)

preservative: Chemical or natural substance used to preserve food

and keep it from decaying; oil, salt, spices, sugar, etc., are all preservatives.

preserve: Any food kept from spoiling by some canning or preserving process; in preserves, fruits and berries cooked with sugar retain their shapes; in jam they lose their shape and become a pulpy mass; in jellies, the pulp is strained out, leaving only the fruit juice to flavor the gelatin.

preserve jar: Jar or pot for holding homemade preserves.

Presskopf: (German—headcheese)

pressure cooker: Airtight utensil for cooking by steaming under pressure.

pretzel: Brittle biscuitlike tidbit made in characteristic bends, circles, or sticks; pretzels are glazed by being dipped in an egg mixture before they are baked and coarsely salted.

pretzel bender: Baker accomplished in bending pretzel dough into pretzel shapes or a machine which performs this task mechanically.

pretzel press: Utensil for shaping pretzel dough.

prezzemolo: (Italian—parsley)

prickly pear: Any of several species of cactus, whose leaves or fruit are edible; sometimes prickly pears are used in making alcoholic beverages or candy; some are also cooked and eaten like other vegetables.

prima colazione: (Italian—first collation; breakfast)

prime beef: Finest grade of beef, according to the U.S. Department of Agriculture standards.

primeiro almoço: (Portuguese—first luncheon) Breakfast.

primost: A creamy Norwegian whey cheese.

primula: A mild creamy Norwegian cheese often flavored with bacon, tomatoes, or shrimp.

Primus: Trademarked name for a portable oil stove popular with campers, outdoor cooks, and explorers; some models burn gasoline, coal oil, or kerosine.

printanière: (French—springlike) Term for a dish of mixed vegetables cut into decorative shapes or scooped out with a melon baller and dressed with butter.

profiterole: (French—small profit) Small dough puffs filled with a sweet or savory filling.

proke: Galubtsy.

promessi: (Italian—promised) Soft cream cheese.

proof: Measure of the alcoholic strength of a liquid; each degree represents 0.05 percent of alcohol: 100-proof straight whiskey is 50 percent alcohol; most blended whiskeys are 82 to 86 proof; fortified wines are 36 to 40 proof; table wines, 20 to 28; beers, 8 to 28.

proost: (Dutch—cheers) A toast.

prosciutto: (Italian—thin-sliced smoked ham)

prosciutto cotto: (Italian—cooked ham)

protein: Amino acid combination containing elements essential to all living cells: carbon, hydrogen, nitrogen, oxygen, etc.; proteins are plentiful in fish and meat but also present in beans, cheese, eggs, milk, peas, and many other foods.

provolone: Stringy-textured Italian cheese often presented in pear-shaped molds suspended by cording.

prugna: (Italian—plum)

prugne cotte: (Italian—stewed prunes)

prugne secche: (Italian—dried plums) Prunes.

prune: (French—plum)

prune: Plum of a variety which can be dried without fermenting.

pruneau: (French—prune)

prune butter: Prunes sweetened, boiled, sieved, and flavored with cinnamon and cloves, used as a spread like apple butter.

prune de damas: (French—damson plum)

prune de Reine-Claude: (French—queen Claudette plum) Greengage.

prunelle: Small yellow plum usually sold in dried form and also the name of an Alsatian plum liqueur.

prune whip: Dessert made of strained prune pulp, sugar, and white of egg.

pt: Abbreviation for pint.

pua'a: (Polynesian—pork)

puchero de carne: (Spanish—meat stew)

pudding: Name for several kinds of dessert: a baked or boiled cereal such as rice pudding or bread pudding; a spongy or creamy dish such as chocolate pudding or tapioca pudding; a baked suet pudding such as orange puff or plum pudding.

puerco: (Spanish—pork)

Puerto Rican molasses: Dark-colored molasses, tasting slightly of rum.

puff paste: Rich flaky pastry dough lightened by elaborate kneading and rolling to work in butter and air.

pulë me orrë: (Albanian—chicken with walnuts)

pullet: Young female chicken less than a year old.

pulpeta: (Spanish—slice of meat) Veal steak spread with a mixture of hard-boiled egg, garlic, olives, parsley, and sherry, browned in olive oil, and baked in a moderate oven.

pulse: Legume seeds such as beans and peas.

pultost: (Norwegian—desk cheese) Rennet type of sour-milk cheese.

pumpernickel: Sour bread made with unbolted rye flour to produce a dark color.

pumpkin: Gourd plant yielding a large orange-gold fruit; in France the pumpkin is used as a vegetable or made into a preserve, salad, or soup; in America its flesh is made into pie filling, and its seeds are salted and eaten as a snack.

pumpkin-pie spice: Fine-ground blend of cinnamon, clove, and ginger used in flavoring pumpkin pies, cookies, gingerbread, breakfast buns, and sweet-potato pies.

pumpkin seed: Seed of the pumpkin roasted and salted for eating.

punch: Party drink made with fruit juices, carbonated water, and ice; often sparkling wine and small pieces of fresh fruit are added.

punchbowl: Large bowl for mixing and serving punch, usually with matching cups and ladle; punchbowls are most commonly made of glass but sometimes of porcelain, silver, or fine plastic.

punch cup: Handled cup containing 4 to 5 ounces of liquid.

punch-type can opener: Utensil for punching wedge-shaped openings in can tops.

punsch: (Swedish—punch) Liqueur made of flavored and sweetened arrack, popular throughout Scandinavia.

purée: (French—thick soup) Thick paste, or smooth-textured sauce, or soup, made by forcing cooked ingredients through a sieve.

purpoo mulligatawny: (Hindi—lentil mulligatawny) Curry soup popular in Ceylon and India.

purslane: Herb of the portulaca family used as a potherb and salad vegetable, sometimes in soups and sauces.

pusher: Piece of bread or roll, or a broad-bladed hoe-shaped eating utensil with which a small child can push food onto a fork.

Pyrex: Trademarked name for heat-resistant glassware used in baking and cooking.

qt.: Abbreviation for quart.

quahog: Common hardshell clam of the Atlantic Coast; small quahogs are eaten on the half shell, large ones minced for use in seafood cocktails or chowders.

quaich: Two-handled drinking cup or porringer.

quaker bread: Twin loaves of bread baked in a double bread pan.

quantity cooking: Preparing food in amounts much larger than usually needed for a family meal; institution-type equipment and special recipes are required.

Quark: (German—curds)

quark: German type of white cottage cheese.

Quarkkäse: (German—cottage cheese)

Quarkkloss: (German—cottage-cheese dumpling)

quart: Liquid measure containing 2 pints, 4 cups, or 32 ounces.

quarter: One-fourth part of a meat carcass, including a leg—the forequarter or hindquarter; quarter alone usually means hindquarter.

quass: Kvass.

quassia bitters: Surinam bitters made from the bark, roots, and wood of the *Quassia amara* tree.

quatre quarts: (French—four-fourths) Pound cake consisting of equal parts of its four ingredients: butter, eggs, flour, sugar.

que aproveche: (Spanish—may you enjoy it) Good appetite.

queen conch: Helmet shellfish of tropical coasts; the flesh is used in chowders, seafood cocktails and stews, and the shell is used to make cameos.

queen olive: Large oblong Spanish olive with elongated pit, usually pickled while still green.

Queensland nut: Macadamia nut.

queen's ware: Cream-colored glazed wedgwood china.

queijadinha de amêndoas: (Portuguese—almond cheese cupcake)

queijo: (Portuguese—cheese)

queijo da ilha: (Portuguese—island cheese) Slightly firm cheese made in the Azores.

quenelle: (French—dumpling) Small ball of minced fish or meat mixed with eggs, used in sauces or garnish.

quenelle de veau: (French—veal quenelle) A dumpling of minced veal.

queso: (Spanish—cheese)

queso de bola: (Spanish—ball cheese) Dutch ball cheese such as edam.

queso de crema: (Spanish—cream cheese)

queso gallego: (Spanish—Galician cheese) Soft creamy cheese of a type made in the Spanish province of Galicia.

quetsch: Dry white Alsatian brandy made from fermented damson plums.

queue: (French—tail)

queue de boeuf: (French—oxtail)

queue de veau: (French—calf's tail)

quiche: Pastry shell filled with egg and cream or milk mixture, containing grated cheese and bits of fried bacon, baked and served hot, usually as an *hors d'oeuvre*.

quiche lorraine: Popular dish of Lorraine in northeastern France, usually served as an appetizer.

quick bread: Biscuits or muffins leavened with baking powder so they can be baked immediately without kneading, and will rise during baking.

quick freeze: Process of preserving food by rapid freezing which forms ice crystals too small to damage the cells; much of the natural color, flavor, and texture are retained by this process.

quick-lunch counter: Off-the-street diner where customers eat standing.

quick oven: Hot oven.

quignon: (French—chunk of bread)

quillet: Cakelike confection coated with an egg cream flavored with orgeat and vanilla.

quince: Small tree of the apple family yielding an astringent pear-shaped fruit used in preserves or liqueurs.

quince compote: Quinces cooked in vanilla syrup.

quince jelly: Jelly made from equal parts of quince juice and sugar.

quince water: Ratafia liqueur flavored with quince.

quinine water: Carbonated water containing quinine extract; used in preparation of many summer highballs.

quinnat: King salmon.

raab: Broccoli rab.

rabanada: (Portuguese—stroke of the tail) Fried bread dessert.

rábano: (Spanish—radish)

rabarbersuppe: (Danish—rhubarb soup)

rabbit: Edible rodent smaller than a hare, many varieties of which are considered good eating; rabbit is eaten stewed, roasted, boiled, and in many other ways.

racahout: Arabian beverage of acorns, spices, and sugar.

racine: (French—root; root vegetable)

rack: Rib section of meat, or the neck and forequarter, particularly of lamb or mutton.

raclette: Swiss dish of cheese melted over an open fire and eaten with boiled potatoes.

radicchio: (Italian—chicory; endive)

Radieschen: (German—radish)

radikia me ladi: (Greek—boiled dandelion greens)

radis: (French—radish)

radish: Pungent fleshy root vegetable eaten as a relish and in salads.

ragbröd: (Swedish—ryebread)

ragoût: (French—stew)

ragoût de mouton: (French—mutton stew)

Rahm: (German—cream)

raie: (French—ray)

raifort: (French—horseradish)

rainbow trout: Food and game fish of Pacific Coast streams.

Rainier: American beer brewed in Seattle, Washington.

raisin: (French—grape)

raisin: Sun-dried grapes of a special variety, eaten as a kind of fruit candy and widely used in baking, cooking, and salad making; raisin grapes are grown in southern California, Spain, Hungary, Greece, and the Middle East.

raisin biscuit: Baking-powder biscuit with raisins mixed into the dough before baking.

raisin sec: (French—dried grape) Raisin.

rakia: Yugoslavian brandy.

ram: Male sheep.

ramekin: Small individual lidless casserole; ramekin is also the name of a small pastry made with some kind of cream-cheese filling.

ramequin: (French—ramekin)

rampion: A plant native to Europe but also grown in other parts of the world which has an edible tuberous root and leaves that are used as salad greens.

r and r: Slang abbreviation for rock and rye.

range: Kitchen stove.

rangette: Small range, usually portable, with or without an oven.

rangiport: Cheese somewhat like port du salut, originating in Rangiport, a small town near Paris.

rangpur: Sour variety of mandarin orange.

rapa: (Italian—turnip)

rarebit: Welsh rabbit.

rasher: Thin slice of fried bacon or ham.

raspberry: Red, black, purple, or yellow fruit of a prickly shrub of the rose family, valued for its delicate flavor; raspberries are eaten raw or in cobblers, pies and preserves, with ices, puddings, etc.

raspberry vinegar: Sweetened vinegar flavored with raspberries, often served with Yorkshire pudding.

rassolni: (Russian—salted cucumber soup)

ratafia: Homemade liqueur made by infusing fruit or herb flavoring with brandy or liquor.

ratatouille: (French—a type of stew) Vegetable stew of eggplant, squash, tomato, and onion cooked in olive oil.

ration: Food allowance or portion, usually determined on a per diem basis.

ravanello: (Italian—radish)

rave: (French—root vegetable)

ravigote: (French—revive; cheer up) Highly seasoned white sauce served hot or cold; ravigote is also the name of a salad dressing of chopped green herbs, garlic, olive oil, and wine vinegar.

ravioli: Pasta pockets filled with seasoned savory mixtures and cooked in tomato sauce.

ravioli alla fiorentina: (Italian—ravioli in Florentine style) Cheese ravioli.

ravioli alla vegetariana: (Italian—ravioli in vegetarian style) Vegetable-stuffed ravioli in tomato sauce.

ray: Cartilaginous fishlike creature related to the shark and the skate; the pectoral fins or ray wings are esteemed by many gourmets who have them steamed and served with some kind of sauce such as burnt butter.

razorback: Wild pig, descendant of domestic pigs run wild; razorbacks are hunted in many parts of the South although their hams are much tougher than those of domestic swine.

reblochon: (French—creamy cheese)

réchaud: (French—reheater) Chafing dish or hot plate used by waiters to keep food warm or for preparing sauces or crêpe suzettes at the table.

recheio de castanha: (Portuguese—chestnut forcemeat) Poultry stuffing popular in Brazil as well as in Portugal.

recherché: (French—sought after; in great demand) Choice or rare.

Rechnung: (German—bill; check; reckoning)

recipe: Formula and instructions for preparing a food dish.

red bordeaux: Claret produced near Bordeaux in southwestern France.

red-cabbage casserole: Classic stew dish of red cabbage cooked with apple, onion, bacon, vinegar, and sometimes caraway seeds and red wine.

Red Delicious: Mildly tart bright-red apple.

red drum: Channel bass.

red grouper: Tasty food fish whose flesh reddens as the creature matures, taken by fishermen from the Virginia capes to the bulge of Brazil.

red gurnard: European saltwater food fish prepared like mullet; red gurnard is also the name of an Australian fish which is related to the European species.

red herring: Any herring cured with saltpeter to give its flesh a reddish color.

Red Malaga: Large purplish-red grape of a type first grown around Málaga in southern Spain.

red pepper: Capsicum pepper.

Red Pontiac: Red-skinned roundish white potato.

red snapper: Brightly colored food fish taken in the Atlantic from Long Island to Brazil.

red table wine: Red burgundies, cabernets, chiantis, clarets, rosés, etc., served with cheeses, chops, game, and all dark or red meats.

reduce: To boil down—to cook until food or mixture becomes concentrated or otherwise diminished.

reflector oven: Oven whose dry heat is intensified by reflection from the inner metal surfaces; most standard home ovens employ the reflected-heat principle, as do portable units designed for use on the beach or in the desert where the cooking is done by reflected sunlight.

refresco: (Spanish—refreshment) Cold drink.

refrigerator: Home appliance, operated electrically or by gas, for preserving perishable foods at temperatures near freezing; most modern refrigerators contain freezer compartments for frozen foods and ice cubes, crispers for fresh vegetables, storage racks, etc.

refrigerator bag: Plastic bag for storing salad greens and other foods; keeps food moist and prevents it from picking up or giving off offensive odors.

refrigerator dish: Covered bowl or other container made specifically for storing food in the refrigerator.

Reh: (German—roe; venison)

rehoboam: Wine bottle containing five to six quarts.

reindeer cheese: Reindeer-milk cheese of the rennet type made in Finland, Norway, and Sweden where reindeer herds are tended and milked just as cows are milked in other lands.

reine: (French—queen) French variety of chicken hence a term applied to sauces, purées, and soups made with cut-up chicken.

reine Claude: (French—Queen Claudette) Greengage plum.

reinsdyrstek: (Norwegian—reindeer roast)

Reis: (German—rice)

rekening: (Dutch—bill; check; reckoning)

relish: Condiment used as a side dish to add zest to a meal; relishes are made in many ways, usually of chopped vegetables or fruits pickled or uncooked.

relleno: (Spanish—filled; stuffed)

relyenong hipon: Philippine-style stuffed shrimp.

remoulade: (French—remolded) Mayonnaise enriched with anchovy paste, capers, gherkins, chopped herbs, and mustard.

rendan santan: (Malay—chicken or meat dish flavored with coconut and ginger)

render: To clarify fat by melting it, or to melt the solid fat away from the surrounding meat tissues.

rennet: Substance composing the lining membrane of the fourth stomach of calves, used in curdling milk for cheese making; most cheeses are started with rennet.

repollo: (Spanish—cabbage)

restaurant: (French—restorative) Public eating place—a word that means the same thing in many languages, including the Scandinavian and Germanic ones.

restaurante: (Portuguese or Spanish—restaurant)

restaurateur: Operator or owner of a restaurant.

restauratiewagen: (Dutch—dining car)

restauratvagn: (Swedish—dining car)

restoran: (Russian—restaurant)

restoran: (Turkish—restaurant)

restorán: (American-Spanish—restaurant)

resutóran: (Japanese—foreign-style restaurant)

rotoo toozta: (Hungarian—plain cake) Strudel.

Rettich: (German—radish)

Rheingold: American beer brewed in Brooklyn, New York.

Rhenish: Pertaining to the Rhine River valley and its wines.

rhine wines: Light dry dinner wines of a type vinted in Germany's Rhineland; rhine wines are served with fish, fowl, and seafood courses.

Rhode Island Greening: Green or yellow cooking apple.

Rhode Island Red: American breed of domestic poultry, valued for its meat and as a good layer, and characterized by its handsome brownish-red plumage.

rhubarb: Coarse herb of the buckwheat family, whose succulent stalks are used in pies, marmalades, stews, sherbets, and preserves.

rhubarbe: (French—rhubarb)

rhum: (French—rum)

ribaude: (French—slut; debauchee) Baked apple dumpling.

rib-eye steak: Choice steak cut from prime ribs of beef.

Ribier: Large black grape of a type originally developed in France.

riblette: (French—rasher; collop)

rib roast: Roast of beef cut from the outer side of the ribs and usually cooked with the ribs attached.

ribs: Contraction for spareribs.

rice: Cereal grass cultivated in well-irrigated tropical and subtropical areas; in many lands it is the staple, often the only food, and is eaten rough; for others it is parboiled to preserve its nutritive qualities, and then is husked and polished by machine, cooked in boiling water or steamed.

rice: To force, usually a purée, through a perforated utensil.

rice boiler: Double boiler.

rice flour: Flour milled from rice, usually made from the broken kernels left after husking and polishing.

rice milk: Rice and milk gruel or porridge.

ricer: Utensil for ricing cooked vegetables and fruits by forcing them through a perforated container; it is called a ricer because the pressed food resembles strings a rice grain in diameter.

rice water: Beverage made by boiling rice in water and adding lime juice flavoring and brown sugar; plain rice water is often served to infants and invalids.

ricotta: Italian sheep's-milk curd cheese used by cooks and confectioners.

ridge grill: Ridged solid-aluminum pan provided with a heatproof handle, for grilling fish or meat without using charcoal; it can be used over a range top, in an open fireplace, or over a campfire.

rieska: (Finnish—flat bread) In western Finland: flat rye bread made without yeast; in eastern Finland *rieska* is also a casserole.

riesling: White wine made from riesling grapes, originally vinted along the Rhine but now produced in places as remote as California and Chile.

rigatoni: (Italian—little stripes) Ribbed or fluted pasta.

rijsttafel: (Dutch—rice table) Meal built around a mound of rice garnished with condiments and curried bits of chicken, seafood, vegetables, etc.

Rinderbraten: (German—roast beef)

Rindfleisch: (German—beef)

Rindfleisch mit Ananas und Kirschen: (German—beef with pineapple and cherries)

ring mold: Ring-shaped food mold of glass, plastic, or metal.

Rinnen: (German—furrows; grooves) Caraway-seed and sour-milk cheese of a type originally made in Pomerania.

riñón: (Spanish—kidney)

ripe olive: Black olive preserved in a can in salt brine or in a wooden cask where it is semi-dry except for some oil and salt, which keeps olives from mildewing.

ris: (Danish, Norwegian and Swedish—rice; French—sweetbread)

ris de veau: (French—calf sweetbread)

rishtaya: Syrian lamb, lentil, and noodle dish.

risi e bisi: (Italian—rice and beans)

riskrem: (Norwegian—rice cream) Dessert made of boiled rice, whipped cream, blanched almonds, vanilla, and sugar.

riso: (Italian—rice)

rissole: (French—turnover) Pastry filled with a savory mixture and either fried in deep fat or baked.

rissolette: Small rissole.

risotto: (Italian—rice dish) Rice cooked in meat broth and then flavored in various ways, according to different recipes.

ristorante: (Italian—restaurant)

riz: (French—rice)

riz au lait: (French—rice with milk) Variety of rice pudding.

roast: To cook something, usually in an oven or a dutch oven, in its own juices.

roaster chicken: Chicken 5 to 9 months old, weighing more than 3½ pounds, and tender enough for roasting.

roasting jack: Electric-powered or hand-driven device for turning a roasting spit.

roasting pan: Enamel or metal pan for roasting food in an oven, usually supplied with a lid although this is often not used.

roasting rack: Wire rack placed inside a roasting pan to support the roast above its drippings.

roast slicer: Sharp-bladed knife for carving poultry and meats.

róbalo: (Spanish—haddock)

robust herbs: Strong-flavored herbs such as dill, mint, sage, and savory, often mixed with fine herbs to dilute their strength.

rock and rye: Mixture of rock candy and rye-whiskey, often served with lemon or lime.

rock cake: Hard cookie made with nuts, dried fruits, and spices.

rock cod: Name applied to various types of fish including the rockfish, any of several species of groupers, and a cod which is a variety of the true cod.

rockfish: Name applied to many different species of fishes, including the striped bass, the Caribbean groupers, the killifish, and to a rock dweller found along the Pacific Coast.

rockfish muddle: North Carolinian fish stew made of rockfish, salt pork, butter, beaten eggs, soda crackers, onions, and tomatoes.

rødgrød med fløde: (Danish—red compote with cream) Summer dessert consisting of berry juices thickened with potato flour and served with cream and sugar.

rødkal: (Danish—red cabbage)

roe: Fish or seafood eggs; processed sturgeon roe is called caviar; lobster roe, or coral, is used in making certain fine sauces; shad roe is considered one of America's finest dishes.

rognon: (French—kidney)

Rohkostplatte: (German—raw-food plate) Vegetable plate or vegetable salad.

rökt al: (Swedish—smoked eel)

roll: Small yeast bread usually prepared in some fancy or special form; butterfly roll, butterhorn, braided, or hard roll, etc.

roll cheese: English rennet cheese made of whole milk of cows and molded in nine-inch cylindrical rolls.

rolled oats: Husked oat kernels flattened with heated rollers; rolling breaks down the kernel so that it can be cooked into oatmeal or baked into cakes and cookies.

rolling pin: Wooden roller with handles, used for flattening dough; some modern rolling pins have a hollow cylinder, which may be filled with ice if dough is to be kept chilled.

rollmop: Boned herring marinated in white wine, stuffed with onion, salted cucumber, and spices, and rolled up.

rolpens: (Dutch—roll paunch) Minced beef and tripe served with fried apples.

roly-poly: Sheet of biscuit dough spread with jam, and rolled up like a jelly roll before it is baked.

romaine: Long-leaved cos lettuce.

romano: (Italian—Roman) Type of cheese used for cooking and seasoning salads and soups.

rombo: (Italian—turbot)

Rome Beauty: Long-keeping reddish-yellow cooking apple developed near Rome, New York.

ron: (Spanish—rum)

room: (Dutch—cream)

roomijs: (Dutch—ice cream)

root beer: Carbonated soft drink containing root extracts and sweetening.

rootie: (Hindi and Malay—bread)

root vegetable: Carrot, parsnip, radish, turnip, or other plant whose roots are the chief portion eaten.

roquefort: Soft, spicy, pungent cheese with bluish-green marbling; French roquefort is always made from sheep's milk, whereas American roqueforts are of cow's milk.

rosbif: (French, Italian, and Spanish—roast beef)

rosé aux fruits: (French—fruit-style pink) Pink dessert wine imported from France.

rosefish: A large saltwater food fish found along the northern coasts of the U.S. and Europe; the mature rosefish is a bright rose red or orange red, hence the name.

rose hip: Rose-seed capsule used in making jellies and in flavoring exotic ice creams and sherbets.

rosemary: Aromatic evergreen shrub of the mint family, whose leaves are used for flavoring preserves, sweet pickles, sauces, cuts of meat, and stews.

rosemary wine: Wine made from rosemary flowers and leaves.

Rosenkohl: (German—brussels sprouts)

rose syrup: Oriental concoction of rose coloring and rose flavoring, used in flavoring puddings, iced drinks and sherbets.

rosette: Sugar-coated fried cake or waffle made in a rosette-shaped iron.

rosette iron: Long-handled baking iron shaped like a rosette; it works like a waffle iron but is much smaller and not electrified.

Rosine: (German—raisin)

rostbiff: (Swedish—roast beef)

Rostbraten: (German—pot roast)

Röstkartoffeln: (German—home-fried potatoes)

rotary beater: Egg beater or electrical mixer; interlocking open-bladed or open-wired cages revolve in opposite directions, as they are turned by a crank or by the motor.

Röte Rübe: (German—red turnip; beet)

rôti: (French—roasted)

rôtisserie: (French—cookshop) In France, a restaurant specializing in barbecues and roasts; in the United States, a charcoal, electric, or gas-fired barbecuing device with a turning spit.

Rotkohl: (German—red cabbage)

Rotkraut: (German—red cabbage)

Rotwein: (German—red wine)

Rouennaise: (French—in the manner of Rouen)

rouget: (French—red mullet)

roulade: (French—something rolled up) Slice of meat, covered with forcemeat or other savory filling, rolled up, and cooked.

round: Meat cut from the center of the hind shank of a meat animal.

round bone: Hip bone, often used in stewing or in stock making.

round clam: Hard-shell clam.

roundfish: Round whitefish of the Great Lakes; the term roundfish is also applied to all other fishes other than flatfish.

round potato: Irish potato.

round radish: Turnip radish.

round steak: Beef cut from the hind round; the inside portion is called top round, the outside is called bottom round; round steak is usually ground for use in hamburgers or forcemeat.

roux: (French—reddish-brown; rust) Mixture of butter and flour used in thickening sauces and soups; brown *roux* is made by browning the mixture in the pan; white *roux* is not browned.

royal fizz: Carbonated gin fizz made with eggs, gin, and soda water.

royal macadamia: Hawaiian-grown macadamia nut.

Royal Worcester: Fine English china or porcelain made in Worcestershire, England, since the 18th century and called Royal by virtue of royal warrant.

royan: (French—large sardine)

røyktlaks: (Norwegian—smoked salmon)

rsvp: Abbreviation for *répondez, s'il vous plaît* (French—please reply) which often appears on formal invitations—a request that the invitee let his host know whether or not he accepts.

ruby port: Blend of young port wines with older vintages; unlike tawny port, ruby port is aged only partly in the cask, continuing to improve when bottled.

rue: Strong-scented woody herb whose bitter leaves are finely chopped and used sparingly in salads and stews.

rugbrød: (Danish—ryebread)

Rührei: (German—scrambled egg)

rum: Alcoholic beverage distilled from molasses or other sugar-cane residue, chiefly in the Caribbean area; the flavor of a particular rum varies according to the country or even the island of origin; rum is used in many cocktails and is a popular flavoring in baking and candy making.

rum an': Slang for rum and Coca-Cola.

rum and Coke: Highball of rum and Coca-Cola.

rum baba: Cake made of sweet yeast dough and soaked in rum sauce, sometimes served with whipped cream.

rum ball: Confection consisting of cocoa powder, corn syrup, crushed graham crackers or vanilla wafers, powdered sugar, and rum.

rum collins: Tom collins containing rum instead of the usual gin.

rum crustas: Iced rum served in a glass lined with lemon or lime peel.

rumnog: Slang for an eggnog flavored with rum.

rump: Cut of meat taken from the back of the sirloin of a meat animal.

rump roast: Roast cut from beef rump.

rum rickey: Highball of carbonated water, lime juice, and rum.

rum toddy: Toddy made with rum.

runcible spoon: Not a spoon but a fork with three broad curved prongs, used for serving appetizers; the name was coined by Edward Lear in his nonsense verse "The Owl and the Pussycat."

Ruppert: American beer brewed in New York City.

rusk: Slice of baked bread that is dried and rebaked in an oven until it is golden brown; zwieback is a rusk.

russet: Brown-mottled green eating apple.

Russet Burbank: Fine white potato named in honor of its producer, Luther Burbank.

russian dressing: Salad dressing made of mayonnaise, chili sauce, and some sharp ingredient such as horseradish, pickle, relish, or barbecue sauce; sometimes caviar, hard-boiled eggs, pimientos, and onions are added.

Russian service: Method of serving a meal in which the food is prepared and cut in the kitchen, then presented on silver or stainless-steel platters by the waiter who approaches from the left and serves counterclockwise around the table.

russian turnip: Rutabaga.

russian walnut: English walnut.

russinkaka: (Swedish—raisin cake)

rutabaga: Large yellow turnip.

rutmus: Mashed potatoes and turnips seasoned to taste and served with hot butter sauce.

℞: Ancient symbol for recipe, now used exclusively in pharmaceutical prescriptions.

rye: Cereal grass cultivated as a food grain in many northern countries, the main ingredient of most black breads and pumpernickels; in the United States it is distilled into rye whiskey.

rye and indian: Slang for bread of rye flour and Indian cornmeal, a favorite of many early American settlers.

ryebread: Bread made with rye flour; ryebreads include most blackbreads, *knäckebröd,* pumpernickel, rye crackers, and caraway-flavored ryebreads.

rye whiskey: Straight whiskey made from rye grain or a blended whiskey in which rye grain predominates.

ryoríya: (Japanese—Japanese-style restaurant)

sabayon: (French—zabaglione)

saccharin: Calorie-free sweetener several hundred times sweeter than sugar but with no food value whatsoever; saccharin is an antiseptic white crystalline compound manufactured from coal tar, widely used as a sugar substitute by diabetics, dieters, and people who prefer its flavor to that of sugar.

Sachertorte: (German—Sacher cake) Rich pastry filled with preserves and topped with chocolate icing; *Sachertorte* is said to have been invented by the Sacher family, Viennese hotel and restaurant owners, and it has been the subject of a famed Austrian lawsuit.

sack: English term for any strong white wine.

saddle: Upper back portion of a meat carcass, including both loins, or the lower back and hind legs of poultry and frogs.

safflower: Herb of the thistle family, whose seeds yield a cooking oil; drugs and dyes are also manufactured from the florets of the safflower.

saffron: Yellowish substance obtained from a species of crocus and used in many East Indian curries and rice dishes, as a flavoring and coloring agent; it takes some 8,000 blooms to produce 3 ounces of saffron, so saffron is one of the most expensive of seasonings.

sage: A shrublike mint with grayish-green pungent and aromatic leaves which are widely used for seasoning.

sago: Starchy substance obtained from the pith of the sago palm, used to thicken puddings and soups; formerly sago was as much a dietary staple in the Moluccas, Indonesia, as rice is in mainland Asia.

sago pudding: Easy-to-digest pudding made of eggs, milk, and sago starch.

sagou: (French—sago)

saguin: Philippine banana.

Sahne: (German—cream)

saignant: (French—bloody; underdone)

Saint-Germain: (French) Term applied to various kinds of thick pea soup.

sake: Japanese alcoholic beverage derived from rice; sake is usually served warm.

sal: (Spanish—salt)

salad: Cold dish garnished with a dressing of some kind; green vegetables are the usual basic ingredients of a salad, but the variations are endless: meat, fish, cheese, potatoes, poultry, macaroni, etc.

salad basket: Wire or plastic collapsible basket for holding salad leaves while they are rinsed and drained.

sala da pranzo: (Italian—dining room)

salad bowl: Large bowl of china, glass, plastic, porcelain, or wood for mixing salads; salad bowls come in a variety of shapes, sizes and styles, and are usually paired with matching fork-and-spoon sets; small salad bowls for individual servings are also common.

salad dressing: Cold sauce used in salads: mayonnaise, French, Italian, roquefort, etc.

salade: (French—salad)

sala de jantar: (Portuguese—dining room)

salade de laitue: (French—lettuce salad)

salade niçoise: (French—salad in the style of Nice) Mixture of potatoes, string beans, tomatoes, anchovy fillets, capers, and olives.

salade variée: (French—mixed salad)

salad fork: Small flat-tined fork for eating salad or a large serving fork, usually part of a fork-and-spoon set for tossing salads.

salad oil: Any oil except olive oil used in dressing a salad: corn, peanut, safflower, etc.

salad plate: Small dish for serving an individual portion of salad.

salad soup: Gazpacho.

salamana: Italian sheep's milk cheese spread sometimes cooked with cornmeal.

salamander: Chef's utensil for browning and glazing cooked foods; some are rods and some are rods with disks set crosswise at the tip like ski poles; they are heated and passed close to cooked foods for browning; the name comes from an old superstition that a salamander could live in fire.

salame: (Italian—salami)

salami: Spicy Italian sausage made with meat, garlic, capers, and other seasonings; hard salami, which is air-dried, will keep without refrigeration, but fresh or soft salami must be kept chilled.

Salat: (German—salad)

salata: (Greek—salad)

salçali köfte: (Turkish—beef balls in tomato sauce)

salchicha: (Spanish—small sausage)

salchichón: (Spanish—large sausage)

salcochado: (Spanish—boiled)

sale: (Italian—salt)

saleratus: Baking soda.

salisbury steak: Hamburger of top-grade beef, served as an entree.

salle à manger: (French—dining room)

sally lunn: Yeast-raised English semisweet tea cake, named for the woman who once sold them in Bath, England.

Salm: (German—salmon)

salmagundi: Exotic hash or unusual mixture of foods, including leftovers.

salmi: Dish of game made by first roasting the flesh, then stewing it, sometimes in wine.

salmis: (French—salmi)

salmon: Food fish prized for its tasty reddish meat, prepared in many ways, including baking, broiling, stewing, and cold in salads; canned salmon is very popular and sold in all food markets.

salmón: (Spanish—salmon)

salmon paste: Smoked salmon reduced to a spreadable paste for making canapés and other appetizers.

salo: (Russian—salt pork)

salon teh: (Malay—tea room)

salonu nerede: (Turkish—dining room)

salpicon: (French—a rich croquette mixture)

salsa: (Italian and Spanish—sauce)

salsa picante: (Spanish—highly seasoned sauce)

salsiccia: (Italian—spiced sausage)

salsifis: (French—salsify)

salsify: A European plant with an edible turniplike root, the flavor of which suggests oyster.

salt: Sodium chloride, a mineral produced by the evaporation of seawater or the mining of underground deposits; salt is an essential seasoning in nearly all recipes and is present in all bodily fluids; rock salt is used in freezing ice creams and sherbets.

salt butter: Salted butter; salt was originally added to butter as a preservative, but today many people prefer the flavor of salted butter to that of fresh.

salt cellar: Container, usually decorative, for holding salt at the table; small scoop is provided for sprinkling on food; salt cellars are not to be confused with salt shakers.

salted nuts: Edible nuts of any kind baked in a pan with butter or oil and sprinkled with salt.

saltimbocca: (Italian—veal and ham wrapped together and braised with anchovies)

salt of soda: Sodium bicarbonate.

saltpeter: Nitric acid and potassium salt used in curing hams.

salt pork: Fat portion of a pork carcass cured in brine, used to moisten and flavor vegetables, meats, and many other dishes.

salt-rising bread: Bread prepared with dough leavened with a fermented mixture of flour, salted milk, soda, and sugar.

salt shaker: Perforated container for holding and sprinkling salt; some are decorative and made of glass, wood, metal, etc.

salt spoon: Small spoon, sometimes perforated, used for serving salt from a salt cellar.

saltwater taffy: Pulled taffy made of boiled-down white sugar or molasses with added flavors, individually wrapped and sold as a candy confection—a specialty of many seaside resorts.

salud, pesetas, y amor: (Spanish—health, wealth, and love) A toast often followed by *y tiempo para gozarlos* (and time to enjoy them).

salute: (Italian—health) A toast.

salver: Tray for serving beverages and food.

Salz: (German—salt)

Salzgurke: (German—pickled cucumber)

Salzkartoffel: (German—salt potato) Boiled potato.

Salzstange: (German—salt stick) Vienna-style poppyseed roll sprinkled with rock salt.

sambal: Indonesian-style curry sauce made with peppers and spices.

sambal goreng: Indonesian green pepper and shrimp dish served with sautéed onions.

samovar: Russian utensil for preparing tea; a samovar is a large urnlike vessel with a central tube for live charcoal, and equipped with a spigot for drawing off the boiling water; samovars are made of brass, copper, or silver, and are often the family's most prized possession.

sancocho: (Spanish—half-cooked meal) Latin-American souplike stew containing fish, fowl, meat, seafood, vegetables, and spices.

sand dab: Name for any of several flatfish such as the rusty dab of the Atlantic coast and several species of small food fishes of the Pacific coast; sand dabs are usually dipped in cornmeal before frying, or pickled in salt brine, onion rings, and vinegar.

sandía: (Spanish—watermelon)

sandwich: Sweet or savory filling between two slices of bread; food spread on only one slice of bread is called an open-face sandwich.

sandwich glass: Pressed glass made at Sandwich, Massachusetts, in the 19th century.

sandwich knife: Long-bladed knife for cutting and slicing through filled or open sandwiches.

sandwich skillet: Square-egg skillet.

sandwich spreader: Wide-bladed spatula strong enough to cut cheeses, sandwiches, and vegetables with its serrated edge, yet flexible enough to frost cakes and apply sandwich spreads.

sandwich tray: Ceramic, glass, or metallic tray for serving sandwiches, canapés, cookies, etc.

sangría: (Spanish—bleeding) Spanish summertime beverage, bloodlike in color, made of red wine, lemon juice, and sweetening usually served in a pitcher containing crushed or cubed ice.

Sanka: Brand name for a caffeine-free coffee.

santé: (French—health) A toast.

sanwiche: (Mexican-Spanish—sandwich)

sapodilla: Tropical American tree yielding a sweet brown-fleshed fruit called a sapodilla plum.

sapsago: Unripened greenish American cheese thought to be patterned after its German counterpart *Schabzeiger.*

saratoga chips: Potato chips first made at Saratoga Springs, New York.

saratoga water: Any of several mineral waters bottled at their source in Saratoga Springs, New York.

sarawak pepper: White pepper from Sarawak on the island of Borneo.

sardina: (Italian and Spanish—sardine)

sardine: Young pilchard taken from the Mediterranean, especially near the island of Sardinia; closely related species are also fished from the Atlantic and Pacific Oceans; nearly all sardines are canned and preserved in some kind of oil or sauce, and are popular in canapés, sandwiches, and snacks.

sardinha: (Portuguese—sardine)

sarma le umplute: (Roumanian—stuffed cabbage)

sarriette: (French—the herb savory)

sarsaparilla: Tropical American plant of the cat-brier family; the dried roots yield an extract used in making a carbonated soft drink.

sas: Abbreviation for sodium aluminum sulfate, a baking powder ingredient.

sassafras: Dried root bark of the North American sassafras tree, used as a flavoring extract in soft drinks, candies, meats, soups, and aromatic bitters.

sate: Indonesian dish consisting of meat skewered on bamboo splints.

satsuma: Variety of mandarin orange grown in Florida and Alabama.

sauce: (French—gravy; sauce)

sauce: Semiliquid solution of condimentlike ingredients for garnishing and flavoring foods; many people believe sauces are the heart of fine cooking, and hence there are countless recipes for sweet and savory sauces.

sauce-alone: Garlic mustard.

sauce béarnaise: (French—Béarn-style sauce) Butter sauce filled with egg yolks, chopped onions, and vinegar.

sauce béchamel: (French—Béchamel sauce) White cream sauce named for Marquis Louis de Béchamel, 17th-century courtier.

sauce boat: Gravy boat.

sauce bordelaise: (French—Bordeaux-style sauce) Brown sauce flavored with bordeaux wine.

sauce bretonne: (French—sauce in the Breton manner) Sauce made of consommé, *sauce espagnole,* and slightly browned fried red onions.

sauce dish: Small shallow dish for serving stewed fruit.

saucepan: Small cooking vessel used for boiling and stewing.

saucer: Small concave dish designed to hold and catch the runover from a matching cup.

sauce suprême: (French—supreme sauce) Rich white sauce made from poultry stock and cream.

sauce tureen: Covered sauce boat, sometimes paired with a matching ladle.

saucière: (French—sauce boat)

saucisse: (French—small sausage)

saucisson: (French—large sausage)

saucisson de bologne: (French—bologna)

saúde e gozo: (Portuguese—health and happiness) A toast.

sauerbraten: (German—sour roast) Beef marinated in vinegar, water, garlic and other seasoning for several days, then braised like pot roast.

sauerkraut: Finely shredded cabbage fermented in its own juice; sauerkraut is traditionally served with hot dogs, mashed potatoes, and pig's feet or pig's knuckles.

saumon: (French—salmon)

saus: (Norwegian—sauce)

sausage: Mixture of minced and seasoned meats, packed into a prepared casing — usually an animal intestine or artificial casing—then preserved by pickling, smoking, or other means; popular sausages include bo-

logna, frankfurters or hot dogs, liverwurst, and salami.

sausage beef: Cutter beef.

sausageburger: Hamburger made of sausage meat.

sauté: To cook or lightly fry food rapidly in small amount of shortening, turning or stirring frequently.

sauterne: White wine originating near the town of Sauternes in the Bordeaux region of southwestern France.

sautoir: (French—sauté pan)

savarin: Sweetened egg bread baked in a ring mold and moistened with rum before serving.

saveloy: Sausage made of pork brains, spiced and dried; another name for it is cervelat.

savory: Aromatic herb of the mint family; the leaves are used in seasoning appetizers, sauces, roasts, and stuffings, etc.; savory is also an English term for a light dish following dessert.

savoy finger: Ladyfinger.

sayadiah: (Lebanese—fish and rice dish)

sazerac: Cocktail made of bourbon, Pernod, sugar, and angostura bitters.

scaillín: Irish beverage made of butter, sugar, hot milk, and whiskey heated together.

scald: To heat liquids below the boiling point as in scalding milk; scald also means to immerse food briefly in boiling water to loosen skins, peels, etc., from fruit and vegetables.

scale: Balance for weighing items; culinary scales include kitchen spring scales, even the bathroom scale if large weights are involved.

scallion: Young onion pulled before its bulb has enlarged, usually eaten raw; scallion can also refer to a shallot or a leek.

scallop: Bivalve mollusk found in shallow seas and along sea beaches; only the muscle hinge is eaten—usually fried, sautéed, deviled, or included in seafood cocktails; the finest scallops are said to be those fished from Peconic Bay off the eastern end of Long Island.

scallop: To bake in a sauce topped with bread or cracker crumbs.

scaloppina: (Italian—collop)

scampo: (Italian—prawn; large shrimp)

scarlet runner bean: Tropical high-climbing bean popular in the British Isles.

scarole: (French—escarole)

Schabzeiger Käse: (German— scraped whey cheese) Hard greenish cheese used in cooking and somewhat like sapsago, its American counterpart.

Schaumtorte: (German—foam tart) Pastry consisting of layers of fruit placed between layers of baked meringue.

schav borsht: (Russian—sorrel soup) Cold summer soup made of sour-grass sorrel, egg yolks, onions, and sour cream.

Schellfisch: (German—haddock)

Schinken: (German—ham)

Schinkenbrot: (German—ham sandwich)

Schlagsahne: (German—whipped cream)

Schlitz: American beer brewed in Milwaukee, Wisconsin.

Schlosskäse: (German—castle cheese) Pungent cheese somewhat like camembert or its American equivalent, liederkranz.

Schmalz: (German—melted fat; drippings)

Schmalz Hering: (German—fat herring)

Schmierkäse: (German—soft cheese) To Germans, any soft cheese; to Pennsylvania-Germans, cottage cheese.

schmierwurst: (German—soft sausage) Easy-to-spread sausage.

Schnapps: (German—alcoholic drink) Brandy, gin, or some other flavored ethyl alcohol.

Schnitzel: (German—cutlet)

schnitz und gnepp: (Pennsylvania-German—apples and buttons) Mixture of dried apples, dumplings, and ham cooked together.

Schokolade: (German—chocolate)

schooner: Large beer goblet.

Schwarzbrod: (German—black bread) Dark-brown rye bread.

Schwarzbrot mit Butter: (German —rye bread and butter)

schwarzer Kaffee: (German— black coffee)

Schwein: (German—pig; pork; swine)

Schweinebraten: (German—roast pork)

scone: Leavened flat Scots hot bread made of oatmeal, barley, or other meal, and baked on a griddle.

scoop: Small deep-sided shovel of plastic, metal, or wood, for scooping up coffee, flour, salt, sugar, and other powdered substances.

score: To cut narrow gashes on the surface of foods; meat is scored to keep it from curling during cooking; pastry covers are scored to release steam from the filling; and so on.

scotch broth: Rich soup made of beef or mutton and vegetables, thickened with barley.

scotch hands: Pair of scored wooden paddles for knurling and shaping balls of butter.

scotch mist: Cocktail made of scotch whisky served with a lemon twist.

scotch oatmeal: Unrefined ground oats for making cookies, porridge, Scots oatcakes, and scones.

Scotch whisky: Malt-and-grain whiskey distilled in Scotland.

scotch woodcock: Eggs served on toast with anchovies.

scrambled eggs: Whole eggs seasoned, beaten, diluted with water or milk, and sautéed in a frying pan, the mixture being stirred, or scrambled, constantly while cooking.

scraper: Pliable spatula of plastic or rubber for scraping bowls and plates clean before washing.

scrapple: Bricklike food combination composed of bits of pork cooked up with cornmeal and herbs; scrapple, supposedly a Philadelphia specialty, is usually sliced and baked or fried for breakfast.

scratchin's: Slang for cracklings.

screwdriver: Highball consisting of vodka and orange juice.

scrod: Young fish, usually a cod.

scullery: Old term for a storage area for culinary utensils or an area adjacent to the kitchen where the cleaning, polishing, and scouring was performed.

scuppernong: Yellow-green American grape developed from the muscadine and yielding a popular homemade wine.

sea bass: Large perchlike food fish, of which there are many varieties, both freshwater and marine; groupers, hinds, white and yellow freshwater bass, and many perch all belong to this important group of food and game fish.

sea bread: Hardtack.

sea clam: Surf clam.

sea cole: Sea kale.

sea ear: Abalone.

seafoam: Candy made with brown sugar and white of egg.

seafood bar: Counter or restaurant specializing in seafood.

seafood cocktail: Cold dish of crab, lobster, shrimp, or mixed seafood, served with catsup or other sauce as an appetizer course.

seafood fork: Small three-tined fork for picking crab or lobster meat from its shell, for eating clams or oysters, or for eating seafood cocktails.

sea kale: A European herb, the large oval leaves of which are sometimes used as a potherb.

sea lettuce: Any of several varieties of green seaweed; used in soups and stews, and in many Japanese recipes.

sear: To brown the surface of meat, using a high heat so it will retain its juices throughout a later, slower process of cooking, usually roasting.

seasoning: Condiment, spice, herb, salt, or anything added to improve the flavor a dish.

seawater: Brine; some recipes call for boiling food in seawater, but if this cannot be obtained, it may be simulated by mixing 95 parts of water with 5 parts of common salt.

sec: (French—dry) Lacking in sweetness, usually applied to tart wines.

sèche: (French—cuttlefish)

Seckel: Small yellowish-brown pear named for the Pennsylvania horticulturist who first developed it.

seconds: Slang for second helpings of drinks or food.

sedani alla Parmigiana: (Italian— celery in the manner of Parma)

sedano: (Italian—celery)

Seezunge: (German—sea tongue) Sole fish.

sel: (French—salt)

Sellerie: (German—celery)

seltzer: Carbonated mineral water named for the spa from which it was originally drawn, Nieder Selters, in the Rhineland.

semillon: White wine grape originating in Semillon in the Bordeaux region, southwestern France.

semolina: Purified middlings of hard, or durum, wheat, used in making alimentary pastes such as macaroni, noodles, and spaghetti, as well as for thickening gravies, sauces, and soups.

senape: (Italian—mustard)

Senf: (German—mustard)

Sercial: Fine dry madeira wine served as an apéritif.

server: Any utensil or implement used for serving: tray, serving spoon or fork, tongs, etc.

serviette: (French—napkin)

sesame: East Indian herb whose seeds are used in decoration and flavoring on or in breads, buns, and cookies.

sesame oil: Oil expressed from sesame seeds and used in cooking and in salads.

seta: (Spanish—mushroom)

seviche: (Ecuadorean- and Peruvian-Spanish—fish cooked in citrus juice)

sfogliata: (Italian—foil) Thin flaky pastry.

sg: Abbreviation for *selon grandeur* (French—according to size), menu term meaning an item is priced according to its size.

sgombro: (Italian—mackerel)

shad: Saltwater fish taken as it swims up coastal rivers to spawn; the roe is especially delicious, and the shad's delicately flavored flesh is served baked, broiled, or stewed.

shadbush: Name applied to several North American trees and shrubs which comprise the genus *Amelanchier* and have an edible red or purple fruit; shadbush is also called juneberry.

shaddock: Pear-shaped citrus fruit, somewhat similar to a grapefruit but of coarser, drier flesh; shaddocks are named for a Captain Shaddock who first brought this fruit to the Western Hemisphere in 1696.

shaker: Lidded container for mixing and dispensing certain foods or liquids: salt shaker, cocktail shaker, etc.

shallot: Onionlike herb of the lily family, whose root forms small clusters of bulbs; shallot bulbs have a delicate flavoring, which is used in salads, soups, sauces, and many other flavored dishes.

shandygaff: Mixture of beer and ginger beer in equal parts.

shank: Upper part of the foreleg of a meat animal; the same cut from the hindleg is called the hind shank.

Shashlik: (Russian—skewered lamb or mutton)

shchi: (Russian—sauerkraut soup)

sheep: Bovine mammal domesticated many thousands of years ago for its wool, its meat, its milk used in cheese making, and its hide.

sheepshead: Large striped fish taken along the Atlantic and Gulf coasts of the United States; sheepshead is also a name for the black drum of West Indian waters, and the dollarfish.

sheffield: Silver-plated flatware of the kind made in Sheffield, Yorkshire, England.

shell bean: Bean shelled before eating: kidney, lima, mung, etc.

sheller: Nutchacker, or a commercial machine for shelling nuts.

shepherd's pie: Leftover meat baked with a mashed-potato crust.

sherbet: Iced dessert made of a flavored water-ice, gelatin, and beaten egg whites; sherbets are flavored in many ways, berry and citrus fruit flavors being the most popular.

sherbet cup: Footed glass cup for serving sherbets and other desserts.

sherry: Dry fortified wine of a type originally produced in Jerez de la Frontera in Spain.

sherry cobbler: Mixed drink of sherry wine, brandy, curaçao, and a slice of orange.

sherry glass: Footed wine glass holding 2 to 2½ ounces of liquid.

ship's biscuit: Hardtack.

ship's galley: Kitchen aboard a ship.

shirr: To bake (opened) eggs in a cream-filled pan; sometimes

shirring is done in two stages—first on top of the stove, and then in the oven.

shish kebab: Levantine dish of broiled skewered beef or lamb cubes.

shivowitza: (Hungarian—slivovitz)

shoestring potato: Very thin french-fried potato.

shokudo: (Japanese—dining room)

shortbread: Butter-rich Scots cookies.

short broth: *Court bouillon.*

shortcake: Dessert made of sweetened rich biscuit dough, split, buttered, and filled with berries or other sugar fruit, and sometimes topped with whipped cream.

short crust: Flaky, fragile, but rich pastry made by using generous amounts of butter or other shortening.

shortening: Butter, fat, lard, or any fat suitable for foods to be baked.

short ribs: Beef cut from between the plate and the ribs.

shot glass: Small glass for serving a shot, or one portion, of whiskey.

shoulder roast: Cut of meat, including the upper joint of the foreleg and adjacent parts.

shredder: Flat metal plate with sharp-edged perforations, used for shredding and grating various foods.

shrimp: Small marine crustacean taken from tropical and subtropical waters; shrimp are eaten fried, cold, in soups, in seafood cocktails, and in many other dishes.

shrimp à la créole: Shrimp cooked in highly spiced tomato sauce and served with rice.

shrimp biscuit: Baking-powder biscuit containing chopped and seasoned shrimp.

shrimp cocktail: Seafood cocktail made of boiled shrimp served cold in a spicy sauce.

shrimp pilau: Highly seasoned shrimp stew favored by old-time residents along the coastal waters of the South.

shuck: Outer covering, husk, pod, or shell, or the shell of a clam or an oyster.

shuck: To remove the outer covering from any edible food.

side: Half a carcass of a meat animal.

sidecar: Cocktail made of brandy, cointreau, and lemon juice.

side meat: Bacon or salt pork cut from a side of pork.

sidra: (Spanish—cider)

sieve: Mesh-bottomed kitchen utensil used in separating liquids from solids; sieves come in all shapes, sizes, and fineness of mesh.

sift: To cause some substance to pass through a sieve, thus removing lumps, large masses, and foreign objects; flour is sifted to remove lumps and to ensure that it becomes thoroughly blended with the other dry ingredients.

sifter: Kitchen utensil for sifting flour, usually with a hand-operated forcing paddle.

sild: (Danish—herring)

silent butler: Portable trash receptacle with a handle and a hinged lid, into which table crumbs are swept, along with discarded cigars and cigarettes, and similar debris.

sill: (Swedish—herring)

sillbullar: (Swedish—herring balls) Herring croquettes.

silver fizz: Hot-weather mixed drink composed of carbonated water, gin, and egg white.

silverware: Eating and serving utensils made of silver or silver plate: knives, forks, spoons, salad bowls, platters, salt-and-pepper shakers, and the like.

simmer: To cook or boil slowly over a low flame.

simple syrup: Sugar and water boiled until syrupy.

singapore sling: Mixed drink of kirsch, gin, lime juice, sugar, angostura bitters, and soda water.

singe: To touch lightly with flame, as in singeing chickens to remove fine hairs.

singing teakettle: Whistling teakettle.

sinigang na isda: (Filipino—fish chowder) Mackerel stewed in clam juice with peppermint, watercress, and tomatoes.

sink: Kitchen wash basin usually provided with hot and cold water, a drain, a drainboard, a working surface, and sometimes a garbage-disposal apparatus.

siphon bottle: Bottle for making and/or dispensing carbonated water; in many, the aeration material comes in a small cylinder inserted in the neck of the bottle; pressing a valve forces the water out through the neck and it emerges as soda water.

sirloin: Overloin or superloin of a side of beef, usually the portion immediately behind the porterhouse.

sirloin chop: Rib portion cut from the sirloin of a meat animal.

sirloin steak: Beef steak cut from the sirloin.

sirnaya: (Russian—cottage-cheese pudding) Dish made of butter, cottage cheese, hard-boiled eggs, flour, raisins, sugar, vanilla, and egg white.

sirniki: (Russian—dessert fritters)

sis kebabi: (Turkish—shish kebab)

six-pack: Carton holding six bottles or cans of some liquid such as a beer or soft drink.

sizzling platter: Restaurant term for a metal platter backed with a wooden plank, used for bringing freshly grilled chops, steaks, lobster, etc., to the diner's table.

skål: (Danish, Norwegian and Swedish—bowl) A toast.

skate: Specialized kind of ray, found in both Atlantic and Pacific Oceans and off both European and American shores; the skate's winglike fins are baked or steamed and served with black butter or some other sauce.

skewer: Metallic or wooden pin used to keep meat in form while it is being cooked.

skewer: To fasten meat together with a skewer.

skillet: Spider, or frying pan on legs, usually made of cast-iron; skillet is also sometimes used to mean an ordinary frying pan of modern materials.

skilly: Watery porridge.

skim: To remove something from the top of a liquid—cream from milk, scum from broth, grease from soup, etc.

skinkestek: (Norwegian—roast ham) Fresh-ham roast.

skip mackerel: Bluefish.

sla: (Dutch—lettuce; salad)

sladky perezs: (Russian—sweet-pepper salad)

slàinte: (Gaelic—health) A toast.

slaw: Coleslaw.

slicer: Hand- or motor-operated utensil for slicing foods such as breads, meats, vegetables, etc.; slicers come in many varieties, including those with long-bladed knives, rotating wheels, electrically vibrated blades, and circular blades moved by crank action.

sling: Mixed drink made of brandy, gin, or whiskey, ice (or sometimes hot water), powdered sugar, and a twist of lemon or lime.

slipcote: Unripened rennet cheese of English type, made from cow's milk.

slivovitz: Plum brandy, usually colorless, from any of the Slavic countries, particularly Yugoslavia.

sljivovica: (Yugoslavian—plum brandy)

sloe gin: Gin distilled from grain and flavored with sloe plums rather than juniper berries, as is true gin.

sloe gin fizz: Highball made of sloe gin, sugar, lemon juice, and soda water.

sloke: Edible seaweeds such as dulse, Irish moss, red laver, sea lettuce, etc.

slotted server: Slotted spoon.

slotted spoon: Perforated cooking and serving spoon for draining excess juices from fruits and vegetables being dished up.

smallage: Wild form of the domesticated celery.

small teacupful: About four fluid ounces.

smältost: (Swedish—melting cheese) Soft cheese of a Scandinavian variety.

smash: Crushed-fruit drink similar to lemonade, or an alcoholic drink made with crushed mint, powdered sugar, plain or carbonated water, and some strong liquor such as gin, rum, or whiskey; the same drink made with bourbon is called a mint julep.

smelt: Small marine and riverine food fish of the salmon family taken off both American coasts; smelts are usually fried or baked as they are delicately flavored.

smetana: (Russian—sour cream)

smitane: (French—sour cream) Sauce of sour cream and onions.

Smithfield ham: Ham from pigs specially reared, near Smithfield, Virginia, the meat carefully smoke-cured and aged; the specially fine flavor of these hams comes from the acorns and peanuts on which the animals are fed.

smoke: To cure food by subjecting it to smoke; smoke cures by drying and by killing the bacteria that cause spoilage, through various chemical compounds in the smoke; many kinds of fish, meat, poultry, and cheese are cured by smoking.

smoked beef: Chipped beef.

smoked fish: Any fish cured by smoking.

smoked ham: Ham cured by smoking.

smoked salmon paste: Canapé mixture usually packed in metal tubes for easy use in making appetizers.

smör: (Swedish—butter)

smörgas: (Swedish—buttered bread)

smörgasbord: (Swedish—bread-and-butter board) Buffet laden with appetizers of every kind: cheese, cold meats, pickled fish, eggs, shellfish, salads, etc.

smørkage: (Danish—butter cake) Rich pastry.

Smørrebrød: (Danish—buttered bread) Smörgasbord—appetizers and delicatessen dishes in many varieties.

snack: Light or quick meal taken between main meals or while traveling or in the midst of some activity.

snack bar: Place where light meals are served with beverages.

snack table: Portable table, often tray-top, for holding casual beverages and snack foods.

snail: Land-dwelling mollusk commonly found in Europe and many warm countries; snails are usually baked or cooked in wine or *bouillon,* and are popular as *hors d'oeuvres,* served in a special holder accompanied by a long-tined snail fork.

snail shell: Shell of an eating snail, usually cleaned and stuffed with snail flesh, then baked.

snap bean: Any bean grown primarily for its pod, such as wax or string bean.

snapper: Basslike marine food and game fish found off the southern states and in the nearby Caribbean; inshore species tend to be green or gray, while fish from deeper waters are often colored brilliantly.

snickerdoodle: Nutmeg-flavored Connecticut cookie made of butter, flour, sugar, eggs, milk, and baking powder.

snoek: Large marine food fish, related to the mackerel-like escolar, common in South African waters; snoek are often canned for export to other parts of the British Commonwealth.

snowball: Any cake or cooky that has a round shape and is coated with some kind of white frosting, particularly coconut, or an ice-cream ball covered with grated or shredded coconut.

snow pea: Light-green pea, eaten pod and all, used in Chinese stir-fry dishes and in salads; the French call it *mange-tout* (eat all).

soak: To cover a food with a liquid; soaking softens hard foods, desalinates very salty ones, and impregnates others with special flavors.

so ba: (Japanese—noodles) Thin green buckwheat variety of noodles.

sockeye: Salmon of the Pacific Northwest; famed for its deepred flesh and flavor, the sockeye is a medium-sized fish highly prized by commercial fishermen and sportsmen.

soda: Bicarbonate of soda or soda water.

soda cracker: White cracker made of yeast dough neutralized with soda.

soda fountain: Counter where ice-cream sodas, and many other ice-cream and soda-pop refreshments are concocted and served; a soda-fountain counter is usually provided with dispensing, mixing, and refrigerating equipment.

soda pop: Any flavored drink of carbonated water, such as ginger ale, root beer, sarsaparilla, colas, fruit pops, etc.

soda water: Carbonated water.

sodium bicarbonate: Baking soda or bicarbonate of soda; baking soda is sometimes used as a leavening agent, especially in devil's food cake.

soep: (Dutch—soup)

sofrito: (Spanish—lightly fried) Puerto Rican term for combination of green peppers, sweet chili peppers, onions, tomatoes, and seasoning fried in olive oil.

soft-ball stage: Candy-making step when a driblet of syrup dropped into cold water forms a soft ball, usually at about 238 degrees Fahrenheit (114 degrees Celsius); the soft-ball stage is sometimes called the thread stage, because the syrup will form a thread when it is dribbled from a spoon.

soft-shell clam: Thin-shelled North American edible clam, usually steamed.

soft drink: Any nonalcoholic beverage, usually a carbonated one bottled under a trade name: Coca-Cola, Pepsi-Cola, Orange Crush, etc.

soft-shelled crab: Molting stage of the blue crab.

sogliola: (Italian—sole fish)

soirée: Evening party.

sole: Flatfish highly popular among fish eaters; sole is usually boned before serving, and is prepared in many ways and served with many sauces.

sole: (French—sole fish)

sole frite: (French—fried sole)

sollo: (Spanish—pike; sturgeon)

solomillo: (Spanish—sirloin)

somen: (Japanese—noodles) Thin noodles made of wheat flour.

sommelier: (French—wine steward)

soor dook: Scots name for buttermilk.

sopa: (Portuguese and Spanish—soup)

sopa à Portuguesa: (Portuguese—soup in the Portuguese manner) Fish soup.

sopa borracha: (Spanish—wine sop) Puerto Rican tipsy cake consisting of white of egg, sponge cake, sugar syrup, and muscatel, often sprinkled with tiny candies.

sopa clara: (Spanish—clear soup; consommé)

sopa de albóndigas: (Spanish—meatball soup)

sopa de almendras: (Spanish—almond soup)

sopa de cebollas: (Spanish—onion soup)

sopa de fideos: (Spanish—noodle soup)

sopa de habas: (Spanish—lima bean soup)

sopa de legumbres: (Spanish—vegetable soup)

sopa de mariscos: (Spanish—shellfish soup)

sopa de mondongo: (Spanish—tripe soup)

sopa de pescado: (Spanish—fish soup)

sopa de pollo: (Spanish—chicken soup)

sopa de verduras: (Spanish—green-vegetable soup)

sopa espesa: (Spanish—thick soup)

soppa: (Swedish—soup)

sorbais: Pungent French cheese made from whole milk.

sorbet: (French—sherbet)

sorbetto: (Italian—sherbet)

sorghum: Name applied to numerous species of cereal grasses such as grain sorghum, which is cultivated for forage and stock feeding, and sorgo, the source of sorghum molasses.

sorghum molasses: Syrupy derivative of sorgo, similar to molasses.

sorgo: Sorghum cereal grass cultivated for its sweet juice used in making molasses.

sorrel: Herb of the dock family whose acidy leaves are used in soups, purees, and with spinach and egg dishes; there are many species and varieties of sorrel.

sosaties: South African skewered lamb with cornstarch and curry sauce.

sotol: Desert plant of the American Southwest and Mexico; used to produce an alcoholic beverage.

soubise: White sauce made by puréeing a mixture of cream, sugar, and onions.

souchong: Large-leafed black tea grown mainly in China; lapsang souchong, a variety, is noted for its smoky flavor; in India and Ceylon the coarser leaves, obtained by firing, are also sometimes called souchong.

soufflé: (French—puffed up) Spongy baked dish made either sweet as a dessert or savory as a main dish.

sound: Fish swim bladder.

soup: Liquid food, often containing solids in suspension; the French distinguish between two main types of soup: *consommé* or *potages clair* (clear soups), and *potages liés* (bound soups;

thick soups); *consommés* may be served plain, with garnish added, or cold; *potages liés* are of three types: *potages crèmes* (cream soups) in which *sauce béchamel* and cream are added to the basic mixture; *potages purées* (purée soups) to which thickening of pasta, barley, tapioca, etc., have been added; and *potages veloutés*, consisting of *velouté* mixture thickened with egg yolk, cream, and butter; *soupe* is a term usually used of a provincial, peasant, or foreign (non-French) soup.

soupa: (Greek—soup)

soupbone: Marrow-filled knuckle, neck, or shin bone suitable for soup-stock preparation.

soupçon: (French—suspicion; conjecture) Tiny pinch or slight trace of some ingredient, usually a condiment, herb, or spice.

soup cup: Double-handled cup for serving soup; a consommé cup is slightly smaller than a cream-soup cup.

soup dish: Large shallow bowl or deep plate for serving the soup course.

soupe: (French—soup)

soupe à la fausse tortue: (French —mock turtle soup)

soupe à l'oignon: (French—onion soup)

souper: (French—supper)

soup ladle: Serving spoon with a very large deep round bowl for dipping.

soup spoon: Round-bowl spoon for eating broths, chowders, and soups.

soup tureen: Large deep covered bowl for serving soup at the table; soup tureens often have matching ladles.

sour: Any of many alcoholic mixed drinks made sour by the addition of lemon or lime juice.

sourball: Tart sugar candy.

sour-cake: Oatmeal or rye bread made in a cake shape.

sour cream: Cream soured by lactic acid and used as a dressing for fruits, pancakes, and soups, and as a base for many cocktail dips.

sour-cream biscuits: Baking powder biscuits made with sour cream instead of milk.

sourdough: Fermented yeast dough, used in making camp bread; a piece of fermented dough is usually saved from each batch of bread to act as a starter for the next batch, thus eliminating the need for yeast.

sourdough bread: Bread made with a starter of sourdough.

soursop: Large, irregularly ovoid, succulent fruit of a small tropical American tree related to the sweetsop.

sous cloche: (French—under bell) Baked under a closed lid, as in a glass casserole.

souse: (Pennsylvania-German— something pickled) Mixture of pork and veal jellied in a vinegar solution.

soused anchovies: Anchovies fried, dried, and marinated in a pickling solution.

soused herring: Pickled herring.

sowbelly: Salt pork taken from the undersides of a pig carcass.

sowens: Scots flummery.

soybean: Pealike legume used in soups, made into flour, fermented to make soy sauce, and processed for its oil.

soybean oil: Oil expressed from soybeans and used chiefly in commercial food processing.

soybean synthetics: Engineered foods.

Soyer, Alexis (1809-58): French gastronome and reformer, the author of many culinary works including one with more than 1,000 recipes and *The Pantropheon, or History of Food.*

soy-protein fiber foods: Engineered foods.

soy sauce: Oriental condiment made from fermented soybean and other ingredients; Chinese soy sauce comes in several grade or weights having a variety of uses in Chinese cooking; there is also a Japanese soy sauce, somewhat different from Chinese.

spaghetti: (Italian—little cords) Pasta made in solid strands of medium to small size with any of a variety of sauces.

spaghetti fork: Three-tined fork with outer tines scalloped for holding slippery strands of spaghetti.

spaghettini: Thin rods of pasta somewhat thicker than vermicelli but thinner than spaghetti.

Spam: Trademarked name for a canned pork product.

spanakopeta: (Greek—spinach rolls) Spinach rolled up in pastry.

spanish chestnut: Large sweet chestnut grown along the Mediterranean.

spanish cream: Molded dessert made of eggs, gelatin, sugar, and milk.

spanish licorice: Extract of the dried root of the licorice plant, used in flavoring.

spanish lime: Genip of the West Indies.

spanish mackerel: Any of several species of mackerel with elongate dorsal fins, one is common in the Atlantic, another in the Pacific.

spanish omelet: Omelet served with a sauce of green peppers, onions, and tomatoes.

spanish onion: Large but mild-flavored onion.

spanish paprika: Pimiento of a type grown in Spain.

spanish peanut: Peanut with a small round pod, originally imported from Spanish Guinea on the coast of West Africa.

spanish pear: Avocado.

spanish potato: Sweet potato.

spanish rice: Rice prepared with garlic, green peppers, onions, tomatoes, salad oil or bacon fat, and seasonings.

spanish salsify: Oyster plant.

spanish toast: French toast, highly colored and seasoned.

spareribs: Rib ends, usually of pork separated from the bacon strip.

Spargel: (German—asparagus)

sparkling water: Soda water.

sparkling wines: Wines allowed to complete their fermentation process after bottling, producing an effervescent beverage: sparkling burgundy, champagne, pink champagne, asti spumante, etc.

spatula: Blunt broad-bladed implement used by pastry chefs and others in preparing fancy sugar icing, usually on a marble slab.

Spätzle: (German—small Swabian dumpling)

spearmint: Aromatic true mint whose leaves are used in mint sauce, mint juleps, candy, and chewing gum.

Speisekarte: (German—the menu)

Speisewagen: (German—dining car)

Speisezimmer: (German—dining room)

spencer steak: Choice steak cut from prime ribs of beef.

Sperrkäse: (German—block cheese) Dry hard German cheese.

spezzatino di manzo: (Italian—beef stew)

spice: Vegetable substance, usually in the form of a powder, of a hot sharp flavor, used sparingly as a flavoring agent; a spice differs from an herb chiefly in being more sharply flavored; herbs are usually derived from herbaceous plants (bay leaf is an exception), and are found in all climates throughout the world; spices are usually derived from a tree or woody vine (ginger is an exception), and are found only in the tropics (*see* herb).

spiced vinegar: Cider vinegar flavored with various spices, such as allspice, clove, mace, etc., and used in sauces and salad dressings.

Spice Islands: Moluccas of eastern Indonesia, source of many spices such as clove, mace, and nutmeg.

spice shelf: Special shelf for storing herbs and spices; some come with matching sets of small glass and porcelain containers.

spider: Cast-iron frying pan for open-fire cooking, having short legs just high enough to hold the pan above a bed of live coals.

Spiegelei: (German—fried egg)

spinach: Leafy vegetable eaten raw in salads and cooked in many attractive ways.

spinacio: (Italian—spinach)

Spinat: (German—spinach)

spiny lobster: Crustacean distinguished from the true lobster by its spiny carapace and unenlarged first pair of legs; the spiny lobster is also called rock lobster.

spirit lamp: Small alcohol lamp used to heat a chafing dish, coffee or tea pot.

spirits: Distillate containing ethyl alcohol, such as brandy, gin, rum, whiskey, etc.

spisestue: (Norwegian and Danish —dining room)

spisevogn: (Danish and Norwegian—dining car)

spit: Pointed metal rod for impaling fish, meat, or poultry to be barbecued or roasted.

Spitzkäse: (German—sharp cheese) Rennet cheese imported from Switzerland.

split: Liquid measure containing a half pint or 8 ounces.

split peas: Green peas dried, split, and used in soups.

sponge cake: Close-textured yellow cake made without shortening or leavening but with beaten eggs.

spoon: Essentially, a shallow bowl affixed to the end of a handle— one of the oldest culinary utensils known to man.

spoonbread: Cornmeal bread of a custardlike consistency, needing to be served with a spoon.

spoon rest: Range-top receptacle with indentation for holding spoons, to be handy when needed again.

sprat: Small variety of European herring, usually smoked or pickled in brine and canned.

sprig: Small shoot of an herb such as mint, parsley, or other herbs used as an aromatic garnish.

Springerle: (German—little leaper) Anise-flavored cookie bearing a design imprinted in the dough by a carved rolling pin.

spring-form pans: Baking-pan molds held together by a hinged clamp, so they can be opened to release the contents easily; pâtés are made in round, rectangular, or oval spring-forms, cheese cakes in round ones; large cakes can be baked in pans whose bottoms are removable—some spring-form, others detached.

spring lamb: Young lamb born in the late winter or early spring and brought to market while still tender.

spring water: Water from a spring or natural well.

spritz: (German—spurt, squirt) Butter cookie made by squirting the dough onto a cookie sheet.

spritzer: White wine and carbonated water.

spruce beer: Beerlike beverage made from spruce twigs and leaves boiled with molasses and then fermented with yeast; sometimes spruce beer means a spruce-flavored soft drink.

spud: Slang for potato, which is harvested by being dug up with a spud or shovel.

spumone: Italian frozen custard dessert.

spun sugar: Confection prepared by boiling sugar and water to the thread stage, then using it to decorate cakes and cookies.

spuntino: (Italian—snack) Coffee counter.

squab: Young bird, usually a pigeon between 3½ and 4½ weeks old.

square-egg skillet: Square sandwich-size (4½-inch) skillet for frying an egg to be used as a sandwich filler; square-egg skillets, some electrically operated, are used for preparing any kind of hot sandwich.

squash: Gourd vegetable such as winter squash grown to ripen for winter use (acorn, hubbard, turban squash); musk squash (canada, cushaw, winter crookneck), or summer squash (scallop, summer crookneck, zucchini); the method of preparation depends upon the variety, to some extent, but most squash can be baked, boiled, sautéed, or made into various desserts.

squaw dish: North Dakotan treat made of fried cube bacon topped with beaten eggs and golden corn kernels.

squeezer: Any utensil for squeezing or extracting juice: garlic press, lime, lemon, or orange squeezer, etc.

squid: Ten-armed cephalopod; considered a delicacy; Italian and Spanish recipes for squid are numerous.

staff of life: Bread, in Jonathan Swift's phrase (Tale of a Tub).

stag: Male of the European red deer.

stainless steel: Acid-resistant kitchenware: cutlery, coffee and tea pots, frying pans, mixing bowls, stew pans, etc.; stainless does not keep an edge and is less easily sharpened than carbon steel, but it requires less care.

stainless-steel sponge: Scouring pad of stainless-steel shavings for cleaning pans and pots.

stalk: Main stem of a plant, like celery.

standard beef: Fourth-best grade of beef, as classified by the U.S. Department of Agriculture.

starch: Complex ingredient that is the chief storage form of carbohydrate; starch is found in many foods: bread, cake, cereal, flour, fruit, root vegetables, as well as stems and tubers; in the natural state, starch is white, odorless, tasteless, and insoluble in cold water.

Starr: Juicy yellow apple used for cooking and eating.

station uval: (French—grape station) Counter where fresh grapes and grape juice are sold; during the ripening season many stations uvales appear in Paris railway depots and throughout the vineyard sections of France.

Stayman Winesap: Reddish cooking and eating apple, named for its American developer, J. Stayman.

steak: Cross-section of meat from the main part of a carcass; steak is usually used for beef chuck steaks, flank, rib, loin, round, porterhouse, sirloin, tenderloin, etc., but can also mean a cross-section of a large fish (codfish steak, swordfish steak, etc.).

steak-and-kidney pie: Pastry of rump steak and beef kidney layered in a casserole with minced parsley and shallots, and covered with a layer of pastry.

steakburger: Hamburger made of ground steak.

steak griller: Thermostatically controlled electric grill for cooking chops, hamburgers, steaks or waffles; most are Teflon coated and hence require a minimum of shortening.

steak hammer: Implement with a spike-studded face for tenderizing meat by pounding and thus breaking down the muscle tissue.

steak knife: Sharp-bladed individual knife with a serrated edge for cutting steaks and other firm meats.

steam: To cook by exposing food to steam; food can be steamed in a pressure cooker, in a covered container, or in a special steamer.

steam-bake: To cook by a combination of steaming and baking; the pan of food is placed in the oven; steam-baking keeps food moist during slow cooking.

steamer: Two-level utensil for steaming food; the food rests on a perforated platform above boiling water in the lower compartment.

steel: Fluted rod used for edging knives; a carving set usually contains a knife, a fork, and a steel.

steel wool: Scouring pad of fine steel threads, often impregnated with soap, for cleaning pots and pans.

steep: To extract the essence of some food by letting it stand in liquid just below the boiling point.

steer: Castrated bull calf raised for meat production.

steer beef: Meat of an altered bull calf, considered superior to cow or bull meat.

steerburger: Hamburger.

stegt al: (Danish—fried eel)

stein: Earthenware mug or tankard for serving beer.

Steinbutt: (German—turbot)

Steinpilz: (German—stone mushroom [an edible variety])

stemware: Drinking glasses and goblets mounted on a footed stem.

sterilize: To destroy harmful microorganisms in foods and cooking utensils; in home canning this is done by heating to the boiling point (212 degrees F or 100 degrees C); this kills most bacteria (although not their spores); in commercial canning, sterilization is done by steam (248 degrees F or 120 degrees C), and is followed by immediate sealing against the entry of air, so even if aerobic bacterial spores have survived, they cannot grow.

sterilizer: Lidded kettle provided with a rack for sterilizing home utensils such as babies' milk bottles, home canning jars, dishes used by sick people, etc., under live steam.

sterlet: Small sturgeon of the Caspian Sea and its tributaries; the roe is made into a caviar widely regarded as the best in the world, superior even to that of other Caspian sturgeon.

sterling: Silverware containing 92 percent silver and 8 percent copper.

Sterno: Trademark name of a portable stove fired by solidified alcohol.

stew: Anything cooked slowly in its own juices, plus added liquid; usually a stew consists of meat browned and stewed, the liquid thickened, and vegetables added.

still wine: Nonsparkling wine of any kind.

stilton: Cheese of the gorgonzola or roquefort type, originating in Huntingdonshire, England.

stinger: Mixed drink of brandy and *crème de menthe,* served as an after-dinner liqueur or as a cocktail.

stir: To mix with a beater, spoon, wire whisk, etc., using a steady circular motion.

stirabout: Oatmeal cooked in hot drippings and stirred constantly.

stir fry: To cook rapidly over high heat, stirring and tossing ingredients constantly; many oriental dishes are stir fried.

stirrer: Swizzle stick.

St. John's bread: Edible pod of the carob tree.

stoccafisso: (Italian—stockfish) Dried codfish.

stock: Broth resulting from cooking fish, fowl, meat, or vegetables; stock is the basis of so many dishes that the French call it *fond de cuisine* (foundation of cooking).

stock pot: Large pot for cooking beef, chicken, fish, or other stock; many cooks and chefs keep a permanent stock pot to hold cooking juices and waters.

stollen: German-style loaf cake baked in a bread tin, studded with nuts and dried fruit.

stolovaya: (Russian—dining room)
stone: Whetstone for sharpening
cutlery; some stones work best
with oil, others with water.

stoneware: Coarse pottery of
dense and well-fired clay, usually in the form of crocks, bean
pots, flagons, "mountain dew"
jugs, etc.

stör: (Swedish—sturgeon)

store cheese: Domestic cheddar
cheese.

stout: Malt liquor, brewed with
roasted malt and hops; stout is
stronger and sweeter than its
milder form, porter, and is usually served half and half with
some lighter ale or beer.

stove: Kitchen appliance for cooking; stoves are heated by electricity, gas, oil, coal, or wood;
some by reflected sunlight; most
modern ranges include an oven
for baking and roasting as well
as open burners for boiling,
braising, frying, sautéeing, etc.,
and an open-flame apparatus for
broiling.

stracciatella: (Italian—little rags)
Chicken soup with egg drops.

strainer: Sieve.

strapazzate al pomodoro: (Italian
—scrambled [eggs] in tomato
style) Tomato omelet.

straw: Originally, a stalk of grain
after threshing, now a commercially made hollow tube of paper or plastic for sipping liquids;
straws are sold in various lengths
and in many decorative colorings.

straw bass: Large-mouthed black
bass.

strawberry: Ground-growing herb
of the rose family, yielding a
juicy red aggregate fruit; straw-

berries are used in preserves, in
baking, in shortcake, and as flavoring in numerous confections.

strawberry bass: Freshwater calico
bass.

strawberry guava: Subtropical
shrub related to the true guava
and yielding a dark-red fruit
used in making preserves.

strega: (Italian—witch) Italian
cordial with a unique aroma and
orange flavor.

streusel topping: Blend of flour,
sugar, and cinnamon mixed with
butter until crumbled, used to
top kuchen and coffeecake.

string bean: Green snap bean,
called string because of the
stringlike fibers along the seams
of its pods.

strömming: (Swedish—riverling)
Small species of herring taken
from the Baltic Sea.

Strong Ale: Eleven-percent beer
brewed by Mitchell and Butler
brewery in Birmingham, England, probably the world's
strongest.

Strudel: (German—eddy; whirl-
pool) Fruit pastry made of layers of tissue-thin dough filled
with chopped apples, nuts, currants, and appropriate spices.

stud: To force cloves, bits of garlic, or other seasoning into the
surface of a food, usually a meat.

stufato: (Italian—stew)

stuffed cabbage rolls: Forcemeat
or other savory mixture wrapped
in cooked cabbage leaves and
baked in a casserole.

stuffed camel: Bedouin wedding
dish consisting of a whole roast
camel stuffed with a whole roast
sheep stuffed with as many
cooked chickens as it will hold;

in turn each chicken is stuffed with fish and these in turn are stuffed with eggs.

stuffed derma: Beef casings stuffed with bread or meat dressing and roasted.

stuffed potatoes: Baked potatoes with meat removed from the shell, mashed and mixed with cheese or sour cream, and replaced in the shell for a final browning.

stuffing: Filling for the inner cavity of fish, fowl, and other meats; stuffing is usually composed of bread, condiments, seasoning, and central ingredients such as sausage, oysters, chestnuts, etc.

sturgeon: Armored fish of ancient order, found in all north temperate seas, valued for its roe which is used in making caviar; in England the sturgeon is regarded as a royal fish, and when caught in English waters, it must be offered to the monarch.

sturgeonburger: Hamburger made of sturgeon meat.

suave: (Spanish—soft; smooth) Soft *taco.*

succotash: American Indian dish of green corn cooked with beans.

sucre: (French—sugar)

sucre à la crème: (French—sugar in cream style) Canadian confection made with melted butter, cream, sugar (brown or maple), and chopped walnuts.

sucrerie: (French—confections; sweetmeats)

sucrose: Any sugar derived from sugar beets, cane, maple syrup, palm, sorghum, etc.

suet: Hard fat found around the kidneys and loins of such creatures as sheep and steers, used

as a larding or a shortening agent.

sugar: Sweet crystalline substance high in energy-producing carbohydrates; sugar is derived principally from sugar beets and sugar cane, but also from other plant sources such as maple trees and palms.

sugar beet: White-rooted beet grown for its sugar, the second most important source of sugar; sugar-beet sugar is available commercially only in refined form as the crude sugar has an unpleasant flavor.

sugar bowl: Dish for holding sugar; some sugar bowls are provided with a special sugar spoon fitting into an indent in the rim.

sugar cane: Principal source of sugar, cultivated extensively in many tropical and subtropical countries, where people cut ripe stalks into segments and chew them like candy; raw cane is mashed between rollers, the juice filtered and crystallized by evaporation into crude brown sugar; refined brown sugar becomes granulated white sugar, and the residue of filtering becomes molasses.

sugar cube: Cube sugar.

sugar shell: Sugar spoon whose bowl is shell-shaped, sometimes provided as a sugarbowl accessory.

sugar tongs: Ornamental tongs for dispensing cube sugar.

suimono: (Japanese—clear soup)

sukiyaki: Japanese dish consisting of thin-sliced beef, bamboo shoots, onions, mushrooms, and other vegetables cooked on the diner's table.

süllö: (Hungarian—fish)

sultana: Yellow seedless grape grown for raisins and wine making.

summer flounder: Small edible marine flatfish taken along the Atlantic seaboard, widely fished by commercial and game fishermen.

summer savory: Savory.

sundae: Ice-cream dessert consisting of a mound of ice cream topped with flavored syrup of some kind; nuts, whipped cream, and maraschino cherries are often added as garnishes.

sunfish: Collective name of many American freshwater fishes including the bass, bluegill, and crappie; all are fine panfish; the ocean sunfish is a huge marine oddity whose body is nearly all head and is not valued as food.

sunflower: Towering American herb of the thistle family whose seeds are dried and salted for eating, or are processed for their oil; sunflower seeds are also favored by parrots and poultry.

sunny side up: Slang for method of frying an egg on one side only, so the yoke resembles the sun surrounded by white sky.

suolasilli: (Finnish—pickled herring)

suomalainen pannukakku: (Finnish—Finnish pancakes)

superburger: Large-size hamburger.

Superior: Small round white potato.

supermercado: (American-Spanish—supermarket)

Suppe: (German—soup)

supper: Last meal of the day, usually eaten around sundown; when dinner is served at mid-

day, the evening meal becomes supper; when dinner is served at the end of the day, a late-evening meal becomes supper.

suprême: (French—superb) Breast and wings of poultry, cooked according to a variety of recipes.

surf clam: Large clam found on New England beaches.

surinam bitters: Bitters made from a Surinam tree called the *Quassia amara*.

surlonge: (French—upper loin) Neck end of beef.

sushi: (Japanese—rice sandwich) Dish containing boiled rice, which is wrapped in either brown kelp, purple seaweed, or sometimes fresh raw fish.

susina: (Italian—plum)

Sussex: Dark-red beef cattle of a type first bred in Sussex, England; also a breed of domestic poultry, red or speckled, raised for meat.

sutliash: (Bulgarian—rice pudding)

svíčková pečene: (Czechoslovakian—sirloin of beef) Pickled beef with sour cream.

svinestek: (Swedish—roast pork)

swan: Long-necked aquatic bird related to the geese and the ducks; in the Middle Ages swan meat was considered a delicacy but today it is considered too oily and too tough.

swedish meatballs: Meatballs seasoned with nutmeg and served with a cream sauce.

swedish turnip: Rutabaga.

sweet: Candy or confection.

sweet and sour: Made of a mixture of sweet and sour ingredients, as in sweet-and-sour spareribs.

sweet basil: Basil.

sweetbread: Thymus gland of the calf or the lamb, considered the most delicate of all meats; the two-part gland consists of the *noix* (or kernel) and the *gorge* or throat; because of its two-part structure, the gland is often called sweetbreads.

sweet butter: Unsalted butter.

sweet cicely: European herb of the carrot family with an aromatic root; the same name is applied to related American species of the same family.

sweet corn: Eating corn.

sweet flag: Marsh herb whose pungent rootstock is sometimes candied.

sweet marjoram: European herb of the mint family whose aromatic leaves are used fresh in salads and fresh or dried as seasoning for meats, poultry, cheeses, sauces, etc.

sweetmeat: Candy.

sweet potato: Vine of the morning-glory family widely cultivated for its sweet tuber; sweet potatoes are served baked, candied, boiled, souffléed, stewed, and sautéed.

sweet roll: Danish pastry.

sweetsop: Sweet pulpy fruit of a tropical American tree; sweetsop is also called custard apple.

sweet sorghum: Sorgo.

swine's cress: Evil-smelling herb of the mustard family.

swiss chard: Succulent herb of the goosefoot family related to the beet; the large leaves and stalks are cooked and served as a potherb.

swiss cheese: Large-eyed cheese originally imported from Switzerland but now produced in Wisconsin and other dairy states.

swiss nut: Pastry biscuit shaped like a golden almond in its shell; filled with creamy chocolate or almond paste.

swiss roll: Jellyroll.

swiss steak: Floured round steak pounded, browned, and served with vegetables.

swizzle: Mixed drink containing bitters, lime juice, sugar, ice, and brandy, gin, rum, or whiskey, etc.

swizzle stick: Stirring rod of glass, plastic, or wood for stirring mixed drinks.

swordfish: Large oceanic fish prized for its delicate flavor; the upper jaw of this fish has become fused and elongated into a beaklike sword; swordfish steaks are baked, broiled, or smoked.

syllabub: Dessert beverage of milk and wine or cider, sweetened with sugar and topped with whipped cream.

sylt: (Swedish—jam)

syrian coffee: Black coffee sweetened to taste and flavored with black cardamom seeds.

syrup: Sugar and water cooked together and often flavored, or any liquid sweetener such as corn, maple, or molasses syrup, and so forth.

szekely: Hungarian cheese sold in sausage skins and made from ewe's milk.

T: Abbreviation for tablespoon.

t: Abbreviation for teaspoon.

Tabasco: Trademarked name for condiment of hot pepper and vinegar.

table à manger: (French—dining table)

tablecloth: Covering for a dining or luncheon table; tablecloths come in many different forms, elegant to simple, for a variety of occasions.

table d'hôte: (French—host's table) Restaurant term meaning a complete meal offered at a fixed price.

table jelly: British term for commercial gelatine colored and flavored like Jell-O.

table knife: Eating knife.

table linen: Napkins and tablecloths, center cloths, place mats of cloth, etc.

table salt: Eating and cooking salt.

tablespoon: Dry measure equal to 3 teaspoons or ½ ounce.

tableware: Any kind of pottery, china, or flatware, used in setting a table.

table water: Bottled water either still or carbonated.

table wine: Still wine, red or white, for serving with meals; a table wine is dry and of not more than 28 proof.

tacchino: (Italian—turkey)

taco: (Spanish—wad; roll) *Tortilla* filled with mixture of beans, cheese, fish, fowl, or meat and vegetables; tacos are served soft (*suaves*) or crisp (*tostados*).

taffy: Old-fashioned pull candy, made with molasses or corn syrup, sugar, and water; cooked porous with air bubbles, and any desired flavor can be "pulled in" during the process.

tafia: Unrefined rum of a type made in the West Indies and the Guianas.

Tagesplatte: (German—today's plate) Dish of the day.

tagliatelle: (Italian—thin egg noodles)

tagliatelle verdi: (Italian—green noodles) Spinach macaroni.

tagliatini: (Italian—very little things cut off) Very thin pasta strips.

taglierini: (Italian—long narrow noodles)

tallow: Renderings of mutton or beef suet.

talmouse: (French—cheesecake)

tamago-yaki: (Japanese—baked egg roll)

tamale: Corn cake stuffed with chopped chicken, fish, meat, seafood, or a vegetable combination, then wrapped in a banana leaf or corn husk and steamed.

tamara: Italian seasoning, a combination of aniseed, cinnamon, clove, coriander, and fennel seed.

tamarin: (French—tamarind)

tamarind: Tropical tree yielding a podlike fruit which is used in preserves, chutneys, soft drinks, and candies; the seed is ground into meal or cooked whole, and in some parts of the world the leaves and flowers are also eaten.

tamarind balls: Jamaican confection made of brown sugar and tamarind, sweet and tart.

tangelo: Tangerine + grapefruit —hybrid tasting of both these citrus fruits.

tangerine: Loose-skinned citrus fruit, a cultivated variety of the mandarin orange, originally imported from China.

tango: Mixed drink composed of gin, vermouth, and orange juice.

tangoa: Tangerine liqueur.

tankard: Tall drinking vessel with a handle and, usually, a hinged lid.

tansy: Aromatic herb of the thistle family, whose bitter leaves were once much used as a flavoring agent.

tansy mustard: American herb of mustard family whose leaves smell and taste somewhat like true tansy.

tansy pudding: Baked dessert made of butter, cream, eggs, and sugar, and flavored with herbs and rose water.

tapang baboy: (Filipino—cured pork)

tapang baka: (Filipino—cured beef)

tapioca: Substance obtained from cassava starch and used to make puddings and provide a light thickening for soup.

tappit-hen: Scots tankard with a knob on its lid, containing 2 Scots pints (3 imperial and about 3.6 U.S. pints); the name comes from a supposed resemblance to a crested hen, called tappit in Scotland.

taro: Tropical plant of the arum family, grown throughout the tropics for its starchy root; taro is used in making the fermented paste known as poi, a favorite dish of Hawaiians.

tarragon: Spicy and tangy herb used to season fish, fowl, meats, and salads, very popular because it does not obliterate the taste of other herbs and spices.

tarragon vinegar: White vinegar flavored with tarragon.

tart: Fruit pie of some kind; to the French and Pennsylvania-German: a large pie without a top or with a lattice crust; to Americans: a small individual pie; to the English: any fruit pie.

tartar sauce: Mayonnaise filled with capers, gherkins, onions, parsley, and seasoning.

tarte: (French—tart)

tartine: (French—little tart) Slice of bread spread with jam, jelly, or other preserve.

tartlet: Small tart.

tartufo: (Italian—truffle)

Tascherin: (German—little pockets) Austrian stuffed turnovers containing cheese, chopped meat, chopped nuts, jam, or some other filling.

tassau: Haitian veal cutlet cooked with orange and lemon juice.

tasse: (French—cup)

tavern: Barroom or combination barroom and restaurant.

tawny port: Port fully aged in the cask, losing some of its natural red color in the process.

T-bone: Steak with a T-shaped bone cut from the short loin of beef.

tbs: Abbreviation for tablespoon.

te: (Danish and Norwegian—tea)

tè: (Italian—tea)

té: (Spanish and Swedish—tea)

tea: Tropical evergreen plant, related to the camellia, whose leaves have been used since antiquity to produce a stimulating infusion; all tea comes from the same plant, but regional differences in climate and soil produce a variety of qualities and types; however, the product is chiefly classified by the process which prepares it for market: black tea (china congou, english breakfast, darjeeling, pekoe, orange pekoe, etc.), fully fermented between rolling and firing; green teas (hyson, gunpowder, pan- and basket-fired, etc.), not fermented at all; and oolongs (formosa, foochow, etc.), partially fermented; tea is served hot or iced, with sugar or lemon, with milk or cream or plain, and mixed with alcoholic beverages to make punch.

tea bag: Cloth or filter-paper sack containing tea leaves to be immersed in boiling water; tea bags permit the leaves to steep without remaining behind as grounds.

tea ball: Perforated metal ball made in two parts so it can be opened and filled with tea; it then serves the same function as a tea bag.

tea biscuit: English term for a sweet light cookie made to be served at tea.

tea bowl: Chinese or Japanese style handleless teacup.

tea bread: Sweet bread, buns, or cakes made to be served at tea.

tea caddy: Small box or chest for holding dry tea.

teacake: Cookie or light, flat, pastrylike cake served at tea.

tea cart: Elegant serving wagon for transporting tea or coffee refreshments from the kitchen to wherever they are to be served.

tea cloth: Small decorative tablecloth for a light meal.

tea cozy: Heavily insulated cloth overcoat to encase a teapot and keep it warm between servings.

teacup: Drinking cup, usually part of a table service, provided with a matching saucer; teacups are usually taller and narrower than coffee cups.

tea kettle: Kitchen utensil for boiling water, provided with a top handle, a tight lid, and a pouring spout; some tea kettles have whistles to announce when water has reached the boiling point.

tea maker: Tea ball in the shape of a shell-bowled spoon.

teapot: Spouted vessel, usually of earthenware, provided with a handle and a lid; for formal servings, tea is made in a pot, then poured out into individual cups; teapot is not to be confused with the kitchen utensil, tea kettle.

tea service: Set of ceramic or metallic utensils, usually decorative, for serving tea; if of metal (usually silver): teapot, tray, caddy, creamer, sugar bowl, hot-water pot, alcohol lamp and lamp stand, etc.; if of ceramic (usually fine china of some kind): teapot, sugar bowl, creamer, teacups, saucers, and tea plates.

tea set: Tea service, particularly a ceramic one that includes cups, sauces, and plates.

teaspoon: Dry measure containing ⅙th ounce

tea tray: Tray large enough at least to hold a tea service, if not the cups, saucers, and plates as well.

Tecate: Mexican beer brewed in Tecate, Baja California Norte.

tee: (Finnish—tea)

Teegebäck: (German—tea cake)

teflon: Commercial term for a compound of tetrafluoroethylene, a nonsticking plastic used to face cooking utensils and reduce the need for fats and oils in cooking.

te-komplet: (Danish—complete tea) Light meal usually including bread, cake, and tea.

telur: (Malay—egg)

temp: Abbreviation for temperature.

tempura: (Japanese—foods dipped in batter and deep-fat fried)

tenderloin: Tender section of pork or beef on either side of the vertebral column.

tequila: Mexican alcoholic beverage made from distilled pulqué —fermented sap of the maguey cactus; tequila is usually served with fresh lime and salt.

teriyaki: Marinated strips of beef, chicken, fish, pork, or veal broiled over charcoal and served with a pungent sauce.

ternera: (Spanish—veal)

tête-à-tête: (French—face-to-face)

tête de veau: (French—calf's head)

texel: Green sheep's-milk cheese, originating on the island of Texel in the Netherlands.

thé: (French—tea)

thé-complet: (French—complete tea) Light meal usually including bread, cake, and tea.

thee: (Dutch—tea)

Thee: (German—tea)

thermometer: Instrument for measuring temperatures; culinary thermometers include: oven thermometers, usually regulating heat thermostatically; meat thermometers imbedded in roasts to determine cooking progress; candy thermometers clamped over the side of saucepans to measure the temperature of boiling syrups.

Thermos: Trademarked name for a vacuum container.

Thompson: Large variety of California seedless grape.

Thompson Pink: Pink-fleshed juicy grapefruit covered with smooth light-yellow skin.

thon: (French—tuna)

thousand-island dressing: Russian dressing garnished with green pepper, pimiento, pickle, and chive.

Thunfisch: (German—tuna)

thuringian caraway: Sour-milk hand cheese flavored with caraway seeds.

thyme: Garden herb of the mint family, widely used in seasoning foods.

tidy: Perforated, triangular sink receptacle of metal or plastic, used for straining garbage so it does not clog the drain.

tiffin: Luncheon or midmorning snack.

tiger meat: Gourmet exotica— meat from surplus tigers (of circuses and zoos) sold in tiger-striped cans.

tillamook: Sharp-flavored cheddar cheese originating in Tillamook, Oregon.

tilsit: Popular rennet cheese, originating in the old Prussian town of Tilsit, now Sovetsk, U.S.S.R.; today it is manufactured in Denmark, Hungary, Yugoslavia, Switzerland, and other European countries.

timbale: (French—kettledrum) Any savory preparation served in a cup-shaped mold.

timbale iron: Long-handled metal mold for shaping and baking shells for timbales; many are embossed with crescent, diamond, star, and other designs.

timer: Clockwork device for timing baking, cooking, or roasting; many timers can be preset to ring when food is cooked.

tini: Slang for martini.

tinware: Kitchen articles made of tinned steel: cake pans, pie plates, graters, sifters, strainers, etc.; however, aluminum is largely replacing tinware in utensils of this kind.

tipsy cake: English dry cake soaked in sherry, cooked with a custard sauce, and chilled.

tipsy pudding: Tipsy cake.

tisane: Originally barley water, but now any herb tea made from camomile, linden blossom, or other such plant material.

tiste: (Nicaraguan-Spanish— name for a soft drink) Beverage made of toasted corn, cocoa, and annatto.

tj: Slang abbreviation for tomato juice.

tjener: (Danish—waiter)

tjoklat: (Malay—chocolate)

toad-in-the-hole: Australian and English dish of meat baked or fried in a batter.

toast: Toasted bread.

toast: To brown by direct heat as in a toaster or under an open flame.

toaster: Electric appliance for toasting bread, rolls, etc.; most modern toasters are fitted with timing devices to pop up the toast when it is done.

toasting fork: Very long handled implement for toasting foods over an open flame.

toby: Jug or mug shaped like a fat old man attired in 18th-century clothes and topped by a three-cornered hat; tobies are sometimes used for serving ale beer, and other beverages, but usually are ornamental pieces of porcelainware.

tocană: (Roumanian—stew) Creamed chicken.

tocino: (Spanish—bacon)

toddy: Beverage made of brandy, rum, or whiskey, hot water, and sweetening, sometimes with some citrus flavoring.

toffee: Chewy English candy made by cooking butter, sugar, and cream to the hard-ball stage, then adding nuts.

toffy: Toffee.

toheroa: Giant edible clam of New Zealand.

Tokay: Amber-colored sweet wine originally made in Tokay, Hungary.

tom and jerry: Hot mixed drink of rum, boiling water, and eggs, spiced with cinnamon and clove.

tomat: Slang for tomato.

tomate: (French—tomato)

Tomate: (German—tomato)

Tomatensaft: (German—tomato juice)

tomato: Perennial herb of the nightshade family, yielding a succulent large red berry; tomatoes are used in salads, sauces, soups, and stews; are fried, squeezed for their juice, combined with herbs and spices to make sauce for pasta, and eaten raw; they range in size from tiny cherry tomatoes to gigantic beefsteaks.

tomato biscuit: Baking-powder biscuit whose dough contains tomato juice instead of milk.

tomato bouillon: Beef bouillon with tomato juice.

tomato juice: Juice extracted from ripe tomatoes; tomato juice is high in vitamin C and low in calories, is good as a chilled drink or mixed with other juices, and is used in a variety of cooking recipes.

tomato ketchup: Catsup.

tomato paste: Concentrated tomato purée.

tomato sauce: Purée of tomato flavored with onions, parsley, shortening, and sugar.

tomcod: Small species of codfish found in the Atlantic and the Pacific.

tom collins: Highball made of gin, soda, lemon juice, and sugar, with a slice of lemon and a maraschino cherry.

tommy: British military slang (after Tommy Atkins, the British soldier personified) for a ration of bread.

tongue: Tongue of a meat animal, especially beef or lamb; tongue is braised, pickled, or smoked, and eaten hot or cold, in sandwiches and in salads.

tonic water: Quinine water.

tonno: (Italian—tuna)

ton yuk kui: (Korean—broiled pork)

toothpick: Sliver of plastic, poultry quill, or wood used to remove food particles from between the teeth; toothpicks are also useful for spearing gherkins, olives, and other miniature *hors d'oeuvres,* and for pinning together double-decker sandwiches.

torrone: (Italian—nougat)

torsk: (Danish and Norwegian—codfish)

torta: (Italian—cake or pie; Spanish—round cake or loaf)

torta de banana: (Spanish—banana cake)

torta di mandorle: (Italian—almond tart) Venetian pastry.

torta di noci: (Italian—nut tart)

Torte: (German—torte; tart-cake) torte: Round cake made with bread crumbs and little or no flour, often enriched with dried fruit and nuts.

tortellino: (Italian—tartlet) Macaroni stuffed with meat.

tortello: (Italian—fritter)

tortilla: (Spanish—omelet; American-Spanish—thin flat pancake made of corn)

tortilla de camarones: (Spanish—shrimp omelet)

tostado: (Spanish—toasted) Crisp taco.

tostón: (Spanish—toast dipped in oil) Venezuelan term for a fried green plantain, which, when cut before frying, resembles a long stick of toast.

tot: Small drink.

tournedo: (French—choice beef fillet)

tourte: (French—round meat-filled pie)

tourtière: (French—pie dish) Canadian term for a meat pie.

toyo: (Filipino—soy sauce)

tragacanth: Tropical plant of the pea family which yields a gum used in candy making as an emulsifier, as well as in ice creams and gelatins.

trails: Slang for entrails or intestines.

trammel: Adjustable pothook for a fireplace crane; the shank is notched for various heights so that a cooking pot can be raised or lowered as desired.

tranche: (French—slice)

trappist cheese: Cheese made in the Trappist Monastery of Port du Salut in France.

treacle: English word for molasses.

treble palma: Top-quality sherry.

tree platter: Ceramic or silver serving platter for roasts with a tree pattern deeply engraved in the base; gravy collects in the channels of the pattern and is easily scooped up.

trefah: (Hebrew—animal torn by wild beasts) Forbidden foods, chiefly: animals not killed according to the dietary laws; the meat of the pig, shellfish, and fish without scales; forbidden parts of kosher animals; and any practice which violates dietary laws such as mixing milk and meat.

trenton cracker: Oyster cracker.

trepang: Bêche-de-mer.

triclinium: (Latin—dining room or table) Roman-style dining room with three three-place couches set on three sides of the table, leaving the fourth side free for serving.

trifle: English dessert made of several layers of sponge cake spread with jam and the whole soaked in liqueur, rum, or wine, and garnished with custard or whipped cream.

tripe: Stomach walls of a meat animal, chiefly beef; plain tripe is taken from the rumen or cud-holding stomach, honeycomb tripe from the reticulum or true stomach; both are eaten well cooked, and are prepared according to a number of recipes.

triticale: New high-yield grain created by crossing triticum wheat with secalis rye, developed by the University of Manitoba, Canada, and the National Institute of Agricultural Research, Chapango, Mexico.

trivet: Three-legged metal stand for holding a hot dish on a table-top; modern trivets are often electrified to maintain the heat.

Trockenkäse: (German—dry cheese) Hard dry cheese.

tronçon: (French—fragment) Chunk of fish or meat cut longer than it is wide.

trota: (Italian—trout)

trotters: Feet of calves, pigs, sheep, etc., used for food and in making calf's foot jelly.

trout: Fast-swimming members of the salmon family found in lakes and mountain streams, very bony and very tasty; trout are prepared in many different ways.

trucha: (Spanish—trout)

truffe: (French—truffle)

truffle: Subsurface European fungus with a dark warty surface and a characteristic odor; the French esteem truffles as a delicacy, using dogs and pigs to detect their smell; they are used in a variety of gourmet recipes.

truite: (French—trout)

trunkfish: Small food fish taken from the coastal waters of the southern Atlantic states where it is often baked in its three-sided shell.

truss: To fasten a fowl with skewers or twine before cooking so its body will retain the juices.

Truthahn: (German—turkey)

try: To render.

tsp: Abbreviation for teaspoon.

tuba: (Filipino—fermented palm sap) Wine of the Philippines.

tube pan: Deep ring-shaped pan for baking angel cakes, and other deep light batter cakes; cooking in a tube pan allows deep cakes to cook in the middle as well as around the edges.

tubetti: (Italian—little trumpets) Thinnest elbow macaroni.

Tuborg: Danish beer brewed in Copenhagen.

tuckahoe: Name applied to two different American plants, both of which have rootstocks used by the Indians for food: arrow arum, a plant of the genus *Peltandra,* and golden club of the genus *Orontium.*

tuica: Rumanian rum-flavored plum liqueur.

tumbler: Stemless drinking glass, usually for water or milk, containing 8 to 12 ounces of liquid.

tumeric: Turmeric.

tun: Hooped wine cask containing 252 gallons.

tuna: Prized food and game fish of the tunny family, mackerel-like in shape but immense in size—sometimes reaching 10 feet and 1,000 pounds; tuna is a favorite in salad and sandwich combinations, and is also made into croquettes, served à la king, baked, and broiled.

tunge: (Danish—tongue)

tunie: Slang for a frankfurter made of tuna meat.

turbot: Large European flatfish, nearly circular in shape, highly regarded as a food fish.

tureen: Soup tureen.

turkey: Large handsome fowl native to North America and successfully domesticated for its meat; turkey, the symbol of Thanksgiving or plenty, is nearly always served roasted, but there are many recipes for preparing leftover turkey meat.

turkeyburger: Hamburger made of turkey meat.

turkish bean: Scarlet runner bean.

turkish coffee: Pulverized coffee cooked in a sugar syrup; the coffee is thrice boiled in a nickel- or pewter-lined racquie or brass pot; when the racquie reaches its third boil, the coffee is ready to be served.

turkish delight: Confection made of gelatin and sugar, quick boiled and flavored, then cut into squares and dusted with powdered sugar.

turkish paste: Turkish delight.

turkish pepper: Bonnet pepper; this also refers to paprika, which is made from the bonnet pepper.

turkish walnut: English walnut.

turk's head pan: Fluted tube pan, whose ringlike shape was thought to resemble a Near Eastern turban.

turmeric: East Indian herb of the ginger family, whose aromatic root is ground and used as a golden-yellow condiment; turmeric is used for flavoring pickles, meats, and eggs.

turner: Broad-bladed perforated implement for turning food being fried.

turnip: Herb of the cabbage group whose edible root is eaten as a vegetable and grown as a fodder crop; rutabagas or swedish turnips have long yellow roots; plain turnips are shorter, broader, and wider; young turnip leaves, or greens, are eaten as a vegetable and often are boiled with bacon.

turnip cabbage: Kohlrabi or rutabaga.

turnip radish: Variety of radish with a bulbous root.

turnover: Semicircular pie made

by folding a round pastry sheet in half and filling it.

turnover coffee maker: Drip coffeepot in 4 levels: pot, insert strainer, spouted server, and lid.

turrón: (Spanish—nougat) Candy of a type dating back to the Moorish conquest of the Iberian peninsula.

tutter: (Dutch—to your health) A toast.

tutti-frutti: (Italian—all fruits) Term applied to anything flavored with a variety of preserved mixed fruits, particularly ice creams and candies.

tv-tray: Portable tray-topped table for serving individual meals to people watching television.

TW & FS: Abbreviation for the Wine and Food Society.

Twenty-ounce: Full apple of yellowish-red.

twin-spout teapot: Teapot with two compartments and two spouts, so that tea may be poured from one and hot water from the other.

twist: Wedge of lemon, lime, or orange peel served with a drink; twist also refers to bread, pastry, or roll formed of twisted strips.

twister: Cruller.

two-bean succotash: Iowan mixture of green beans, lima beans, and yellow corn.

tybo: Mellow-type Danish cheese.

tyrolienne: (French—in Tyrolean manner)

tyrol sour cheese: Pungent hand cheese of a type made in the Austrian, German, Italian, or Swiss Tyrol.

tzimes: (Yiddish—complicated casserole stew) Combination of carrots, raisins, or prunes, baked and in a casserole.

udang karang: (Malay—coral shrimp)

udder: Pendant milk sac of certain mammals such as the cow, goat, sheep, etc.; udders are sometimes served braised, salted, or smoked.

udon: (Japanese—noodles) Thick corn or wheat noodles.

ugli: Jamaican tangelo, a citrus fruit 4 to 5 inches in diameter having the flavor of grapefruit, orange, and tangerine; the ugli was developed in Jamaica and has a lemon-yellow skin splashed with green.

uisgebeatha: (Gaelic—water of life) Whiskey; the English word whiskey comes from *usquebaugh*, a corruption of the Gaelic.

uitsmitjter: (Dutch—thrower-out; bouncer) Sandwich topped with a fried egg.

ukha: (Russian—fish soup)

ullage: Amount a bottle, flagon, flask, or other container lacks of being full.

ulva: Sea lettuce gathered and eaten in many oriental countries and by many orientals living in other lands; ulva is popular in many salads, soups, and stews.

umbles: Deer entrails, made into umble, or humble, pie; the expression *"to eat humble pie"* comes from the custom of assigning the inferior parts of a game carcass to the servants, to whom they were served in a pasty.

umido: (Italian—stew)

uncork: To remove the cork from a bottle; uncorking wine requires some skill as the cork must be withdrawn intact, and the bottle must not be agitated in the process, or sediment will be stirred up.

unfermented tea: Green tea.

unfermented wine: Grape juice.

univalve: Edible mollusk with a single shell: abalone, conch, snail, whelk, etc.

uovo: (Italian—egg)

uovo affogato: (Italian—poached egg)

uovo al latte: (Italian—egg in milk style) Soft-boiled egg.

uovo bollito: (Italian—boiled egg)

uovo farcito: (Italian—stuffed egg) Deviled egg.

uovo fritto: (Italian—fried egg)

uovo sodo: (Italian—hard egg) Hard-boiled egg.

uovo strapazzato: (Italian—scrambled egg)

upper crust: Pastry cover, top crust.

upside-down cake: Cake made by lining a pan with butter, brown sugar, nutmeats, and canned fruit (usually pineapple, peach, or apricot), then pouring an egg batter on top and baking; when baked, the cake is inverted so that the sugar-and-fruit mixture is on top.

urda: Roumanian sheep's-milk cheese.

USDA: Abbreviation for the United States Department of Agriculture.

uszka: (Polish—stuffed dough pockets)

utensil: Any implement or vessel of household, particularly kitchen, use; any number of ingenious, handsome, and well-made utensils are on the market today.

utensil tray: Shallow compartmented tray of wood or plastic, to keep flatware and other utensils sorted while stored.

utility beef: Sixth-best grade of beef as classified by the U.S. Department of Agriculture.

utrennii: (Russian—breakfast)

uunijuusto: (Finnish—cheese dish) Milk dish made by taking a cow's first milk after freshening, sweetening it, and baking it in a slow oven.

uva: (Italian, Portuguese, and Spanish—grape)

uva passa: (Italian—dried grape) Raisin.

uva seca: (Spanish—dried grape) Raisin.

úzhin: (Russian—supper)

vaca: (Spanish—cow)

vache à lait: (French—milk cow)

vacherin: Swedish cheese used as a spread, creamy and aromatic.

vacuum bottle: Bottle-shaped vacuum container.

vacuum carafe: Vacuum-insulated jug for keeping ice water cold.

vacuum coffee pot: Glass or metal coffeepot consisting of a gasket-sealed upper bowl and a connecting lower receptacle joined by a filter, used with extra-fine ground coffee.

vacuum container: Container with
an inner and outer wall and
a sealed-off vacuum between
them for keeping liquids at
about the temperature (hot or
cold) they were when poured
in.

vaffel: (Norwegian—waffle)

vagão restaurante: (Portuguese—
dining car)

vagone ristorante: (Italian—dining car)

vagon-restoran: (Russian and
Turkish—dining car)

vainilla: (Spanish—vanilla)

Valencia: Sweet summer-ripening
orange, widely cultivated in the
U.S.

Valenciana: (Spanish—in the
style of Valencia)

valentine: Heart-shaped cake,
candy, cookies, etc., made for
presentation on Valentine's Day,
February 14.

valesniki: Russian-style cream-
cheese croquettes.

valio: Light-golden Finnish cheese
distinguished by its sharp nutty
flavor.

valpolicella: Italian-type dry red
wine.

vand: (Danish—water)

van der hum: (Africaans—what's-
his-name) South African tan-
gerine-flavored liqueur.

vaniglia: (Italian—vanilla)

vanilla: Tropical American climbing orchid whose podlike capsule is aged, cured, and used in
making vanilla extract—perhaps
the favorite flavoring agent of
American bakers and dessert
makers; many people prefer to
use finely cut bits of the pod instead of the extract or its many
synthetic imitations.

vanilla bean: Dried pod of the vanilla plant; beans are soaked in
ethyl alcohol to produce vanilla
extract.

vanilla sugar: Flavored sugar produced by burying a vanilla bean
in an airtight jar of sugar; when
sugar has taken on a vanilla flavor, it is used in baking and dessert making.

vanille: (French—vanilla)

vann: (Norwegian—water)

vareniki: (Russian—dumplings
stuffed with cottage cheese)

variety meats: Brains, feet, hearts,
kidneys, knuckles, livers, lungs,
tails, tongues, and other discards
or entrails such as intestines and
their tripe.

varm kartoffelsalat: (Danish—
warm potato salad)

vatapá: (Brazilian-Portuguese—
name for a seafood) Flour-based
stew of shrimp, fish, or chicken
seasoned with coconut milk and
palm oil.

vatroushkis: (Russian—open-
faced tart)

vatten: (Swedish—water)

V.D.N.: Abbreviation for *Vin
Doux Naturel* (French—natural
sweet wine) Fortified wine.

veal: Flesh of a calf up to 14
weeks of age; meat from a milk-
fed calf is preferred, since the
flesh of grass-fed animals develops too dark a color.

veal birds: Pounded veal cutlets
spread with a dressing of bread
crumbs and onion, rolled up,
skewered, sautéed in butter, and
finally braised.

vealer: Milk-fed calf, suitable for
veal.

veau: (French—veal)

vegalinks: Vegetable sausage links, a kind of engineered food.

vegeburger: Vegetarian-style meatless hamburger made of edible spun-protein fiber plus coloring and flavoring.

vegetable: Herbaceous plant grown for the sake of an edible part: root, stalk, leaf, flower, fruit, etc.; any living thing not classified as an animal is a vegetable.

vegetable brush: Coarse-bristled brush, usually in loop form, for scrubbing vegetables which are to be cooked whole.

vegetable butter: Vegetable caviar.

vegetable caviar: Russian vegetarian dish made by combining finely chopped baked eggplant with finely chopped onions, parsley, and tomatoes, then cooking in olive oil; vegetable caviar is served cold.

vegetable cheese: Bean curd.

vegetable chowder: Hearty soup made of assorted raw vegetables sautéed in butter, then cooked in water with canned tomatoes.

vegetable coloring: Coloring matter of such vegetable origins as maple bark, onionskin, butternut balls, etc.

vegetable dish: Large platter for serving simply prepared vegetables such as baked potatoes, corn on the cob, steamed rice, etc.

vegetable egg: Eggplant.

vegetable gelatin: Agar.

vegetable gold: Saffron.

vegetable ice cream: Cherimoya.

vegetable jelly: Pectin.

vegetable marrow: Egg-shaped summer squash popular in England.

vegetable milk: Synthetic milk made principally from soybean.

vegetable oil: Essential oil extracted from any plant, as opposed to animal or mineral oils.

vegetable oyster: Salsify.

vegetable peeler: Parer.

vegetable plate: Restaurant term for a main course consisting of several vegetables served together on one big plate.

vegetable stock: Pot liquor obtained by boiling vegetables, used in making soups and stews.

vegetable strainer: Sievelike strainer to help pour off water from boiled vegetables; the strainer is held against the lip of the pot, keeping vegetables in the pot while the water is poured out.

vegetarian: Person who lives solely on fruits, nuts, and other vegetables; some vegetarians include dairy products and eggs, and hence are called ovolactarians.

velouté: (French—velvety) White sauce made of chicken or veal stock thickened with white roux.

velvet: Beverage composed of equal parts of champagne and porter.

venaison: (French—venison)

venison: Wild-animal flesh, especially deer, elk, moose, and reindeer; venison is often tough and gamey, and only the better cuts are commonly served: saddle, haunch, loin, etc.

verdura: (Italian and Spanish—vegetables)

verenika: (Yiddish—noodle dumpling)

verloren: (German—poached)

verloren Ei: (German—poached egg)

vermicelli: (Italian—little worms) Very thin pasta made in long strands thinner than spaghetti.

vermouth:Fortified white wine with herbs added; Italian vermouth is somewhat sweeter than French.

vermouth cassis: Highball composed of French vermouth, *crème de cassis,* and soda water.

vesi: (Finnish—water)

Vesperbrot: (German—vesper bread; light afternoon luncheon)

viande: (French—meat)

vichyssoise: (French—Vichy style) Cold soup made with butter, leeks, potatoes, chicken consommé, and cream.

vichy water: Effervescent mineral water of a type imported from the spring in Vichy, France.

vienna cream: Finger-shaped arrowroot biscuits filled with creamed icing.

vienna loaf: Crisp and crusty white bread with a braided shape somewhat thick in the middle and with tapered ends.

vienna sausage: Beef and pork sausage thinner than frankfurters and with both ends cut off square.

vienna wafer: Meringue cooky made of powdered sugar, almonds, flour, and egg white.

vikingekaffe: (Danish—viking coffee) Strong hot coffee laced with wine and topped with whipped cream and cinnamon.

vin: (Danish, French, Norwegian, and Swedish—wine)

vinagre: (Spanish—vinegar)

vinaigre: (French—vinegar)

vinaigrette: (French—little vinegar) Salad dressing made with olive oil, vinegar, and seasonings.

vinaigrette sauce: Sauce of oil, parsley, shallot, and vinegar served with fish or cold meats.

vin blanc: (French—white wine)

vin coupé: (French—diluted wine)

vin de table: (French—table wine)

vin d'honneur: (French—wine of honor) Wine served in honor of a distinguished guest.

vin du pays: (French—country wine) Local wine made in the neighborhood.

vin du Rhin: (French—Rhine wine)

vinegar: Sour-tasting acetic-acid solution obtained from the fermentation of beer, cider, wine, and other dilute alcoholic liquids; commercial white vinegar has a chemical base, cider is a derivative of fermented apple juice, malt of beer, and wine of red and white wines; herb vinegar is one of the above with herbs added to it.

vinepress: Winepress for expressing grape juice used in wine making.

vinho: (Portuguese—wine)

vinho de Madeira: (Portuguese —Madeira wine)

vinho do pôrto: (Portuguese— port wine)

vinjak: (Yugoslavian—cognac)

vin mousseux: (French— sparkling wine)

vino: (Italian and Spanish—wine)

vino asciutto: (Italian—dry wine)

vino bianco: (Italian—white wine)

vino blanco: (Spanish—white wine)

vino dolce: (Italian—sweet wine)

vino espumante: (Spanish—sparkling wine)

vinologist: Student of vines and wines.

vinology: Study of grapevines and other vines.

vinometer: Hydrometer for testing the strength and purity of wines.

vin ordinaire: (French—ordinary wine) Common table wine of France, usually cheap claret or Sauterne of inferior quality.

vino rosso: (Italian—red wine)

vino spumante: (Italian—sparkling wine)

vino tinto: (Spanish—tinted wine) Red wine.

vin pur: (French—pure wine) Undiluted wine.

vin rosé: (French—pink wine) Light and slightly sweet rose-colored wine served with cold cuts and salads.

vin rouge: (French—red wine)

vintage: Wine yield of a certain year.

vintage port: Unblended port of a good year allowed to age in the bottle; in bad years true port is not vintaged but is used in fortified port.

vintage wine: Wine grown and processed naturally; because of variations in the weather, and other variables, the vintages of some years are superior to others, and those of certain outstanding years are considered superfine.

vintner: Dealer in wines.

virginia ham: Smithfield ham.

VI rum: Virgin Islands' rum, usually distilled on the island of St. Croix—Cruzan rum.

vis: (Dutch—fish)

viscera: Internal organs: heart, intestines, kidneys, liver, lungs, etc.; culinarily, most of these are included among offal meats.

vitamin: Any of a number of organic substances necessary for animal nutrition; vitamins help regulate the metabolic processes of the body but do not provide energy (carbohydrates) or serve as building units (protein).

vitamin A: Carotene found in butter, carrots, egg yolks, fish-liver oils; it is essential to good eyesight and to growth.

vitamin A_1: Nutritive element present in egg yolk, milk, and milk products such as butter.

vitamin A_2: Nutritive element found in freshwater fish liver.

vitamin B: Nutritive element: essential to digestive and nervous systems, found in breads, egg yolk, lean meat, fruits, nuts, and green vegetables.

vitamin B_1: Thiamin vitamin required for correct metabolic and nerve functions, found in many foods.

vitamin B_2: Riboflavin, growth-promoting element found in milk and liver, also called vitamin G.

vitamin B_6: Pyridoxamine, found in cereals, liver, yeast, and bees' royal jelly.

vitamin B_{12}: Vitamin complex available in kidney, liver, and seafood dishes, used in treating anemia.

vitamin C: Ascorbic acid found in citrus fruits and many vegetables, essential for tooth health and as an antiscorbutic.

vitamin D: Antirachitic vitamin essential in prevention of rickets and formation of good bones and teeth, found in egg yolk and fish-liver oils.

vitamin E: Antisterility vitamin contained in seed oils and leafy vegetables, formerly called vitamin X.

vitamin G: B_2—riboflavin, found in milk and in liver.

vitamin H: Biotin or growth vitamin found in egg yolk, liver, and yeast.

vitamin K: Fat-soluble vitamin necessary for coagulation of the blood.

vitamin M: Folic-acid vitamin necessary to overcome anemia or sprue.

vitamin P: Bioflavonoid, the permeability vitamin found in paprika.

vitamin PP: Pellagra-preventive vitamin present in nicotinic acid.

vitello: (Italian—veal)

vitello al forno: (Italian—veal in oven style) Roast veal.

vitreous china: Nonporous ceramic ware protected by a dense vitrified glaze.

vitrine: Glass-shelved and glass-sided china closet for displaying fine bric-a-brac.

vittles: Colloquialism for victuals or food.

vlattero: Currant-flavored Greek liqueur.

VO: Abbreviation for very old, applied usually to brandy, but sometimes to whiskey.

vodka: (Russian—little water) Liquor distilled from fermented potatoes, rye, or wheat mash.

voileipäpöytä: (Finnish—bread-and-butter table) Appetizer course similar to *smörgasbord.*

volaille: (French—fowl; poultry)

vol-au-vent: (French—flight on the wind) Light patty shell made of puff paste and filled with some creamed savory mixture.

vongola: (Italian—mussel)

Vorspeise: (German—appetizer)

VSO: Abbreviation for very special old (brandy).

VSOP: Abbreviation for very special old pale (brandy).

wachenheimer: One of several varieties of white wine, originating near the town of Wachenheim in the Rhineland, Germany.

Wachsbohne: (German—wax bean)

wafer: Any very thin crisp biscuit or cooky.

Waffel: (German—waffle)

waffle: Large batter cake baked in a waffle iron with an impressed design, usually of simple indentations.

waffle iron: Utensil for baking waffles; most modern waffle irons are electric, but cast-iron models for use with coal or wood stoves are also sometimes found.

wagon-restaurant: (French—dining car)

waiter: One who waits on table —a restaurant employee who serves drinks and meals; waiter can also mean a serving tray for for carrying food or holding a coffee or tea service.

Waldmeister: (German—wood master; forest warden). Woodruff.

waldorf salad: Fruit salad made of diced apples, celery, walnuts, and mayonnaise, first served at the old Waldorf-Astoria Hotel in New York City.

wall-eyed perch: Freshwater food fish characterized by its prominent eyes; because of its size and slenderness, the walleye is sometimes called walleyed pike.

walnut: An edible nut from a tree of the genus *Juglans,* particularly the english walnut; the english walnut is heavily cultivated in California as an eating walnut; the native American black walnut is a flavorful nut used in many ice creams.

ward 8: Bostonian cocktail containing bourbon or rye whiskey, grenadine syrup, some powdered sugar, and lemon juice.

warmer: Chafing dish or hot plate.

warming tray: Tray whose bottom is covered with electric heating element, providing uniform warmth to objects placed upon it.

wasabi: Asiatic herb of the cabbage group, whose thick green root is used in Japan like the horseradish, usually ground and eaten with fish.

wassail: Holiday punch made of ale or beer, flavored with roast apples, sweet spices, lemon, toast, and sugar.

Wasser: (German—water)

waste disposal: Garbage disposal.

wastelbread: Kind of bread made of the finest flour.

water: Odorless, tasteless, colorless liquid essential to life.

water apple: Custard apple.

water biscuit: Biscuit or cracker made with water instead of milk.

water bottle: Carafe, canteen, leather skin, or any container for holding or transporting liquids.

water breaker: Ship's water cask well sealed to prevent contamination by seawater; most lifeboats are kept permanently equipped with water breakers in case of emergency.

water chestnut: Old World aquatic plant related to the myrtle, yielding a nutlike fruit; water chestnuts (no relation to true chestnuts) are widely used in Chinese dishes, and in Western cooking are sometimes sliced and added to meats and stews.

watercress: Aquatic herb of the mustard family, which grows in running water; watercress is used in salads, or for spicing stews, and soups.

water ice: Shaved ice flavored with fruit syrup; sometimes sherbet is called a water ice to distinguish it from ice cream.

water kale: Meatless vegetable broth.

watermelon: African vine of the cucumber family yielding a large round or oblong fruit with sweet, red, juicy flesh; watermelons are eaten raw but the rind is sometimes pickled, and the seeds are roasted, salted, and eaten as a snack.

water noodles: Commercial noodles containing less than 5.5 percent egg solids.

water of life: Whiskey or brandy, from the Latin name given to the first distilled liquor, *aqua vitae*.

water pitcher: Large pitcher, usually of glass, with a broad lip and a large handle for holding a supply of ice water at the table.

water rice: Wild rice.

water softener: Device for softening hard water by neutralizing calcium carbonate deposits with sodium chloride (salt); water softeners are used primarily in industry, but small units are available for the home.

waterzoï: (French—Waterzootje)

waterzootje: (Flemish—water lot) Dish made of several kinds of freshwater fish cooked in butter and seasoned stock; sometimes a chicken *waterzootje* is cooked in similar fashion.

wax beans: Yellow snap beans.

waxed paper: Wrapping paper coated with white wax to protect it from water and grease, used for storing food, for wrapping sandwiches, for covering dishes temporarily, etc.

weakfish: Food fish of the croaker group, taken off the Atlantic and Gulf Coasts; weakfish are so called because their mouths are easily torn by fishhooks.

Wealthy: Bright-red fall apple prized for cooking as well as eating.

wedding cake: Cake served at a wedding celebration as a symbol of the festive occasion; the traditional wedding cake is a dark fruit cake iced with white sugar frosting; today it is more common to serve a commercially baked and deocrated yellow cake (often a sponge or pound cake) several tiers high, frosted with sugar icing, and garnished on top with figurines of a bride and groom or a wedding bell or fresh flowers; it is customary for the first piece to be cut by the bride and bridegroom together.

wedgwood: Cameo-decorated or classically designed pottery of the style perfected by Josiah Wedgwood in 1769.

weenie: Slang for frankfurter.

Weinbrand: (German—wine brand) German brandy.

Weinkaltschale: (German—cold wine soup)

Weintraube: (German—cluster of grapes)

weisse Rübe: (German—white turnip)

Weisswurst: (German—white sausage)

well and tree platter: Tree platter.

welsh bean: Kidney bean.

welsh rabbit: Dish made of melted cheese, beer, and other ingredients, poured over toast or served as a dip for bread sticks; it is also known — incorrectly — as welsh rarebit.

wensleydale: Strongly flavored whole-milk cheese first made in Wensleydale, Yorkshire, England; it is somewhat similar to stilton and easy to distinguish by its deep-blue veins.

Werderkäse: (German — Werder cheese) Rennet cheese originating in this town west of Berlin.

western: Omelet sandwich of ham, onions, and green pepper cooked in an egg mixture and served on bread.

westernburger: Western omelet; a small steak.

west indian gherkin: A small prickly cucumber originating in the West Indies, and grown chiefly for pickling.

Westphalian ham: Ham imported from Westphalia in Germany; Westphalian ham has a distinctive flavor derived from the German method of smoking over a fire of beechwood and juniper.

wether: Castrated male sheep.

wham: Meatless ham; *see also* engineered foods.

wheat: Cereal grass cultivated for its edible seed, which is threshed and ground into flour; about one half the world's cultivated land is used to produce wheat; the three principal types are *Einkorn* (German—one corn), emmer, and common; *Einkorn* is rarely cultivated and then only as a fodder grain; emmer wheats fall into several varieties: the most important is durum (hard) wheat, yielding semolina; common wheat is just what its name implies, and two of its six types,

bread and club wheat, form the bulk of the world's annual wheat crop.

wheat: Slang for wheatcake.

wheatcake: Pancake.

whip: Fruit dessert consisting of fruit pulp, preserves, or fresh fruit whipped up with egg white or whipped cream and sometimes gelatin.

whip: To beat into a broth, with fork, egg beater, or electrical appliance.

whipped butter: Creamed butter.

whipping cream: Cream containing more than 36 percent butterfat; this can be whipped into a froth for use in dessert toppings, and as an ingredient in many sweet dishes and beverages.

whisk: Looped-wire utensil for beating, stirring, and whipping.

whiskey: Strong alcoholic intoxicant made from a mash of fermented grains such as wheat, rye, corn, or barley; spelled with an *e* in the American fashion, whiskey usually means bourbon or rye.

whiskey collins: Tom collins made with whiskey.

whiskey glass: Shot glass.

whiskey sour: Cocktail made of bitters, lemon juice, and whiskey.

whisky: Scotch whiskey.

whistling teakettle: Kettle with a spout provided with a steam-activated whistle to warn users when the water has begun to boil.

whitefish: Important freshwater fish of Eurasia and North America, formerly common in the Great Lakes.

white glass: Clear uncolored glassware produced for kitchen and dining-room use.

white-label rum: Trade term for clear rum.

white malaga: Greenish-white grape popular because of its mild flavor.

white meat: Pork or veal, or the white (breast) meat of poultry.

white pepper: Pepper.

white potato: Irish potato.

white sauce: Milk sauce thickened with butter and flour, used on vegetables or as a base for creamed-meat dishes.

white table wines: Chablis, rhine wines, sauternes, etc.; white wines are served with chicken, fish, omelets, shellfish, and other white meats.

whiteware: Any white pottery.

white yam: White-fleshed variety of yam cultivated in many of the islands of the South Pacific, Indonesia, and the West Indies, eaten in many different ways.

wicker bottle: Rum, wine, or other bottle covered with woven wicker.

wicker flask: Liquor flask covered with woven wicker.

wickerwork: Anything made of wicker: bread tray, trash basket, fruit and vegetable container, etc.

wiener: Frankfurter; originally a wiener was a vienna sausage (*Wienerwurst*) but today it applies to the popular hot dog.

wienerbrød: (Danish — Viennese bread) Coffeecakelike pastry known to many Americans as danish pastry.

Wienerschnitzel: (German—Viennese cut) Pan-fried breaded veal cutlet served with a slice of lemon or lime.

Wienerspritz: (German—lively wine) Mixture of white wine, charged water, and ice—summertime cooler of great popularity.

Wienerwurst: (German—Viennese sausage)

wijn: (Dutch—wine)

wild angelica: European herb of the carrot family found on Cape Breton Island; *see also* angelica.

wild basil: Aromatic herb of the mint family, widely distributed throughout Europe, Asia, and North America.

wildfowl: Any game bird, particularly aquatic: wild duck, geese, snipe, swans, etc.

wild honey: Honey made by wild bees; there is no particular difference in quality between wild honey and hive honey, but the domestic kind is easier to obtain.

wild rice: Tall aquatic grass native to North America where it has long been cultivated and harvested by American Indians; wild rice (not related to true rice) requires longer cooking than true rice but is tastier.

wild sweet potato: Name used for an American morning glory which has a large starchy root.

willow pattern: Chinaware of a type originally imported into England from China; the blue-on-white Nanking pattern featured a willow tree and two young lovers pursued by angry parents; hence willowware, or willow-pattern china, has come to mean any white china with a blue design.

wine: Mildly alcoholic beverage produced from fermented grape juice; wines are of three principal types: vintage wines, standard wines, and fortified wines, which types are subdivided into many brands, regional pressings, growths, etc.

wine acid: Tartaric acid.

wine apple: Large, wine-flavored red apple.

wine bag: Wineskin.

wineberry: Raspberry of China and Japan with an acid red fruit; wineberry also refers to numerous other local fruits: the wine grape, the red currant, the gooseberry, the bilberry, etc.

wine biscuit: Arrowroot biscuit sometimes served with wine but more often to children with cocoa or milk.

wine bottle: Commercial container of varying shape, holding 24 to 30 ounces; wine bottle can also refer to any glass container designed to hold some kind of wine.

wine card: Wine list.

wine cellar: Room, usually in the basement or cellar, for storing wines; wine cellar can also mean simply a stock of wines kept on hand in any convenient storage area.

wine coaster: Rimmed disk of ceramic, metal, plastic or wood in which to set a wine bottle, so that drippings will not spot the tablecloth.

wine cooler: Ice bucket for chilling a bottle of wine before serving.

wine cradle: Serving basket designed to cradle a bottle of wine at a slant so the sediment will not be disturbed.

wine ferment: Wine yeast.

wine glass: Small glass, usually stemmed, in which wine is served; wine glasses hold from 4 to 6 ounces of liquid and vary in shape—tulip-bowled, conical, poppy-shaped, etc.—according to the type of wine.

wine grape: Any grape used in wine production.

wine herring: Pickled herring preserved in a wine-flavored sauce of spices and vinegar.

wine jelly: Molded gelatin dessert flavored with wine.

wine lees: Wine dregs.

wine list: List of wines served in a restaurant, aboard an airplane, ship, or train, or in a bar or hotel.

wine press: Device for expressing grape juice for wine making.

wine rack: Metal or wooden rack for storing bottles of wine at the correct slant.

winery: Place where wine is made.

Winesap: Bright-red slightly tart winter apple.

wine server: Blown-glass table container with a bubble insert for holding ice and a dispensing spigot near the bottom.

wineskin: Bag used as a wine container, usually of goatskin but sometimes of calf- or sheepskin.

wine vault: Underground area where wine is stored.

wine whey: Wine-coagulated milk whey.

wine vinegar: Vinegar made from soured red or white wine; popular in salad dressings and sauces.

wine yeast: Yeast used in making wine.

winged yam: White yam.

winter apple: Apple ripening late in the fall and ready for winter markets.

wintercress: Yellow-flowered cress whose leaves are used as a salad green.

winter flounder: Small flatfish fished from Maine to Maryland, differing from the summer flounder in having its eyes on the opposite (right) side.

wintergreen: Low-growing evergreen herb of the heath family whose aromatic leaves yield oil of wintergreen, used for flavoring candy and chewing gum; however, the natural product is now largely superseded by a similar oil compounded artificially or by a natural oil derived from the birch.

Winterkohl: (German—winter cabbage) Kale.

winter pear: Any late-ripening pear.

winter savory: Aromatic European herb of the mint family; its leaves are used fresh or dried as a flavoring agent.

wintersweet: Wild marjoram.

winter wheat: Wheat sowed in autumn and harvested in spring; sowing winter wheat is a common method of retaining a ground cover on farmland through the winter.

Wirtshaus: (German—inn; tavern)

Wiśniak: Polish cherry cordial.

witloof: Endive.

Wittwenkuss: (German—widow's kiss) Almond-filled pastry.

wonton: Chinese-style stuffed pockets of dough served in soup.

wonton soup: Chicken broth served with Chinese wonton.

wood apple: Crabapple.

woodenware: Kitchen utensils made of wood: bowls, breadboards, buckets, chopping blocks, knife racks, pepper mills, etc.

woodruff: Sweet-scented European herb of the madder family sometimes used to flavor wine.

worcestershire: Condiment sauce originating in Worcestershire, England, and made of soya, vinegar, anchovy, molasses, garlic, and seasonings; Worcestershire sauce is served as a table condiment and as an ingredient in other dishes.

work: To knead or mix slowly.

wormwood: Woody European herb of the thistle family whose bitter leaves are used to flavor absinthe, vermouth, and wine.

wt: Abbreviation for weight.

Wurst: (German—sausage) Big easy-to-slice sausage.

Wurstbrot: (German—sausage sandwich)

Würstchen: (German—link sausages)

Würstspeise: (German—pork product)

Würzburger: Dark beer of a type originally brewed at Würzburg in Bavaria, Germany.

Wyandotte: American breed of domestic poultry derived from interbreeding Brahmas and Hamburgs.

xaintray: French-type goat's-milk cheese.

xanthia: Cocktail concocted of brandy, gin, and yellow chartreuse.

xanthin: Yellow food coloring extracted from the herb madder.

xérès: (French—sherry) Originally a Spanish sherry produced at Xeres, or Jerez, near Cadiz on the southwest coast of Spain.

xeres cocktail: Combination of orange bitters and sherry.

xerophagy: Dry eating—the strict fast observed during Lent by certain members of the Greek Orthodox Church; Xerophagists abstain from all food except bread, salt, vegetables, and water.

Xipe: Aztec god of sowing and ploughing; his health is sometimes toasted in old towns of Mexico.

Xmas cookies: Assorted cookies baked for the Christmas holiday season.

Xmas fruitcake: Christmas fruitcake.

xymase: Enzyme fermenting sugar into alcohol.

xynogala: (Greek—clabber; sour milk that has thickened)

yablouchni: Chilled Russian apple soup served on hot summer days.

yahni: (Greek—method of cooking) Technique for preparing a vegetarian dish by braising in olive oil and then boiling with tomatoes.

yakimono: (Japanese—broiled food)

yam: Tropical climbing vine whose tuberous root is filled with mealy-white potatolike food; yams are a staple in many tropical areas where they are baked,

boiled, fried, and eaten as potatoes are in temperate climes.
yam bean: Tropical pea vine with
turniplike tubers eaten as vegetables; the pod is also edible,
and the seeds are pressed for
their oil.
yam koong: (Thai—shrimp salad)
yam potato: Sweet potato.
yaourt: (French—yogurt)
yarmouth capon: Red herring.
yaupon or yaupon tea: Carolina
tea.
yautia: (Spanish—sweet potato)
yeast: Fungus cells found in simple sugars, used to promote fermentation; yeast causes bread
dough to rise and grapes and
mash to ferment in the making
of beer, wine, and whiskey; baking yeasts are sold in cake and
granular form.
yeast cake: Commercial yeast sold
in small cakes.
yeast granules: Commercial yeast
sold in granular form, usually
in foil-wrapped individual portions.
yeen wor: (Chinese—bird's nest)
yellow cherry: Small variety of tomato, usually preserved; yellow
cherry is also a variety of true
cherry, sweet and eaten raw or
preserved.
yellow perch: Common American
perch, abundant in lakes and
streams; sometimes the smallmouth black bass and red-
breasted bream are also called
yellow perch.
yellow pike: Walleyed pike.
yellow plum: American wild plum.
Yellow Transplant: Tart greenish-
yellow eating or cooking apple.
yellow yam: Sweet potato.
yema: (Spanish—egg yolk)

yerbabuena: (Spanish—good
herb; peppermint)
yerba maté: (Spanish—maté herb)
Tealike beverage made from the
Paraguay tree maté; *see also*
maté.
yerba santa: (Spanish—holy herb)
Any of several plants of the
waterleaf family, native to the
American Southwest.
yiaourti: (Greek—yogurt)
yingling: Candy composed of butterscotch chips, Chinese noodles,
and salted peanuts, boiled and
formed to look like a little hay-
stack.
yogurt: Semisolid partly evaporated and fermented milk food,
often served with fresh berries
or berry preserves.
yokan: (Japanese—beancake
cookies)
yolk: Yellow center of egg, consisting chiefly of proteins, leci-
thin, and cholesterol.
york ham: English cured ham
served in tissue-thin slices, originated in York, England.
Yorkshire: Breed of white swine of
a type originating in Yorkshire,
England, designated small, medium, and large, according to
the type for which the animal
is bred.
yorkshire pudding: English meat
garnish made by baking batter
in the roasting pan with the
meat; Yorkshire pudding is usually served in wedge-shaped
chunks.
york state bean: Bean of a type
cultivated in New York State for
use in making boston baked
beans.
yucca: Any of several plants of the
lily family found in the American Southwest; yucca fruit is

served roasted, and young yucca stalks are eaten like asparagus.

yu chi tong: (Chinese—shark-fin soup)

yule-log cake: Cake baked in the shape of a log and covered with chocolate frosting worked with a fork to simulate bark.

yvette cream: Violet-flavored liqueur.

zab: Slang for zabaglione.

zabaglione: Egg yolks beaten to a froth in marsala wine, served warm and eaten with a spoon.

zabaione: (Italian—zabaglione)

zachtegekookt ei: (Dutch—soft-boiled egg)

Zahlen, bitte: (German—the bill, please)

zakinski: (Russian—appetizers)

zalm: (Dutch—salmon)

zampone: (Italian—pig's trotter)

zanahoria: (Spanish—carrot)

Zante currant: Variety of seedless raisin grape imported from the Ionian island of Zante (Zakinthos), Greece.

Zara: Maraschino liqueur made at port of Zara in Dalmatian sector of Yugoslavia.

zarf: Arabian-style coffee-cup holder made of metal.

zarzamora: (Spanish—blackberry)

zarzuela: (Spanish—musical comedy) Shellfish stew containing as many ingredients as a musical comedy.

zavtrak: (Russian—breakfast)

zdrowie twóje: (Polish—your health) A toast.

zebu: High-humped Indian cattle also called brahma or brahman, imported from India into southern U.S. because of their ability to withstand long hot summers and cattle fevers; they have been interbred with other domestic cattle.

zeevis: (Dutch—seafish; seafood)

zeller-es paradicsomsaláta: (Hungarian—boiled celeriac salad) Boiled celery root served with tomatoes and green peppers.

zenzero: (Italian—ginger)

zéphir: (French—zephyr) Chef's term for any light and frothy preparation.

zeppole: (Italian—fritters)

zest: Orange or lemon peel added to a drink to enhance the flavor.

zesteuse: (French—citrus peeler)

zythos: (Greek—beer) Ancient Egyptian beer brewed of barley.

Zimtstern: (German—cinnamon star) Spicy cooky baked in star shape; sometimes two are put together to form a cooky snow-flake, which is then sprinkled with confectioner's sugar.

zingara: (Italian—gypsy woman) Garnish of finely chopped ham or tongue mixed with mushrooms and flavored with tomato sauce containing tarragon.

Zingiber: Genus of tropical herbs which includes the ginger.

zitoni: (Italian—unfluted macaroni) Biggest unfluted macaroni made.

Zitrone: (German—lemon)

zizanie: (French—wild rice)

zombie: Rum highball seasoned with sugar, lime juice, pineapple and papaya juice, and apricot brandy, served with a pineapple stick and topped with a maraschino cherry.

zoolak: Carbonated fermented milk drink.

zubrowka: (Polish—sweet grass) Greenish vodka flavored with bitter almond.

zucca: (Italian—gourd; pumpkin)

zucchero: (Italian—sugar)

zucchino: (Italian—vegetable marrow) Green variety of summer squash.

Zucker: (German—sugar)

zugo: (Italian—sweet fritter)

zumo: (Spanish—juice)

zumo de uvas: (Spanish—grape juice)

Zunge: (German—tongue)

Zungenscheiben: (German—sliced tongue)

Zungenwurst: (German—tongue sausage)

zupa: (Ukrainian—soup)

zupa grzybowa: (Polish—mushroom soup) Soup made with sour cream, dried mushrooms, meat stock, and seasoning.

zuppa: (Italian—soup)

zuppa di pesce: (Italian—fish chowder)

zuppa inglese: (Italian—English soup) Rum cake covered with custard or whipped cream; this so-called English soup is really a cake dessert.

zurrapa: (Portuguese—cheap wine)

zuurkool: (Dutch—sauerkraut)

Zwaan: (Dutch—swan) Trade name for a canadian-style bacon processed and canned in Holland for export.

Zwetschgenknödel: (German—plum dumpling)

Zweitfrühstück: (German—second breakfast) Late-morning meal, larger than the first (a cup of coffee and a roll) as it also includes a big sandwich or a sausage or even more.

Zwieback: (German—twice baked) Rusk—dry sweet bread sliced and browned to a delicate crisp.

Zwiebel: (German—onion)

Zwiebelrostbraten: (German—pot roast with onions)

Zwiebelsuppe: (German—onion soup)

zymase: Enzyme which ferments sugar into alcohol.

zymi: (Greek—leaven)

zymology: Science of fermentation.

zymurgy: Branch of applied chemistry dealing with brewing and wine making.

zythos: (Greek—beer) Also ancient Egyptian beer brewed of barley.

WITHDRAWAL